Paddling Texas

A Guide to the State's Best Paddling Routes

Shane Townsend

FALCONGUIDES

GUILFORD, CONNECTICUT
HELENA, MONTANA
AN IMPRINT OF ROWMAN & LITTLEFIELD

FALCONGUIDES®

An imprint of Rowman & Littlefield
Falcon, FalconGuides, and Outfit Your Mind are registered trademarks of Rowman
& Littlefield.

Distributed by NATIONAL BOOK NETWORK

Copyright © 2014 by Rowman & Littlefield
All photographs by Shane Townsend
Maps by Alena Joy Pearce

British Library Cataloguing-in-Publication Information available

Library of Congress Cataloging-in-Publication Data

Townsend, Shane.
  Paddling Texas : a guide to the state's best paddling routes / Shane Townsend.
    pages cm -- (Paddling series)
  ISBN 978-0-7627-9126-2 (paperback)
  1. Canoes and canoeing--Texas--Guidebooks. 2. Kayaking--Texas--Guidebooks.
  3. Texas--Guidebooks. I. Title.
  GV776.T42T68 2014
  797.12209764--dc23
                    2014031240

♾™ The paper used in this publication meets the minimum requirements of American National Standard for Information Sciences—Permanence of Paper for Printed
Library Materials, ANSI/NISO Z39.48-1992.

For Abigail, James Riley, Jenny Ruth, and Ruth Riley

Contents

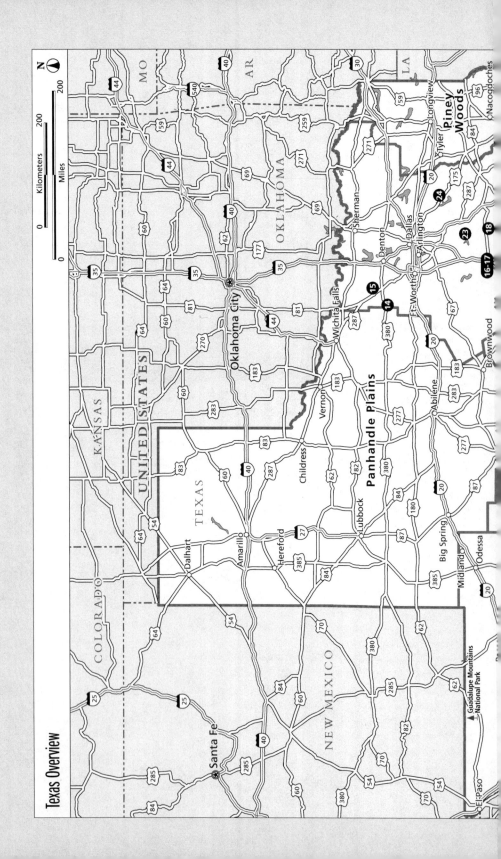

Texas Overview

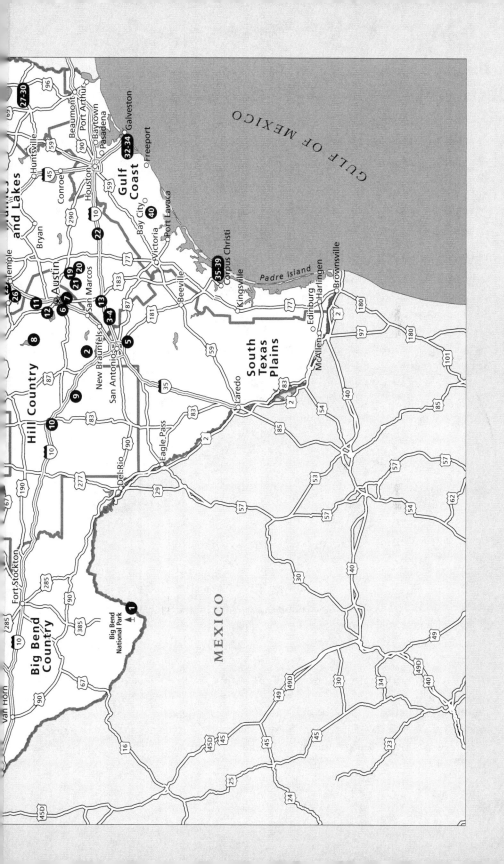

GULF OF MEXICO

MEXICO

Big Bend
Country

Hill Country

South
Texas
Plains

Gulf
Coast

and Lakes

Padre Island

Big Bend
National Park

Van Horn
Fort Stockton
Del Rio
Eagle Pass
Laredo
New Braunfels
San Antonio
San Marcos
Austin
Temple
Bryan
Conroe
Huntsville
Beaumont
Port Arthur
Baytown
Pasadena
Houston
Galveston
Freeport
Bay City
Port Lavaca
Victoria
Beeville
Corpus Christi
Kingsville
McAllen
Edinburg
Harlingen
Brownsville

27-30 **32-34** **35-39** **40** **22** **19** **20** **21** **26** **11** **12** **6** **7** **13** **3-4** **5** **8** **2** **9** **10** **1**

Foreword

I grew up on a slow, muddy stream down on the Texas coast called Oyster Creek. My dad and I built a wooden boat in our garage and I spent every waking moment that I wasn't in school exploring a waterway that was literally at my backdoor. Since those childhood days, now more than fifty years ago, I have run whitewater streams and rivers all over the United States, and in Asia and Antarctica as well. I know with certainty and gratitude that my lifelong love of running rivers goes back to those wonderful days on the creek. One who truly shares that love is Shane Townsend.

I first met Shane when he joined the team here at The Meadows Center for Water and the Environment to help facilitate the creation of a community-based watershed protection plan. During one of the early meetings, I was struck by his unassuming manner, which enabled him to engage people who would otherwise have stayed silent and not voiced their opinions. Shane's easy-going personality makes him immediately likeable, putting people at ease and willing to open up to him. It has occurred to me that this same skill has enabled him to literally navigate all over the state of Texas, negotiating both the tricky currents of our rivers and streams and our many and diverse cultures as well.

Once a Peace Corps volunteer who worked on ecotourism projects with native communities in Bolivia's Amazon region, Shane has paddled in Mexico, Bolivia, Thailand, the Philippines, Texas, Virginia, Mississippi, Louisiana, Alabama, Florida, Minnesota, and New York. He is a certified Texas Master Naturalist and winner of Excellence in Craft awards from state and national outdoor writing associations. Most recently, he has initiated a paddling program within the Meadows Center here at Texas State University to collect water quality data. His unique ability to work with people, keen interest in our state's natural resources, and ability to effectively convey information in writing are invaluable for ensuring the sustainable use of our limited water resources.

And his work could not be more timely.

Paddling, which includes kayaking, canoeing, and stand-up paddling, is one of the fastest growing outdoor activities. With more than 3,700 named streams, 15 major rivers, and some 3,300 miles of tidal Gulf Coast shoreline, Texas offers paddling opportunities for a lifetime, from the iconic reaches of the Rio Grande to the backwaters of streams like Oyster Creek.

Paddling Texas complements the growing body of information about water in Texas. The book is a practical guide written for people who are interested in paddling Texas. It highlights forty paddle trips across Texas waterways, including rivers, lakes, streams, and estuaries. His longest trip is Boquillas Canyon on the Rio Grande, at 37 miles; Bastrop State Park Lake is the shortest, at 1 mile. Other parts of the book have an eye toward conservation, stewardship, volunteer opportunities, bird-watching, fishing, hunting, and more.

Oak Bayou, catch of the day

Paddling Texas is a great resource for river rats of all ages. It will help them get out on the water safely, in beautiful places, where they can learn that the waters of our state are a tremendous source of fun, learning, and inspiration, as well as a resource for which they must take responsibility so that that resource will be there for future generations.

— *Dr. Andrew Sansom is the executive director of The Meadows Center for Water & the Environment, and author of* Texas Lost: Vanishing Heritage, Texas Past, Water in Texas: An Introduction, *and other works. Austin, Texas, 2013*

Acknowledgments

Many people made *Paddling Texas* possible. My wife, Abigail, deserves at least half the credit for this book. It was her "Why don't *you* write that book?" that put me on the water for this project; and it was her selfless encouragement and support that kept me there.

Others who deserve my sincerest thanks are Bastrop River Company; Bergheim Campground; Carey Lange; Chris Hackerd, Joseph Dowdy and the rest of the Austin Canoe & Kayak team; Coastal Conservation Association; Cody Ryan Greaney; Corey Miller; Dan Meacham; Dave Brown; Emily Warren; Howell Canoe Livery; JB Hunting Ranch; Julie and Heath Johnson for their support and encouragement; Julie Schweitert; Kathryn Nichols; Kelly Leff; Larue the Blue Canoebaru; Leland at Island Tackle; Linda Rivelis; Linda who served me a chupacabra burger when I needed it most; Lisa Densmore; Marta Newkirk; Melissa Parker; Meredith Blount Miller; Michael Murphy; MOC Kayaks; Outdoor Writers Association of America; Papa Chops Rod & Reel Repair; Professional Outdoor Media Association; Sheryl, George, Bridget, and Georgey Bey; Steven Rivelis; T. J. Greaney; Texas Master Naturalists; Texas Outdoor Writers Association; Texas Parks & Wildlife; Texas Stream Team; ESPN Outdoor Zone; Kimery Duda and the Expedition School; the Matador Network; The Meadows Center for Water and the Environment; Desert Sports; Theodore Roosevelt and the Civilian Conservation Corps for their contributions to America's public lands and outdoor traditions; Tom Harvey; Travis Tidwell; and William Younger.

At FalconGuides, my sincerest appreciation to Jess Haberman for accepting a stranger's e-mail and directing me to John Burbidge (who worked with me to envision the book), and to Katie Benoit Cardoso, Clyde Soles, and the team that dedicated so much time getting the book ready.

A special thank-you to Dr. Andrew Sansom for his contribution to the book and, moreover, for all he has done to conserve the public lands and waters of Texas.

My best estimation is that I've forgotten to mention at least thirty-three people. If you're one of them, call me immediately and we'll barbecue, throw washers, maybe catch a fish, and talk about how I can make it up to you.

Introduction

There is water enough in Texas for a lifetime of paddling. From the canyons of Big Bend National Park to the cypress swamps of Pine Island Bayou, the waters of Texas have something for most every type of paddler and every paddling mood. You might float the diminutive Comal River, argued to be the shortest river in the world. You might dig deep and follow the four-day, 260-mile route of the Texas Water Safari, which *Canoe & Kayak* magazine referred to as "The World's Toughest Canoe Race." Whitewater is here too. Lakes are as well. And, the Texas Gulf Coast is home to sandy beaches, knobby mangroves, and sea grass flats suitable to fix the briny jones of any salty dog.

Texas is home to some of the fastest growing cities in America, and paddling is the fastest growing outdoor sport in the country. The idea is that *Paddling Texas* will serve as a guide for those who are new to either, and to those who already love both. The goal is to remove as many barriers as possible, so *Paddling Texas* features paddling trips through public lands, such as US Army Corps of Engineers lakes and Texas Parks & Wildlife Department parks and paddling trails, because they offer easy access, secure environments, good facilities, good fishing, great wildlife viewing, and beautiful scenery.

Paddling Texas gives recreational paddlers and anglers all the information they'll need to paddle forty of the best trips in Texas: forty fantastic floats through the Lone Star State

If you're in Texas and you want to paddle, this book will help you do it.

Safety and Laws for Paddling Texas

By Melissa Parker, Texas Parks & Wildlife

It is important that paddlers in Texas follow some basic rules and etiquette to stay safe and keep the waters, banks, and shorelines clean and enjoyable for generations to come.

Safety

Basic laws related to paddle craft in Texas require a personal flotation device for each person aboard the vessel, plus an efficient sound-signaling device. If you're going to be out after dark, then a white light source visible from 360 degrees is also required.

To stay safe, some recommendations are:

- Never paddle alone.

- Always file a "float plan"—tell someone where you are going and when you expect to return.

- Check weather forecasts before heading out.

- Carry a map of the stream or a chart of the bay so you can find your location at any time.

- Carry a cell phone or handheld VHF radio for emergencies, as well as a global positioning system (GPS) unit; it can help you stay on track and allow you to give your position to rescuers in an emergency.

- Wear protective footgear and carry plenty of drinking water, sunscreen, and insect repellent.

- Plan your trip so your paddling skills are equal to the water conditions.

Laws and Navigable Water

Navigation of public waterways in Texas is recognized as a public right in the Texas Constitution. In exercising this right, paddlers must be aware that Texas is predominantly a private land state. It is very important to respect adjacent private and public property when paddling on public waterways. Do not trespass or litter, and keep your noise level down.

Be aware that in some areas, especially in smaller, freshwater streams and along banks and shorelines, the boundary between public and private rights may be unclear. If you are not sure about your rights in a particular location, there are some helpful resources online. See the Texas Paddling Trails website at tpwd.state.tx.us/paddling. On the left side of the main page, click the link "What Laws Apply?"

The answer to your question may be in one of the articles on this site, such as "Overview of Laws Regarding the Navigation of Texas Streams," or "If a River Runs Through It, What Law Applies?" In some cases, however, it may be necessary to consult your local game warden or county sheriff. All Texas game wardens are listed by county at tpwd.state.tx.us/warden.

As you will see in *Paddling Texas*, there are myriad choices for paddling in the state; and each location offers a whole different adventure. You can learn more about places to paddle, Texas river laws, where to rent canoes or kayaks, safety information, and river flow gages on the Texas Paddling Trails website. Paddle safely, and enjoy your trip!

STILL: Five Tips for Getting the Most from Your Time in Nature

By David T. Brown, master naturalist

You're reading this because you like being outside. Whether you're paddling Texas, hiking Kilimanjaro, or gardening in your backyard, immersing yourself in nature, in wilderness, is one of the most rewarding experiences that life on Earth can offer. But with modern life and all its expectations, limited vacation time, money concerns, and other issues, time in the wild is all too rare.

Fluorescent bulbs and cubicles have replaced the campfire and cave. And crowded resort pools too often replace slow paddles on quiet rivers. If you're like me, you are reading this because you want more of life's quiet rivers. You want to make the most of the rare time you have in the wild and want to experience more, in that short time, from nature.

As a naturalist and outdoorsman, I've spent a lot of time in wilderness. And I've picked up some efficient tips to make the most of limited time in places where, if you make the effort, you can gain better perspective of our place, as humans, in the natural world. Places where human noise becomes the minority and where nature shows us things we would never know we're missing—things that can have a profound impact on our lives. The paddles outlined in this book will take you to some of those places and things. Following are five simple steps you can take to make the most of your time in the nature you find there.

I call them the STILL guidelines:

Be *Silent*. Nature often whispers more than shouts. So even as you're preparing to launch, shift your volume. Get quiet. If you're with a partner, allow each other the acoustic space to listen more. It will boost your awareness and help you see and literally hear a lot more.

Take your *Time*. Slow down. Go at a natural pace and not the pace of the city. Time isn't about clocks; it's about moments blending into other moments that all contribute to life. Nature is in no rush, because rushing can waste energy. Simply put, you miss things when you're racing.

Follow your *Intuition*. We all have a sense of intuition inside us that, while we may not be able to explain it, gives us greater awareness. Intuition isn't just some mystical thing. It is an evolutionary product that contributes to survival and is the voice of our instincts. It's there for a reason; we just don't use it as often as our ancestors did. Practically speaking, it's rather simple: If you notice something, give it attention, look at it more closely. Don't question or second-guess yourself. If you feel something "off," or conversely, feel like something special is near, follow the other tips in this list, and see what happens. Acknowledging your intuition can greatly enhance your time in nature . . . and it can save your life.

Look. Be aware. Look in all directions: in the trees and grass on all sides, up in the sky, down in the water, and in the dirt. And look closely. Don't feel obligated to overlook the little things or the common things. There is incredible diversity all around you, in the big and the tiny.

Leave no trace. It takes effort for us to leave no trace, and I think nature knows that and rewards our effort. Just by doing simple things like holding onto empty water bottles, bags, and snack wrappers, you are saving nature a lot of trouble. Baby animals just learning to eat tend to ingest anything that looks different than their natural surroundings. And any animal, especially birds and turtles, can get their necks caught in a plastic loop of any kind. Also, plants and animals rely on a fragile ecosystem balance that can be upset by humans who are either unaware or reckless. Be aware, and try to leave the wilderness nicer than it was when you got there.

All of these contribute to an attitude of being *still*. Literally speaking, it is helpful if you can take even five minutes to just not move around. Stay still for a bit: Look, listen, be aware of your own heartbeat as part of the activity of nature, not separate from it. Or take a moment to express gratefulness for the opportunity to be on the water.

You can be still even if you're moving. For example, the first few times you dip a paddle, breathe deeply, calm your mind, and observe the swirling currents that are moving you forward. Just the attitude of mentally listening, more than chattering, can expand your experience. And when you're still, you might be surprised by how you're moved.

GPS Coordinates: An Overview

By Travis Tidwell, angler, biologist, marine scientist
There are several different ways to record latitude (lat) and longitude (long) with GPS. Here is an overview of the most common.

DD MM SS

One of the most common ways is to record the coordinates in degrees, minutes, seconds (DD MM SS). In this case, each degree is divided into 60 minutes, and each minute is divided into 60 seconds. The seconds can be broken down into fractions for a more accurate location. This type of lat/long coordinate is useful for nautical navigation because 1 minute of latitude equals 1 nautical mile (1.15 statute miles) and each second of latitude equals 1/60th of a nautical mile. Note that for longitude, this is only true at the equator because the distance between longitudes decreases as you move north and south of the equator, until all longitudes converge at both the North and South Pole.

DD MM.MMMM

Another way to record lat/long is in decimal minutes (DD MM.MMMM). In this case, the seconds have been converted into fractions of minutes. For example, a coordinate that has 30" (the double prime stands for seconds) converted to decimal minutes would change those seconds to 0.5000 minute because 30" equal one half of a minute.

DD.DDDD

A third way to record lat/long is in decimal degrees (DD.DDDD). In this case, the minutes and seconds have been converted into fractions of a degree. For example, a coordinate with 30' (where the single prime indicates minutes) converted to decimal degrees would express those minutes as 0.5000 degree because 30' equal one half of a degree. Decimal degrees is a useful way of recording coordinates into datasets such as spreadsheets, and for GIS applications.

One note about decimal degrees: Whereas the other ways to record lat/long use N, S, E, and W to denote hemisphere, the decimal degrees format uses positive and negative numbers. Positive latitude coordinates indicate Northern Hemisphere, while negative latitude coordinates denote Southern Hemisphere coordinates. Positive longitude coordinates indicate the Eastern Hemisphere, and negative longitude coordinates indicate the Western Hemisphere.

Which Is Best?

While this book uses decimal minutes, each form of recording lat/long has its own strengths. It really comes down to personal preference as to which way a person likes the coordinates represented. In some cases though, you may receive coordinates in a format that is different from the type you are used to, or prefer. In those cases, there are ways to convert the coordinates into the form you prefer by doing some simple calculations.

CONVERTING COORDINATES

Example 1: To convert degrees, minutes, seconds to decimal minutes:

N32 21'26.87" / W95 59'40.43"

Take the seconds and divide by 60.

Latitude 26.87" ÷ 60 = 0.4478'

Then add to the minutes: 21.4478'

So … N32 21'26.87" = N32 21.4478'

Now do the same for longitude:

40.43" ÷ 60 = 0.6738'

Add to minutes: 59.6738'

So … W95 59'40.42" = W95 59.6738'

Example 2: To convert decimal minutes to degrees, minutes, seconds:

N32 21.4478' / W95 59.6738'

Take the fractions of the minute and multiply by 60.

Latitude: .4478' x 60 = 26.87" (This is your seconds value.)

N32 21.4478' = N32 21' 26.87"

Longitude: .6738' x 60 = 40.43" (This is your seconds value.)

W95 59.6738' = W95 59' 40.43"

Author's note: All outdoors folk should have a working understanding of orienteering using map and compass, GPS, and natural navigation. The trips in this book require a little of each. Those interested in navigation should see *The Natural Navigator* and FalconGuides' *Outward Bound Map & Compass Handbook, Basic Essentials Using GPS,* or *Backpacker magazine's Using a GPS.*

How to Choose a Kayak

Contributed by Kelly Leff, Austin Canoe & Kayak

With so many options on the market today, the difficult question of "Which kayak is right for me?" plagues most first-time buyers. Recommendations and product reviews are a good start, but it really comes down finding your kayak personality.

There are three simple questions you can ask to help determine your kayak personality.

Why do you want it? Fishing, bird-watching, exercise, camping trips?

Where are you going? Lake, river, rapids, ocean?

How will you get it there? Large or small vehicle? Hand carry?

Now you can begin narrowing down which kayak type is right for you by looking at its key components, benefits, and disadvantages.

Recreational (Sit Inside)

Mostly enclosed with a generous cockpit opening. Feature easy entry/exit, stable, handles smoothly, and affordable. Shorter length makes storage/transportation easier. Great for lakes, rivers (no rapids), and coastal areas (no waves).

Recreational (Sit on Top)

Versatile, stable. and easy entry/exit. Great for fishing, snorkeling, swimming, and/or surfing. Available in a variety of lengths.

Day Touring

Similar to the recreational sit-inside kayak. Medium-size, easy to control, and typically with storage for one- or two-day camping trips.

Multiday Touring

Fast, efficient, and ideal for open water. Long, with large storage areas below the deck to stow gear on multiday trips. Tracks well and cuts through water easily.

Inflatables

Small/compact, less expensive, and easy to store. These are typically sit-inside models, but versions for whitewater and pseudo touring are available.

Next, look at the design differences.

Length

The longer the kayak, the faster it will move and the better it will track (stay on a straight line). But that length also makes the kayak harder to maneuver. Additionally, length has a big impact on weight and space requirements for storage and transportation.

Width (Beam)

The wider the kayak, the greater the stability. But narrower kayaks glide through the water with more efficiency.

Hull Shape

Rounded Hull: Rounded edges give the kayak a "torpedo" shape that results in increased speed and more maneuverability.

V-Shaped Hull: The V shape allows the hull to better cut through the water, making the kayak fast and effective at tracking. However, boats with V-shaped hulls are sometimes considered tippy.

Flat Hull: Based on other factors like length, width, and curvature, a flat hull combines stability and maneuverability. Flat hulls also offer great primary stability.

Pontoon Hull (aka Tunnel): Stability is the key feature of the pontoon hulls, which generally has decent tracking. But pontoon hulls aren't known for speed.

Storage Space

Sit-inside kayaks have greater inside-hull storage, and some have water-resistant bulkheads to seal off an area. Sit-on-top kayaks tend to have greater on-deck storage, and many have hatches to access storage in the hull.

With a basic understanding of the types of kayaks on the market and knowing the pros and cons of different design features, you can easily narrow down the selection to find the kayak perfect for you!

How to Choose a Paddle

Contributed by Kelly Leff, Austin Canoe & Kayak

Based on its intended use, there are three main factors to consider when choosing a paddle. Each alters the performance of the paddle and the effort required by the kayaker.

Paddle Size (Length)

The main factors that will influence your paddle length are:

1. Your height

2. Boat width

3. Paddle stroke

Paddles generally come in four sizes: 210 centimeters, 220 centimeters, 230 centimeters, and 240 centimeters. It is nearly impossible to give you a foolproof way to size a paddle, but your height can be used as a starting point and then the paddle length adjusted based on the width of the boat and your stroke.

Methods for Sizing Recreational and Touring Paddles

Method #1: Stand with one arm in the air, and select a paddle that is approximately the same height as your reach. If you do not have a paddle to measure against, you can measure from the floor to as high as your arm can stretch and use this chart to help you.

Arm Height	Paddle Size
</=85"	210cm
86"–89"	220cm
90"–94"	230cm
95"+	240cm

Method #2: Sit on a flat floor and measure your torso length from the floor between your legs to your nose. Use this chart to determine the proper paddle length.

Torso Size	Low Angle Stroke	High Angle Stroke
26"–27"	210cm	210cm
28"–29"	220cm	220cm
30"–31"	230cm	230cm
32"–33"	240cm	240cm
34"+	240cm	240cm

Method #3: This chart is the simplest and sometimes the easiest way to determine paddle length.

Height	Boat Width		
	Under 23"	24"–28"	29"+
Under 5'5"	210cm	230cm	230cm–240cm
5' 5"–5'11"	220cm	230cm	230–240cm
6' +	220–230cm	230cm–240cm	240cm

Paddle Weight

Paddle weight is often overlooked, but can have a substantial impact on the paddler over the course of a day. Most paddlers lift their paddles (stroke) 500 times per mile. A heavier paddle on a long trek can become very exhausting and inefficient. But paddle weight is a personal preference.

Weight per Mile Equation
Paddle Weight (lbs.) x 500 = Pounds Lifted per Mile

Blade Shape/Stiffness

The shaft of a paddle is very important, but the shape and stiffness of the blade can have just as much of an impact on the performance.

The stiffer the blade, the more effort it will take to move the paddle through the water. But a stiffer blade typically displaces more water, propelling you faster. A flexible blade allows more water to spill over the edges, causing a loss in power.

Generally you will see two blade shapes. One is wider and shorter, while the other is longer and narrower. The size is measured in square inches, and while a narrow, longer blade may appear smaller, it oftentimes has more surface area.

The larger the blade, the more surface area you have to work with and the more water you affect. A long, narrow blade allows for a lower orbital stroke, while a wider blade allows for deeper digging. Consult the experts at your paddle sports store for any questions about shaft design and importance.

A Taste of Kayak Fishing

I spotted the flash from the corner of my eye. Something big was hunting the shallows off the river's main current, and it sent fry in mirrored sprays. I back-paddled to slow my float, aligned my bow, and traded paddle for rod. My lure swooped down toward the flitting fish. This was going to be good.

Just then my lure nipped a limb, wrapped three times around another and perched on a third. I swore to myself. The fish fled. Fumbling, I tucked my reel between my knees and paddled toward the overhanging limbs. There, teeter-tottering to free my lure, it hit me: *Fishing and kayaking are the best and the worst of siblings.* There's nothing like it when they work together, but it's also against their natures. Fishing begs for big strikes, surprises, and action—it's always looking for a fight. Kayaking needs balance, fair warning, and no sudden movements.

One demands two hands on the paddle. The other, two on the rod. So there sits the kayak angler—me, the middle child, plopped down with a four-handed job and a balancing act. Neglect the paddle and swim. Or overlook the rod and risk a hook piercing and tetanus shot.

But kayak fishing isn't really so hard, even though my balance isn't particularly good. I can't recall having ever accidentally flipped while fishing. Maybe it's because my dad taught me the two skills separately. When we started fishing from the canoe, I tossed a few rods into Mississippi's Pascagoula River, but we stayed dry.

Here is how you can too:

Technical Instruction and Practice

A basic kayaking class will likely cover paddling, entering and exiting the watercraft, basic water reading skills, and safety. You'll also get time on the water without the distraction of a fishing rod. If you forgo the lessons, launch your kayak from a sandbar. Get your bottom in the seat as quickly and gracefully as you can. Use the first few trips to learn the boat, explore the water, and scout fishing spots. Only bring fishing gear when you are comfortable in the kayak.

Fishing guides are great sources of information and can be found most anywhere. If you'd rather teach yourself, learn to tie a few knots and see how you like it before you buy your gear. Practice fishing from the bank until you're comfortable casting, landing, and releasing fish. Then try fishing from the kayak.

Remember the Basics

Maintain a low center of gravity. Keep yourself and your gear tight to the kayak's centerline. Don't lean heavily to the sides. Move smoothly. Look ahead for rocks, logs, or fishing spots, so you have time to prepare calmly for whatever lies ahead.

Pack Light, Pack Right

Poor gear selection and packing choices can ruin your day. They've ruined a few of mine. Bring what you need and can carry in a comfortable and accessible way. Load your kayak with the heaviest items along the centerline. If the kayak lists, repack.

Casting

Aim the kayak's bow at your target for the most stable casting scenario. Cast forward with your elbow tucked along the boat's centerline. Avoid exaggerated movements. You can cast sideways, but you risk losing accuracy and stability.

Tree Limbs and Tight Lines

I catch a tree limb on every trip. One morning I forgot to pay out the line after hooking a limb. I reached for my paddle; the line tightened and snatched my rod from the boat.

If your hook hangs on something, give out some slack. Otherwise the taut line can set a booby trap. I once saw a tight line send a hook into a guy's neck after he released his lure from a snag. At the hospital the doctor pushed the hook through the other side, clipped the barb and slid the hook out of his neck. They finished him off with a tetanus shot.

Catching

When that big strike comes, instinct screams Rare back! Bury the hook! Instinct will get you wet. The trick is to give a controlled hook set and play the fish to the boat without breaking the centerline or raising your center of gravity too much. Net the fish without leaning over the side of the boat.

Back to my fish story . . . I made two more strokes toward the 100-year-old cypress, then laughed at my tree tangle. A great blue heron stalked the back of the cove.

An easy cast over the bow sent my lure to the base of a cypress knee. Perfect. A congregation of red-eared slider turtles watched from their log pew. Then I felt it. Fish on!

I kept my cool. The boat was steady. I coerced the fish to the kayak with one hand. With the other, I grabbed the net from near my left hip and landed the fish. The reel at my feet, I unclipped the hemostat from my life vest and removed the hook. My camera was tucked near my right hip, making it easy to get a quick photo without distressing the fish. At the water's surface, I cradled the catch. It regained strength and darted off. I rinsed my hands, checked my lure, looked upstream, and picked up the paddle—happy to have the siblings working together and on my side.

Packing for a Paddle Trip

Some paddlers are minimalists, bringing little more than what keeps them afloat and fills their pockets. Others pack their canoes in heaps of gear like giant ice cream scoops. Both extremes can be uncomfortable, so I let conditions dictate and try, like most paddlers, to find balance.

Kayaks are great for day trips, but a canoe suits me best for longer floats. Here are some items to consider when packing:

Float Plan

Study maps, distances, weather, and other information to plan your trip. Create a float plan that includes information about your group, entry and exit points, schedules, likely camping spots, and contact information for local first responders. Give the plan to someone who will take the necessary actions in an emergency. Be sure to monitor your progress against the plan using maps and compass or a GPS unit.

Paddling Gear to Match the Conditions

Thanks to blind trust in my outfitter, a friend and I made a four-day trip down a Bolivian river in little more than an inflatable pool toy. His paddle broke on the first set of rapids; and on the last day, we hit a snag and sunk. Luckily, we only had to swim the last 15 feet of the trip.

When planning your trip, talk to folks at area paddling clubs and outfitters about watercraft, paddles and leashes, clothing, spray skirts, and other gear and accessories they'd recommend for the route you plan to paddle. Their advice will help you choose the right gear for your trip, or the right trip for your gear.

Health and Safety Gear

The US Coast Guard requires all recreational boats to carry a lifejacket for each person aboard. I also sit on a float cushion because it's comfortable, can be used as a pillow, and can be thrown to a troubled swimmer. Nylon rope and an NRS Kayak Rescue Throw Bag are invaluable when you need them. The throw bag is a lifesaving device that you can throw to someone in danger of drowning, without putting yourself in a dangerous position. Other items to include: a hat, sunscreen, sunglasses, bug repellent, first aid kit, hand sanitizer, parachute cord, and toiletries.

Fishing Gear

Fishing is a great partner for paddling and can supplement your provisions. If you plan to fish, check out my suggestions on Matador Network's Essential Packing List for a Fishing Trip (matadornetwork.com/goods/essential-packing-list-for-a-fishing-trip/) and refer to A Taste of Kayak Fishing on page 8 and Packing for a Fishing Trip 101 on page 12.

Bladed Tools

On short trips, a lock-blade pocketknife or a multitool work well for general use. On multiday trips, bring a short machete for cutting fallen wood for fires, a filet knife to use only for preparing fish, and a fixed-blade knife for general use.

Easy Fire Starters

Nothing beats a fire when you're waterlogged. The trick is to start one when you need it most. In a small dry bag, pack a new lighter, tea candles, and strike-anywhere matches you've dipped in wax. Even when dry tinder and kindling are scarce, these three items will help get your fire started.

Headlamps and High-Powered Flashlights

While on a canoe trip down south Mississippi's Red Creek, my dad learned from the radio that a hurricane had developed and was headed toward our hometown. He spent a long night navigating the creek's snags and crooks by headlamp. Bring a small headlamp for convenience, and at least one large flashlight (a Maglite, for example) for candlepower.

Water Shoes

Flip-flops are comfortable and easy to ditch, but they're not very sturdy. Look for a shoe that will protect your feet while portaging, looking for firewood, walking, exploring a gravel bar, or moving across an oyster bed. Water shoes are a must and, sometimes, they are the only thing between you and a visit to the emergency room.

Mesh Bags for Plastic Collection

Plastics are among the greatest polluters of our waterways and, ultimately, our oceans. Take a mesh sack along with you on trips to collect monofilament fishing line, disposable water bottles, and other plastics you find along the way. See 5Gyres.org and NRDC.org/oceans/plastic-ocean/ for more information.

Dry Bags

Dry bags are necessary for keeping gear dry on a trip. They are also great for stowing wet clothing and gear in your vehicle on the ride home.

Travel Guitar

I can't think of anywhere more inspiring than the outdoors, so I often bring a travel guitar on trips. It's small, inexpensive, and packs well in its case. The Martin Backpacker and Washburn Rover are both good options.

Things to Keep in Mind

Conditions should dictate the gear you bring paddling. Climate, terrain, water conditions, and other variables will influence your packing list. When paddling is partnered with other activities, like fishing or camping, what you pack needs to change. Consider food, water, shelter, communication, safety, and the goal of your trip.

Many books are available for those interested in canoeing and kayaking. A bookstore's local authors section often carries books about local waters.

Take only what you need, and refine your gear list after each trip.

Service your equipment before each trip. Bad or broken equipment can put you in real danger.

Paddling and water safety courses are available across the United States. The skills taught in those classes will help you and those around you stay safe.

If you take up paddling, please be an active and dedicated steward to our natural resources.

Packing for a Fishing Trip 101

First published in Matador Network, matadornetwork.com/goods/essential-packing-list-for-a -fishing-trip/.

Ask three fishermen how to get ready for a trip and you'll get four answers.

The idea of fishing is simple: hook, line, and game fish.

The act of fishing though is far more complex. An angler's craft reveals her personality and reflects traditions born of a unique place. One angler sits on an upturned-bucket and uses a cane pole and red worms to take shellcracker from the Pascagoula River. Another casts wooly buggers with a fly rod to wrestle smallmouth bass from under the Nickel Bridge in Virginia's James River. Sculling a dugout canoe, another angler uses a hand line baited with armadillo bits to catch piranha in Bolivia's Rio Pirai.

Whether you're preparing to cast after work or for a five-day float, here are a few things to take along:

Fishing License and Regulations

In the United States, licensing requirements and regulations vary by state. Fishing abroad? Requirements vary by country. For instance, our guide in British Columbia sold licenses on the boat, but in Bolivia, there was no talk of licenses. It's best to check with the local tourism board.

Water and Food

On short trips, a water bottle and snack bar may get you by. Longer trips require more provisions and a water purification system, such as a SteriPEN or iodine tablets.

Gear to Match the Game Fish

Countless species of fish swim the world's waters. There are nearly as many ways to fish for them. Fishing is a broad subject with libraries dedicated to it. Some books teach techniques (for example, fly fishing). Others focus on a species (for example, largemouth bass) or a particular region. The important thing to remember is to let conditions dictate. Get the gear to match your game fish and fishing conditions.

Basic gear includes a fishing rod and reel, a tackle box, line, and some sort of bait. Artificial lures are ready to fish with right out of the box. If you fish with organic bait (for example, worms or minnows) you'll need hooks, sinkers, corks, and swivels, many of which can be stored neatly in film canisters.

Fishing gear (including line and hooks) is specialized. The hook and line intended for freshwater panfish is very different from that used for saltwater king mackerel.

At your local sporting goods store, ask the following questions:

What's biting?

Where?

What are they hitting?

How do I fish it?

Anything else I should know?

Waterproof Bag

Anglers get wet—even when we don't intend to. Use a ziploc bag for your wallet, phone, and other such items. Small dry sacks offer a more environmentally responsible option.

Water Shoes

River rocks are slippery, jetty rocks are sharp, and boat decks are slick. Footwear can prevent puncture wounds, scrapes, and nasty—although potentially comical—spills.

Maps

It's important to know where you are at all times. On short trips, a mental map will do the trick. If preparing for a long or complicated trip, remember you are also packing for a trek and bring the appropriate map, a compass, and/or a GPS unit.

Health and Safety Gear

A hat and sunscreen protect you from the sun. Polarized sunglasses take away the water's glare and improve visibility on the water. A good knife is a must. Other items to carry include a small first aid kit, bug repellent, feminine hygiene products, a cell phone, and biodegradable toilet tissue. When paddling, I take nylon rope and a rescue throw bag.

Camera versus Tape Measure

You just caught the biggest fish ever. Your hands are slippery, your nerves a wreck, and your concentration, shot. A small tape measure gives your tale credence, but not evidence. Consider a waterproof camera. Phone cameras or GoPro cameras are also convenient, and a Nikon D60 digital camera yields great quality.

Pliers and Hemostats

It can be difficult to remove a hook from a fish's mouth. Hemostats work well for small game fish. Needle-nose pliers are good for large and stubbornly hooked fish.

Lanyard

Use a lanyard to carry nail clippers for cutting line and hemostats for removing fish hooks.

Backpack

I carry a backpack with zipping outer pockets and a pocket for water. It's convenient, organized, and doesn't get in the way of fishing.

Things to Keep in Mind

When fishing is partnered with other activities, such as paddling and camping, your packing needs change. Consider food, water, shelter, communication, and safety. Conditions should dictate your gear. Climate, terrain, water conditions, the game fish sought, and other variables will influence your packing list.

As with packing for a paddling trip, check out the local authors section of a bookstore, which usually will carry a couple of books about fishing local waters. Also, local anglers will give you some good information.

Also, as with paddling, take only what you need and refine your gear list after each trip. Service your equipment before each trip. And remember to be an active and dedicated steward to our natural resources.

Tips for a Successful Paddle

Although there's plenty of water to paddle here, Texas was in a serious drought when this guide was researched and written. These trip descriptions cover drought-affected waterways, but the trips are drought resistant. Some waterways, however, will look very different in non-drought years. Be sure to do your homework before heading out on a paddle trip. Again, contact guides, river authorities, or land managers listed in the paddle descriptions to ask about water conditions. It's their job to know the water, and they look at it every day.

Dam releases and flash floods mean water can rise fast, and there is little information about when either will happen. Watch the weather, talk to people whose livelihood depends on the water you want to paddle, do your homework, and prepare.

Always check on *temperature, tide, water levels, water temperament (is the water angry, flooding, etc.), rain, wind, hunting seasons and areas,* and any other variables that may be important before you set out. All of this should inform your decision on whether to paddle and how to approach the paddle. These considerations can make the difference between a great day and a rescue. Do as much homework beforehand as possible, using online resources for Accuweather, Navionix, Weather.com, fish feeding forecast, US Geological Survey, Texas Parks & Wildlife, and others.

Every paddle should be done with a partner and must be done using a *GPS unit and a map.*

Look out for others on the water. In the waterman tradition, we take care of each other. If you're going to be on the water, become part of that tradition.

Hard-soled, close-toed water shoes and UV sunglasses are a must. Buy them. Wear them on every trip. The shoes will protect you from everything from slippery limestone to razor-edged oyster beds that can slice soggy feet like sandwich meat.

When temperatures drop, what would be a reasonable temperature inland can be uncomfortable and dangerous on the water. Protect yourself with a kayak skirt, warm and waterproof gear, and dry bags.

Guitars, drums, and other instruments are essentially just large hollow bodies with an opening that allows them to resonate. Kayaks are the same. When a kayak or canoe hits an oyster bed or something solid, it becomes an instrument that plays music that will send crowds of fish, birds, and other animals fleeing.

Remember, plastics are among the greatest polluters of our waterways and, ultimately, in our oceans. Take a mesh sack along on your trips to collect monofilament fishing line, disposable water bottles, and other plastics you find along the way.

Most important, realize that you are responsible for yourself on the water. There are no guarantees that anyone can help if you get in trouble. Study your route; share your paddle plan; prepare with safety classes; bring the proper gear, including food, water, sunblock, life jackets, sunglasses, and other recommended safety equipment; and pay close attention to landmarks, weather, currents, tides, etc. Also, use natural navigation techniques to stay oriented: Learn how by reading *The Natural Navigator,* which is available at naturalnavigator.com.

If you're a paddler or an angler—or you would like to be—please be a steward to our natural resources and an ambassador for our sport.

How to Use This Guide

Paddling Texas presents forty fantastic floats across the varied waters of The Lone Star State. Each chapter begins with a trip summary followed by an "at a glance" section for your consideration. Trip descriptions highlight waterway attributes to help you select and plan a great outing. The information provided may include:

Length: One-way distance of the route in miles. For lakes, this category will be Size and provide the length and width of the lake and sometimes shoreline and acreage. Angling can affect the listed length of the paddle trips.

Float time: The time it takes to paddle the route at an average pace. Generally it is based on a paddling speed of 2 to 3 mph plus rest breaks. Plan to travel more slowly if your group is large or inexperienced, or if there are difficult rapids to scout or portage, adverse tides, or winds. Paddling time is a matter of mood. Those who fish, paddle slowly. The paddling durations given in this book are in anglers' time.

Difficulty: The general type of skills appropriate for the waterway. For instance, the level of whitewater skills or the ability to perform a self-rescue if capsize occurs on large lakes or ocean waters in rough conditions. Throughout this book, when there is a judgment to make with regard to a paddle's difficulty, I err on the side of caution because beginners and recreational paddlers are the target audience. For example, the International Scale of River Difficulty assigns six levels of difficulty to rapids according to various attributes. In assigning these ratings, I have leaned toward the higher rating when there was some question. Also note that water level is a determinant of the rapids classifications. Not only is high water important; low water levels can reveal steep rock ledges, high drops, and other hazards that would be unseen and, perhaps relatively unimportant, under normal water conditions. It's always very important to talk to local guides or other experts who know the water before you go paddling. Trust them over this or any other book.

Rapids: If rapids exist, this indicates the whitewater class and relative frequency of rapids.

River type: Description of the waterway (e.g. bay, reservoir, etc.)

Current: Subjective gauge of water speed

River gradient: The steepness of the streambed calculated as vertical feet per stream mile.

River gauge: Presents cubic feet per second (CFS) for paddling

Land status: Indicates the general land ownership along the banks as private (no trespassing) or public, such as parks, national forests, or BLM lands.

County: For planning purposes

Nearest city/town: For planning purposes

Boats used: Type of watercraft most frequently used or encountered on this waterway.

Season: Time of year when favorable conditions exist to make the trip. On some streams, rainfall or snowmelt dictates favorable conditions. On other waterways, wind, temperature, or fog may be a greater influence.

Fees and permits: Indicates if money or permit is required to access the waterway.

Maps: Lists detailed maps depicting the waterway. These may include USGS topographic maps, national forest maps, NOAA navigation charts, or local maps. Map illustrations in this book are designed for trip planning to give you a general idea of the water route; they are not meant to be navigational aids. They show only a few of the rapids or navigational concerns.

Contacts: The names, phone numbers, and websites of organizations, agencies, or outfitters that may provide more specific information or answer questions.

Special considerations: Any unusual factors you may encounter that require your attention, planning, or special equipment. You can pay attention before you paddle or pay later when you are delayed or need emergency rescue and/or medical care.

Put-In/Takeout Information: Provides directions for legal approaches to waterways. Some are improved with launch ramps, paved parking, and restrooms. Others are informal sites with roadside parking and streambanks suitable only for hand-carried craft. Most require use fees.

Overview: Describes general features or background information.

Paddle Summary: Describes the suggested route, including some of the features, challenges, or attractions that may be encountered while paddling.

HELP US KEEP THIS GUIDE UP TO DATE

Every effort has been made by the author and editors to make this guide as accurate and useful as possible. However, many things can change after a guide is published—water routes are rerouted, regulations change, techniques evolve, facilities come under new management, etc.

We would appreciate hearing from you concerning your experiences with this guide and how you feel it could be improved and kept up to date. While we may not be able to respond to all comments and suggestions, we'll take them to heart and we'll also make certain to share them with the author. Please send your comments and suggestions to the following address:

Globe Pequot
Reader Response/Editorial Department
246 Goose Lane, Suite 200
Guilford, CT 06437

Or you may e-mail us at:

editorial@falcon.com

Thanks for your input, and happy paddling!

Trip Finder

Best Trips for Scenery
1   Boquillas Canyon Backcountry (Rio Grande)
8   Devil's Waterhole Loop (Inks Lake)
9   Schumacher's Crossing (Guadalupe River)
16 Bosque Bluffs Loop (Bosque River)
36 Redfish Loop (Redfish Bay)

Best Trips for Wildlife
1   Boquillas Canyon Backcountry (Rio Grande)
13 Luling-Zedler Mill Paddling Trail (San Marcos River)
29 Bevilport to Martin Dies Jr. State Park (Angelina and Neches Rivers)
30 B A Steinhagen Lake–Birds to Butch Loop (Neches River)

Best Trips for Fishing
3   Lake Seguin Loop (Guadalupe River)
24 ShareLunker Loop (Purtis Creek Lake)
33 Jenkins Bayou Loop (Galveston Bay)
36 Redfish Loop (Redfish Bay)

Best Trips for Families with Children
6   Red Bud–Barton Creek Loop (Lower Colorado Lake)
8   Devil's Waterhole Loop (Inks Lake)
20 Bass Hog Loop (Buescher Lake)
37 Electric Loop (Corpus Christi Bay)

Trips at a Glance

Trips Under 5 Miles
3   Lake Seguin Loop (Guadalupe River)
8   Devil's Waterhole Loop (Inks Lake)
9   Schumacher's Crossing (Guadalupe River)
12 Sandy Creek's Paddle Hard Loop (Lake Travis)
14 Chupacabra Point Loop (Trinity River at Lake Bridgeport)
15 LBJ Grasslands Loop (Black Creek Reservoir)
16 Bosque Bluffs Loop (Bosque River)
19 New Life Loop (Bastrop State Park Lake)
20 Bass Hog Loop (Buescher Lake)
25 Calamity Jane Loop (Belton Lake on the Leon River)
27 Walnut Slough Loop (Neches River on B A Steinhagen Lake)

Legend

═══(10)═══	Interstate Highway	≋	Boat Ramp
═══(183)═══	US Highway	‿	Bridge
═══(123)═══	State Highway	■	Building/Point of Interest
═[3351]/[FR922]═	County/Forest Road	▲	Campground
───────	Local Road	▲	Campsite
= = = = = = :	Unpaved Road	✪	Capitol
• • • • • • •	Utility/Power Line	—	Dam/Levee
- - - - - - - -	Water Trail	🅿	Parking
· · · · · · · ·	Land Trail	◢	Put-In/Takeout
‖‖‖‖‖‖‖‖‖‖‖	Boardwalk	👣	Ranger Station/Headquarters
–··–··–··–·	International Line	⫽	Rapids
– – · – – · – –	State Line	✺	Scenic View/Viewpoint
───────	Region Line	♠	Small Park
∿∿	Small River/Creek	○	Town/City
-·-·--·-·-	Intermittent Stream	❓	Visitor/Information Center
⁘⁙⁘	Mangrove/Seagrass		
⬭	Body of Water		
▭	National Forest/Park		
⌐ ⌐	State/County Park		

Big Bend

When you think about the Big Bend Region, you're thinking about far west Texas. It's a dry, rugged, stunningly beautiful place wedged between old Mexico and New Mexico. The Big Bend region is home to 800,000-acre Big Bend National Park, 300,000-acre Big Bend Ranch State Park, the Chihuahuan Desert Nature Center, the McDonald Observatory, the Guadalupe Mountains, and a bevy of quirky, historic communities like Terlingua.

The Rio Grande offers some of the finest scenery in the state, if not the world. So, if you have a chance to paddle it, take it. You'll be rewarded with thousand-foot spires, high canyon walls, backcountry solitude, and magnificent night skies. If you only do one trip in *Paddling Texas,* do the Rio Grande in Big Bend National Park. There is nothing like it.

In this section, you will find a perfect Rio Grande, Big Bend, backcountry float.

Rio Grande, floating Boquillas Canyon

1 Boquillas Canyon Backcountry (Rio Grande)

The true measure of a big river's grandeur is not in its volume, but in the cathedral it has, over the millennia, carved into the unholiest of desert places. In Boquillas Canyon, the Rio Grande runs cold, clear, and the color of jade at the foot of 1,200-foot bluffs. Huisache bloom in yellow bursts. Bats pour from crevices at dusk. And candelilla wax mining camps lay dormant on the Mexican bank. The 37-mile Boquillas Canyon float through Big Bend National Park is a rare backcountry paddle that is worthy of experts and fitting for groups with a novice or two. Those new to backcountry camping or paddling should not do this without the company of experienced partners. Desert Sports offers expert service.

Start: Rio Grande Village, Big Bend National Park, N29 10.78'/W102 57.65'
End: Heath Canyon Ranch, N29 27.02'/W102 49.32'
Length: 36.7 miles
Float time: 3–5 days, depending on flow and desire
Difficulty: Moderate to difficult due to backcountry setting, absence of escape routes, sun, strainers, wind, duration
Rapids: Class I/II
River type: Wilderness river running through canyons
Current: Slow to swift, depending on river levels
River gradient: 4.15 feet per mile
River gauge: 54–1,000 cubic feet per second (cfs). Call a guide to confirm. Short portages are required at 54 cfs, but worth it. It's best at less than 200 cfs.
Land status: National park, private
County: Brewster
Nearest city/town: Terlingua
Boats used: Canoes, kayaks; in higher water rafts are an option.

Season: Late summer and early fall. The water is a little lower in late Feb before spring break, but it's really peaceful.
Fees and permits: Big Bend National Park backcountry permit and Lower Canyons release form; Big Bend National Park weekly vehicle access fee; per person Heath Canyon Ranch access fee (call 432-376-2235 for permission). Campers also must get a fire pan and special feces bags (both available from an outfitter), so you can haul out all waste. Talk to a guide or the park for more information.
Maps: TOPO! CD: Texas; USGS Texas, Rio Grande Village, Ernst Valley, Stillwell Crossing; Delorme: Texas Atlas & Gazetteer: page 75
Contact: For information on recreation or river conditions, see the Big Bend Daily Report at nps.gov/bibe/daily_report.htm, call Big Bend National Park headquarters at Panther Junction at (432) 477-2251 or visit nps.gov/bibe/index.htm, or contact Desert Sports at (888) 989-6900 or desertsportstx.com. Call Heath Canyon Ranch at (432) 376-2235 for information about the takeout.

Put-In and Takeout Information

To shuttle point/takeout: From Terlingua, drive northeast on Farm Road 170 south for 4.6 miles. Turn right onto TX 118 south for 21.5 miles. Stay straight on US 385 north for 3 miles. Turn left to remain on US 385 north for 28.4 miles. Turn right onto Farm Road 2627 for 27.9 miles. Take the last left before the La Linda Bridge. A four-wheel-drive vehicle is recommended. Leaving the vehicle overnight is not recommended.

To put-in from takeout: From Heath Canyon Ranch, drive west on Farm Road 2627 for 14 miles. Turn left onto US 385 south for 28.4 miles. At Panther Junction, turn left onto Park Route 12 for 20.4 miles. Turn left at Rio Grande Village in Big Bend National Park.

Overview

The Rio Grande begins in the San Juan Mountains in Colorado, and flows some 1,900 miles south through New Mexico before forming the Mexico–US border and, finally, pouring into the Gulf of Mexico at Brownsville, Texas, and Matamoros, Mexico. The river drains some 176,000 square miles of the countryside in a basin that covers portions of several US states—Colorado, New Mexico, Texas—and Mexican states—Chihuahua, Coahuila, Nuevo Leon, Tamaulipas, and Durango. Thanks to a convoluted equation of sources, tributaries, allocations, and precipitation, nothing could float the length of the Rio Grande, not a leaf. Though it may reach the Gulf of Mexico, says Sally Spener, foreign affairs officer at the International Boundary and Water Commission, parts of the riverbed are bone dry. About 1,200 miles of the Rio Grande make up the southern Texas border.

It is remote. It is beautiful. It is one of the best paddles in Texas. And, there are no guarantees that it will always be here. Paddle it while you can.

Rio Grande, Micah navigating the shallows

Paddle Summary

The 36-mile Boquillas Canyon float is worthy of its own guidebook, six novels, nine dissertations in seven disciplines, at least three films, and lifetimes of dedicated study and contemplation. Here we get 600 words that simply can't convey the experience of floating this river. If you're contemplating your first run of Boquillas Canyon—even if you are top-notch river folk—consider going with a guide, if not for safety or their expertise on the water, for their knowledge and interpretation of place. Anyone who isn't a bona fide river rat should go with an experienced guide. When low, the river doesn't look like much, but it can put an inexperienced or inattentive paddler in a world of hurt quickly. And this is the true wilderness, so if something goes wrong, you only have your fellow paddlers to count on. Call well ahead to plan the trip. Limited backcountry passes are available.

▶ See also: "The Great Unknown of the Rio Grande," a Texas River Guide by Louis F. Aulbach focusing on the Rio Grande; Big Bend river use regulations at nps.gov/bibe/parkmgmt/riverregs.htm; information on planning your trip to Big Bend at nps.gov/bibe/planyourvisit/things2do.htm; and information specifically for backcountry uses at nps.gov/bibe/planyourvisit/backcountry-main.htm.

That's the pitch. We'll use the rest of the words to provide some tips, help you navigate the river, and track your progress, which is no certain undertaking since the canyon walls and general backcountry voodoo here wreak havoc on global positioning systems.

This stretch of river offers one gravel bar after another, riffle upon riffle, and countless Class I/II rapids in its swings and turns. In many long stretches the river slopes several feet. In low water, the new and inattentive do more walking than those who read the river well. Pay attention to sharp turns in the river, where the full volume of the water is forced through narrow stretches that may be only a few feet wide. Here the water accelerates. It crashes into stone walls, churns over submerged trees, or bullies just inches below arms of raking cane. This situation is common—too common to list all the places it might be encountered. You can see these situations coming in plenty time to decide whether to run it or line it. Line it is most often the right answer. For the most part these scenarios are easily addressed. But, taken lightly they can flip the boat, pin you under water, soak your gear, ruin your morning, or otherwise cause problems.

Locals say, "Boquillas is where the wind is born." I'm inclined to believe them; the wind at either end of the canyon can be crippling. On bad days it keeps paddlers from getting into the canyon. At other times, the wind is silent, or it motors you along.

Get to Big Bend National Park a full day before the trip to get permits and handle last-minute preparations. *Note:* Local officials warn against camping or hiking on the Mexican side of the river.

The launch is at the edge of Rio Grande Village, at the end of a long sandy slope. Pull down to the water and unload. Slip the boat into a jade-colored river, which is some 25 feet wide.

At 1.5 miles, the landscape explodes into 50-foot stone cliffs.

At 2.9 miles, the Mexican town of Boquillas del Carmen is on the right.

At 5.6 miles, Boquillas Canyon begins. The river turns and accelerates. Jesus, a vendor from "Boquillas" pueblito, sings and offers hiking sticks, copper scorpions, "paisanos" (roadrunners), and songs. This is a great sandbar for lunch.

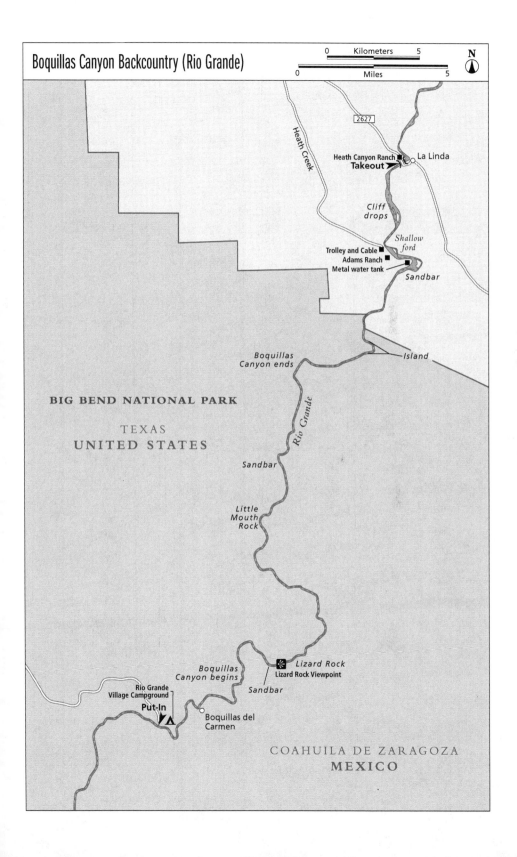

Boquillas Canyon Backcountry (Rio Grande)

0 Kilometers 5
0 Miles 5

N

2627

Heath Creek

Heath Canyon Ranch
Takeout
La Linda

Cliff drops

Shallow ford

Trolley and Cable
Adams Ranch
Metal water tank
Sandbar

Boquillas Canyon ends

Island

BIG BEND NATIONAL PARK

Rio Grande

TEXAS
UNITED STATES

Sandbar

Little Mouth Rock

Lizard Rock
Lizard Rock Viewpoint

Boquillas Canyon begins

Sandbar

Rio Grande Village Campground
Put-In

Boquillas del Carmen

COAHUILA DE ZARAGOZA
MEXICO

FATHER OF BIG BEND: EVERETT TOWNSEND

"I wish you would take a map of the State showing the counties, put your pencil point on the Rio Grande, just where the Brewster and Presidio County line hit that stream; then draw a line due East and at a distance of sixty miles it will again strike the River. My dream is to make the area South of this line into a park and I shall live to see it done."

—Everett Townsend, 1933

Everett Ewing Townsend (1871-1948) was born on October 20, 1871, in Colorado County to Captain William Wallace and Margaret (Long) Townsend.

1891—Joined the Texas Rangers

1893—Appointed deputy US marshal

1894—Tracked a stolen mule into the Chisos Mountains, where he's said to have said that the vista made him "see God as he had never seen Him before."

1918—Elected Brewster County sheriff

1932—Elected representative to the Texas Legislature

1933—Coauthored a bill creating Texas Canyons State Park

1934—Found water in the Chisos Mountains for a Civilian Conservation Corps camp that would build Big Bend State Park

1943—Realized his dream when Governor Coke Stevenson transferred 750,000 acres to the National Park Service

1944—Appointed US commissioner for Big Bend National Park

1948—Died at age 77

1954—Posthumously awarded an honorary park ranger commission on the tenth anniversary of Big Bend National Park's establishment

Even today, only 1 percent of land in Texas is accessible to the public. Over many years, countless people fought to create and preserve Big Bend National Park—a uniquely beautiful place accessible to people from all walks of life. Townsend Point is named in honor of Everett Townsend's commitment to that cause.

Townsend Point Details
Elevation: 7,580 feet
Rank: 19 in Texas; 2 in Big Bend National Park (behind Emory Peak at 7,825 feet)
County: Brewster
Quad: Emory Peak
Coordinates: N29 14.310' / W103 17.436'

At 8.9 miles, a bar of sand and gravel is on the left, with plenty of good camping and firewood.

At 9.25 miles, a good sandbar to camp at is on the left. It has two canyon views from inside the bend.

Mile 9.8 offers the first view of Lizard Rock.

Mile 10.4 marks the base of Lizard Rock. There's a gravel bar on left. The river bends right and then sharply left, then right and left in a Class II with a strainer. Line this. We did not, and the GPS took a swim. Distances and locations from this point reflect that loss.

At mile 18.2, a 30-foot, mouth-shaped stone bites out over the water. Paddle under it.

At about 18.5 miles, the Rabbit Ears formation is on the left. Check out all the animal prints here.

After the long straightaway with a strong headwind, the river seems to end. It's in a left turn. Little Mouth Rock, a large rock formation, resembles a bird mouth.

At 20.5 miles, the bar on the left is a good campground.

At 24.6 miles, the canyon ends. The high canyon wall peaks and drops into flats and the rolling landscape in Mexico. By the next bend, the US side of the canyon has done the same. Big sky. Hot sun. A low mountain makes the horizon ahead.

At 27.1 miles, an island is in the river. Line it to the right.

At 27.7 miles reach another an island. Line it to the right.

At 31 miles, a metal water tank is on the left.

At 31.2 miles is a shallow ford. Look back and see the water tank and the brown ranch house.

Note: There aren't many good camping sites in this area. Some of the bars look good, but they're too muddy.

At 32.2 miles, the left bank offers a good sandbar. The formation on the right resembles an office building. This is about a mile upstream from Adams Ranch. Do not camp at Adams Ranch.

At 33.3 miles, a trolley and cable runs from limestone bluffs across the river. Wind here can be your nemesis or your lover. Heath Creek is to the left.

At 33.7 miles, reach an island. Go right.

At 34.8 miles, reach another island. Line it to the left. On the right the cliffs have ended. On the left are 200-foot cliffs.

At 35.3 miles, the wall drops from 200 feet to 100 feet on the left.

At 36.7 miles, reach the Farm Road 2627 bridge. The low, cobbled bank on the left is one of two exit points. The final exit is 200 yards down, before the base of the industrial complex and to the left of an island and rapids.

If you miss this, you have several more days of paddling to do.

Paddle Information

Organizations

Rio Grande Institute, 3811 Bee Cave Rd. Suite 205, Austin, TX 78746; (512) 422-8200; riogrande.org. This nonprofit organization is focused on all things Rio Grande. Their mission: "The Rio Grande Institute is working to foster appreciation of the unique economic, cultural, and natural resources of the Rio Grande/Rio Bravo border and to facilitate informed action to conserve those resources and use them for the public good."

Contact / Outfitter

Panther Junction Visitor Center, PO Box 129, Big Bend National Park, TX 79834; (432) 477-2251; nps.gov/bibe/index.htm. Stop in for information, books, backcountry permits, and insights on the river and Big Bend National Park.

Desert Sports, PO Box 448, Terlingua, TX 79852; (888) 989-6900 (toll-free); desertsportstx.com—These guys are professionals. They are Big Bend and Rio Grande experts. Even if you're a top-notch paddler, it's worth teaming up with these guys for the Boquillas Canyon float because of what they bring in knowledge of local and natural history. They also offer boat and gear rentals and shuttles.

Local Information

Alpine Texas Chamber of Commerce, 106 N. 3rd St., Alpine, TX 79830; (800) 561-3712; alpinetexas.com.

Visit Big Bend (Brewster County Tourism Council), Brewster County Courthouse, 201 W Avenue, East Alpine, TX 79830; (432) 837-3366; visitbigbend.com. Check out this site to plan your visit. There's a lot to do in and around Big Bend National Park.

Local Events / Attractions

Ghost Town of Terlingua, Terlingua, TX 79852; ghosttowntexas.com. You'll understand once you get there. Plan to stay a few days.

Terlingua International Chili Championship, Terlingua, TX 79852; chili.org. Get a bowl of west Texas!

South Texas Plains

The South Texas Plains region stretches from hill country to the Gulf Coast across some 28,000 square miles and thirty counties. The brushy, humid region hosts six major rivers: the Guadalupe, San Antonio, Nueces, Lavaca, and Rio Grande. It is also home to attractions such as the World Birding Center, and many state and local parks, including the Bentsen–Rio Grande Valley State Park, Choke Canyon State Park, Estero Llano Grande State Park, Falcon State Park, Goliad State Park & Historic Site, Lake Casa Blanca International State Park, Mission Rosario State Historic Site, and Resaca de la Palma State Park. There is plenty of opportunity to fill days with paddling, camping, hiking, cycling, birding, and sightseeing.

In this section, you'll find trips along the Guadalupe River and on Victor Braunig Lake.

Guadalupe Lake Nolte Seguin, at the put-in and takeout

2 Bergheim Campground to Guadalupe River State Park (Guadalupe River)

In the land of 100-degree days and 60-degree waters, the Guadalupe River is a highly regarded head-dunking destination. It curls cellophane-clear and popsicle-cold around ancient cypress. It tumbles over limestone ledges. And it rests in shady pools. Paddle the 8.6-mile stretch above Guadalupe River State Park and run Class II rapids, cast for Guadalupe bass, or photograph wildlife. The park offers kid-friendly swim areas, hiking trails, and a Saturday tour of Honey Creek State Natural Area.

Start: Bergheim Campground, N29 53.56'/W98 33.48'
End: Guadalupe River State Park, N29 52.56'/W98 29.19'
Length: 8.6 miles
Float time: 3–5 hours, depending on flow and effort
Difficulty: Moderate due to the need to navigate several small rapids
Rapids: Countless Class I; two Class II/III
River type: Dam-controlled river
Current: Moderate to swift
River gradient: 4.2 feet per mile

River gauge: 45–1,000 cubic feet per second to run
Land status: State park and private
County: Kendall
Nearest city/town: Boerne
Boats used: Canoes, kayaks, tubes
Season: Year-round
Fees and permits: A fee is charged to access the state park. For shuttle/rental prices, call Bergheim Campground at (830) 336-2235.
Maps: TOPO! Texas; USGS Bergheim TX; DeLorme: Texas Atlas & Gazetteer: page 68

Put-In and Takeout Information

To shuttle point/takeout: From Boerne, follow TX 46 east for 10.2 miles. Turn left onto Farm Road 3351 for 4.9 miles. Look for a line of kayaks set back from the roadside. Turn right onto White Water Road and enter Bergheim Campground.

To put-in from takeout: From Guadalupe River State Park, take State Park Road 31 and turn right onto TX 46 west for 3.0 miles. Turn right onto Farm Road 3351 for 4.9 miles. Look for a line of kayaks set back from the roadside. Turn right onto White Water Road and enter Bergheim Campground.

Overview

Guadalupe River is one of the most scenic rivers in Texas. It is also a river of a forked origin. Its north fork emerges about 4 miles from the Kerr County–Real County line. From here it flows some 20 miles toward the town of Hunt. The south fork of the Guadalupe River begins near the intersection of TX 39 and Farm Road 187, and runs some 20 miles northward. The confluence of the north and south forks of the Guadalupe River is near Hunt. The Guadalupe River continues another 230 miles to

Guadalupe Boerne, Guadalupe River State Park near takeout

its mouth on San Antonio Bay. Along the way, it drains 6,000 square miles and runs from the high limestone bluffs of the Edwards Plateau to the low coastal plains. The path of the Guadalupe River is home to a single major reservoir (Canyon Reservoir), and a succession of smaller ones. The river offers great opportunities for paddling, fishing, wildlife viewing, photography, tubing, and other activities. The river is also home to 1,900-acre Guadalupe River State Park, in Kendall and Comal Counties.

Paddle Summary

Stop at Bergheim Campground to pay your fees, arrange your shuttle, and get the scoop on the river conditions. Ask about "Rock Pile Rapid" and "Dogleg Rapid." The put-in is just below the Farm Road 3351 bridge, on a grass-and-gravel bank that slides into a cypress-lined pool 20 yards across and 50 yards long. Park in the center of the looping drive. Walk to the creek and slide the boat into the pool. Turn left to head downstream.

▶ **When the water is really low, it exposes the craggy limestone river bottom, which in places can drop several feet. Scope out the path ahead. If you're not comfortable, line it.**

Ahead the river widens and slows, then narrows and hastens, beginning a pattern repeated a thousand times. For the duration, the river bottom and banks are various iterations of limestone—some smooth, others craggy, all beautiful. Armies of cypress stand along the banks; their limbs reach for one another like the Arch of Sabers at a military wedding. Deer wade. Hawks, songbirds, herons, and waterfowl are common companions. The waters are filled with game sunfish and Guadalupe bass. The hills are filled with wildlife. Every turn of the river, and half the straightaways, present a riffle or a Class I rapid. They change with the water level. They are easy to navigate and too numerous to count. The more notable, for either navigating the river or tracking float progress, are included below.

▶ **No one knows this stretch of river like the people at Guadalupe River State Park or the Bergheim Campground. Learn as much as you can from them before you get on the river.**

At 0.4 mile, a gravel island splits the river. Bear right.

At 1.25 miles, a creek enters on the left and runs beneath a puckered limestone lip that reaches nearly to midstream. Fern and lichen grow on the stone wall. The creek dwindles into nothing as it moves inland.

At 1.3 miles is a 30-yard Class II/III rapid (depending on water levels). Err on the side of caution and line it. Or, scout before running it. At 45 cfs, the river abruptly drops 3 feet. It would be easy to get sideways and flood. Enter the rapid on the left, cut hard right into an eddy, then turn left hard to drop the fall.

At 1.7 miles, a dry creek enters from the right.

At 2.9 miles, a Class I rapid is to the left and a Class II/III rapid (depending on water levels) is to the right. Approach from the left and work through the shallows gradually. When the river is running at 45 cfs, the rapid along the right bank immediately drops 3 feet and turns a hard left across the main river current. Take the left path.

At 3.7 miles, a dry creek enters on the right.

At 3.9 miles, the Edge Falls Road bridge crosses the river. Immediate after the bridge is a Class I rapid and debris pile. Approach from the right bank. Once beyond the bridge, cut diagonally to the left side of the river for the best path.

At 4.4 miles, a creek enters on the right.

At 4.6 miles, a dry creek enters from the right.

At 5.7 miles, a dry creek is on the left.

At 6.4 miles, a 100-yard stretch of large boulders is in the riverbed. It is easy to navigate.

At 7.1 miles, a culvert is on the left.

At 7.9 miles, a log jam is on the right and a narrow pass on the left. Go left.

At 8.1 miles, some house-size boulders are in the middle of the river. Pass on either side.

At 8.5 miles is a rope swing. Ahead is a 50-foot limestone bluff on the left bank. Don't pass this wall.

Bergheim Campground to Guadalupe River State Park (Guadalupe River)

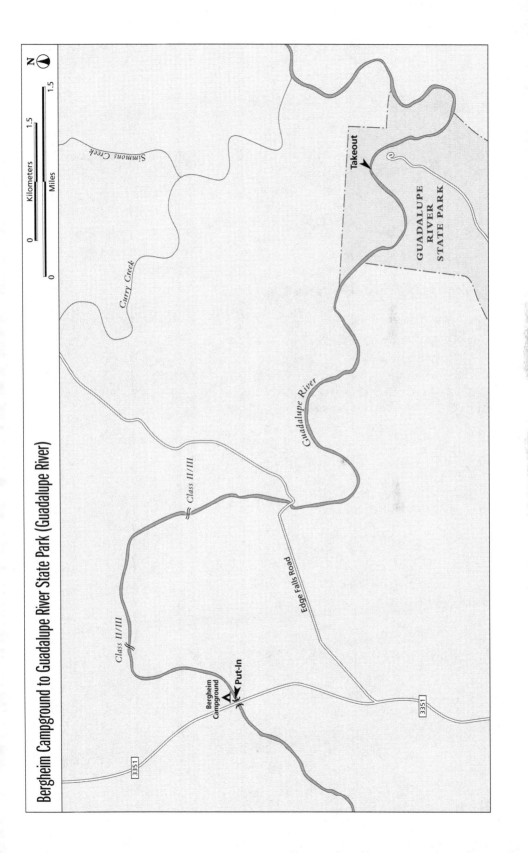

At 8.6 miles, a garbage can is on top of the grass bank on the right. This is the takeout. Climb to the hilltop to see the road where you will be picked up.

Paddle Information

Organizations

Guadalupe Blanco River Authority, General Office, 933 E. Court St., Seguin, TX 78155; (830) 379-5822; gbra.org/conditions/data.aspx. A source for river information.

▶ Want to learn more about the river? Check out Wayne H. McAlister's *Paddling the Guadalupe,* a river guidebook, sponsored by The Meadows Center for Water and the Environment.

Contact/Outfitter

Bergheim Campground, 103 White Water Rd., Boerne, TX 78006; (830) 336-2235; bergheim campground.com. Call about river conditions.

Local Events/Attractions

Boerne Market Days, Main Plaza, 100 N. Main St., Boerne, TX 78006; (210) 844-8193, boernemarketdays.com. This outdoor market tradition stretches back to 1850 and can be experienced on the second weekend of every month.

Cibolo Nature Center & Farm, 140 City Park Rd., Boerne, TX 78006; (830) 249-4616; cibolo.org. This interactive center is dedicated to promoting conservation of natural resources through education and stewardship.

3 Lake Seguin Loop (Guadalupe River)

This 3.8-mile trip through Guadalupe County offers an easy flat-water paddle with good fishing and bird-watching opportunities. Paddle it in January and you'll have a chance to see the reddest cardinal in Texas. The float begins and ends in Max Starcke Park and offers access to recreational opportunities from golf to picnicking. This is one of two paddles in Seguin. They can both be done in a single day. The second paddle is the Lake Nolte Loop. It is highlighted later in the guide.

Start: Max Starcke Park, N29 33.08'/W97 58.30'
End: Max Starcke Park, N29 33.08'/W97 58.30'
Length: 3.8 miles
Float time: 2–4 hours
Difficulty: Easy due to calm, largely protected water
Rapids: None
River type: Dam-controlled river
Current: Mild
River gradient: Not applicable
River gauge: Not applicable
Land status: Municipal park and private

County: Guadalupe
Nearest city/town: Seguin
Boats used: Canoes, kayaks, johnboats, small, motorized craft
Season: Year-round
Fees and permits: None
Maps: TOPO! Texas; USGS Seguin TX; DeLorme: Texas Atlas & Gazetteer: page 78
Special considerations: The water is controlled by an upstream dam and can rise quickly, so before coming to paddle, see gbra.org/conditions/data.aspx or call the Guadalupe–Blanco River Authority at (830) 379-5822.

Put-In and Takeout Information

To put-in/takeout: No shuttle is needed. Put-in and takeout are in the same location. Pass through downtown Seguin on TX 123/South Austin Street. Look for the baseball diamond on the left. On the right is a Max Starcke Park sign. Veer right onto River Drive West. A dog park is on the right. Follow the road toward the water plant, which is clearly labeled "Welcome Max Starcke Park." A blue-and-white Texas Paddling Trail sign is ahead. Turn right. Drive past the parks and recreation office and the Max Starcke Park Golf Course. The road ends at the river. The kayak/canoe launch is behind the blue-and-white Texas Paddling Trails information kiosk.

Overview

One of the most scenic rivers in Texas is the forked Guadalupe River. The river's south fork begins near the intersection of TX 39 and Farm Road 187, and runs some 20 miles northward. Its north fork emerges about 4 miles from the Kerr County–Real County line and flows 20 miles toward the town of Hunt. The confluence of the north and south forks is near Hunt. The river continues 230 miles to San Antonio Bay. It drains 6,000 square miles and runs from the high limestone bluffs of the

Guadalupe Lake Seguin, resident canoe

Edwards Plateau to the low coastal plains. The Guadalupe River hosts a single major reservoir (Canyon Reservoir) and a succession of smaller ones that, along with the main course of the river, offer great opportunities for fishing, paddling, wildlife viewing, photography, tubing and other activities. The river is also home to 1,900-acre Guadalupe River State Park in Kendall and Comal Counties.

Paddle Summary

This trip gives paddlers options: Float it as a standalone; paddle it as one of a pair of trips in a day; or create a Paddle & Putt Party by floating the river and then playing around of golf at the municipal Max Starcke Park Golf Course, which shares the parking lot.

The put-in/takeout is at the base of a set of concrete stairs that leads from near the Texas Paddling Trails signs to the river. At the center of the stairs is a flagpole, which is marked by a plaque reading "National Youth Administration 1937–1938." Carry the boat down the somewhat steep stairs to a 6 by 40-foot concrete platform with a ladder and several metal rings. Slide the boat into the blue-green water and step into the boat.

Lake Seguin Loop (Guadalupe River)

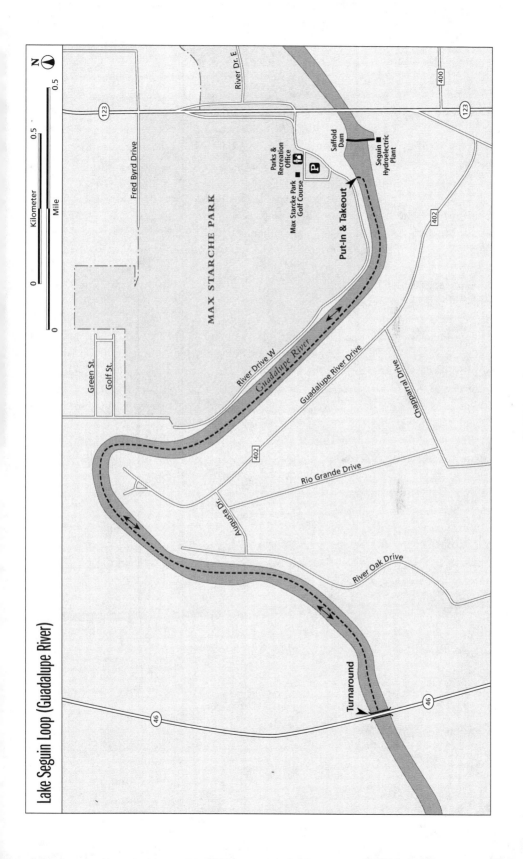

The river is some 40 yards wide. It's deep and slow, so there should be no need to get your feet wet. The swoosh of water falling just downstream will bring your attention to the hydroelectric plant and historic Saffold Dam, the origins of which date back to the 1800s. An orange buoy marks the restricted area that paddlers should avoid. The far bank is lined with docks, cypress, pecans, and other trees that separate the river from manicured lawns and riverside homes. Golf balls ping from the golf course on the right bank.

Turn right and head upstream without concern for the negligible current.

Within a few hundred yards, a cluster of picnic tables marks the end of the park-land on the right. Families fish from the bank and spread blankets and containers across the green slopes. Squirrels bark commentary. At the left bank, pecans hang from limbs, johnboats and rope swings rest, and mallards swim at the foot of 30-foot palms. Some felled trees lay in the water. They do not obstruct the way, but they do offer structure for fish. Cardinals, blue jays, mockingbirds, and tiny brown birds generic in look but brilliant in song work and flitter in and out of brush on the leafy banks and from bamboo stands.

Past the park, homes emerge on the right as the banks lift high. Many johnboats, canoes, kayaks, and pedal boats may be about. When I paddled here, three squirrels played chase and barked around the base of a tree, and a fat black cat watched, seem-ing to contemplate his approach and criticize mine. A 17-foot aluminum boat was wrapped around a cypress tree well above the current water level—a reminder of the quiet river's power.

The reddest cardinal in Texas is in Seguin, and he flits in the brushy banks on the Guadalupe River. Other wildlife includes turtles, deer, great blue herons, teal, wood ducks, and other waterfowl. Fish include Guadalupe bass, catfish, largemouth bass, and sunfish. Along the trip, water vines tangle overhead like a nest of Saigon telephone wires. Stands of bamboo grow in swatches of green and yellow.

At 1.8 miles, a dry creek enters on the left. The current picks up considerably, but not enough to prevent progress.

At 1.9 miles, the TX 46 bridge crosses the river. The river upstream looks a bit more remote and may offer some good fishing and quiet paddling. For this trip, turn around here and head back downstream toward the put-in.

Pass the boat that hangs from the tree. It is now on your left. Look for the picnic tables on the left to mark your reentry to parkland. The orange buoy and whoosh of the waterfall signal the put-in/takeout on the left at 3.8 miles.

Paddle Information

Organizations

Guadalupe–Blanco River Authority, General Office, 933 E. Court St., Seguin, TX 78155; (830) 379-5822; gbra.org/conditions/data.aspx. A source for river information.

Guadalupe Lake Seguin, river near put-in

Seguin Outdoor Learning Center, 1865 US 90 East, Seguin, TX 78155; (830) 379-7652; seguinolc.org. "Our mission is to provide an educational experience for all ages in a natural setting." Hunter's education courses are also offered.

Texas Agricultural Education and Heritage Center, 390 Cordova Rd., Seguin, TX 78155; (830) 379-0933; texagedu.org.

Contact/Outfitter

Austin Canoe & Kayak (ACK), 11604 Stonehollow Dr. #300, Austin, TX 78758; (888) 828-3828; austinkayak.com. Want to rent a boat and take it with you wherever you decide to go? ACK offers boat rentals from locations in Austin, Houston, San Marcos, San Antonio, and Spring. "Take it anywhere you like," says one ACK representative, "Just bring it back."

Local Events/Attractions

Pecan Fest Heritage Days, Tourist Information Center, 116 N. Camp St., Seguin, TX 78155; (800) 580-7322; visitseguin.com. A family event celebrating the area's pecan history and rural heritage.

Max Starcke Park Golf Course, 650 River Dr. West; (830) 401-2490; seguintexas .gov/parks_recreation.

4 Lake Nolte Loop (Guadalupe River)

This 5.3-mile trip through Guadalupe County offers an easy, flat-water paddle with good fishing and bird-watching opportunities. The float begins and ends in Riverside Park, which offers access to recreational opportunities from picnicking to basketball. This is one of two paddles in Seguin. Lake Seguin Loop, featured earlier in the guide, is the other paddle.

Start: Riverview Park, N29 33.51'/W97 57.70'
End: Riverview Park, N29 33.51'/W97 57.70'
Length: 5.3 miles
Float time: 3–4 hours
Difficulty: Easy due to flat water, slow current, and ready access to a residential area
Rapids: None
River type: Dam-controlled river
Current: Mild
River gradient: Not applicable
River gauge: Not applicable
Land status: Park and private
County: Guadalupe

Nearest city/town: Seguin
Boats used: Canoes, kayaks, johnboats, small motorized craft
Season: Year-round
Fees and permits: None
Maps: TOPO! Texas; USGS Seguin TX; DeLorme: Texas Atlas & Gazetteer: page 78
Contact: Riverside Park, (830) 401-2480
Special considerations: The water is controlled by an upstream dam and can rise quickly; before coming to paddle, see gbra .org/conditions/data.aspx or call Guadalupe-Blanco River Authority at (830) 379-5822.

Put-In and Takeout Information

To put-in/takeout: No shuttle is needed. Put-in and takeout are in the same location. Pass through downtown Seguin on TX 123/South Austin Street. Look for the baseball diamond on the left. On the right is a Max Starcke Park sign. Veer right onto River Drive West. A dog park is on the right. Follow the road toward the water plant, which is clearly labeled "Welcome Max Starcke Park." Turn left at the stop sign. Pass under the bridge. Near the baseball complex, turn right onto River Drive East. Pass baseball fields on left and the playground on right. Stay straight and follow the riverbank. Pass the covered basketball courts on left. The kayak and canoe launch is on the right, behind the Texas Paddling Trails sign.

Overview

The scenic Guadalupe River drains 6,000 square miles and runs from the high limestone bluffs of the Edwards Plateau to the low coastal plains. Its north fork emerges 4 miles from the Kerr County–Real County line and flows some 20 miles toward the town of Hunt. The Guadalupe River's south fork rises near the intersection of TX 39 and Farm Road 187 and runs some 20 miles northward. The confluence is near the town of Hunt. From there, the river continues 230 miles to the San Antonio Bay.

The path of the Guadalupe River is home to the 1,900-acre Guadalupe River State Park, Canyon Reservoir, and a succession of smaller reservoirs. The river offers great opportunities for paddling, fishing, wildlife viewing, photography, tubing, and other activities.

Paddle Summary

Lake Nolte (aka Meadow Lake) offers one of two good flat-water paddles on dammed sections of the Guadalupe River in Seguin—the self-proclaimed home of the "World's Largest Pecan." The home of this paddle is Riverview Park, which also offers opportunities for baseball, basketball, picnics, fishing, and other recreational activities. The put-in location is on a low area, alongside a culvert, below a blue-and-white Texas Paddling Trails sign. Park beside the sign and carry the boat some 50 feet downhill to the water. There will likely be bank anglers fishing here, so be mindful of their lines. At the bank, the opaque blue-green water is slow and shallow, but it deepens quickly. The river is about 40 yards wide. On the far side stands a pecan grove.

Find a low spot on the bank and slip into the water. Turn left and head downriver. The public parkland ends some 50 yards down, at a creek on the left. The remainder of the float carries runs slowly through private land, manicured yards, pecan orchards, and under a big, blue Texas sky. Along the way cacti line the ridges, wood ducks swim the brushy banks, and fist-size waterbirds walk on the lily pads with barely a ripple. Kids fish and families paddle along in kayaks, canoes, and pedal boats. The occasional johnboat putts past. Other common

Guadalupe River/Lake Nolte, family fishing

companions include great blue herons, squirrels, songbirds, various ducks, oaks and cypress, turtles, sounds of wind chimes, and Willie Nelson's music from the homes.

The river is used much less in winter, so if you're looking for a cool, quiet paddle, this is a good match. It's a good summer paddle too. Because the current is slow, tubers find this stretch of river less appealing than others.

At 0.8 mile, an octagonal house is on left bank. From here, the sounds of traffic from TX 123 bridge are audible.

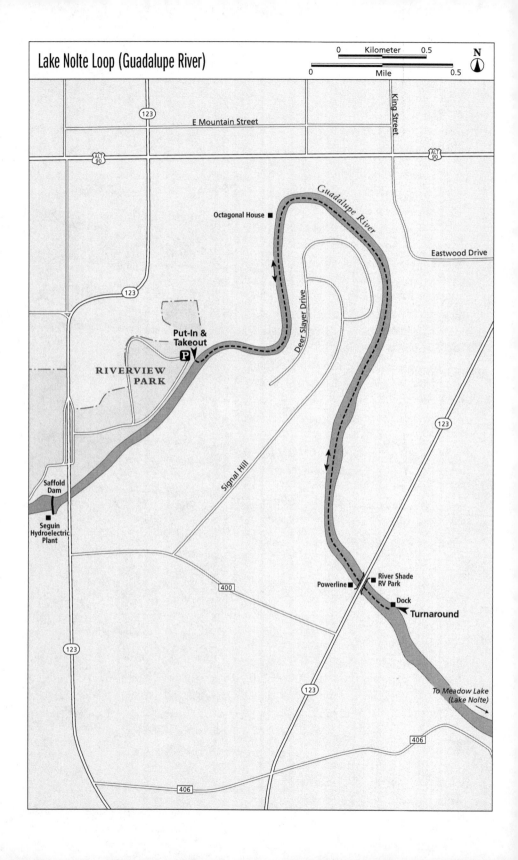

Lake Nolte Loop (Guadalupe River)

0   Kilometer   0.5

0   Mile   0.5

N

123
E Mountain Street
King Street
ALT 90

Guadalupe River
Octagonal House ■
Eastwood Drive

123
Deer Slayer Drive

Put-In &
Takeout
P

RIVERVIEW
PARK

123

Signal Hill

Saffold
Dam

Seguin
Hydroelectric
Plant

400

Powerline ■   River Shade
           ■   RV Park

Dock
■ ► Turnaround

123

123

To Meadow Lake
(Lake Nolte)

406

123

406

At 2.5 miles, the TX 123 bridge crosses the river. Downstream from here appears to be a bit wilder than the upper stretch of this paddle. Just past the TX 123 bridge, River Shade RV Park is on the left. The park offers eighty-seven RV sites and is busy with campers, so expect to see people using the river there. The park also has a store on site that offers fishing supplies, bait, ice, soft drinks, and so on. Turn around at the fishing dock or boat launch and head back to the put-in. The current is slow enough that it is easy to paddle back up stream.

At about 5.3 miles, arrive back at the takeout/put-in.

Paddle Information

Organizations

Guadalupe–Blanco River Authority, General Office, 933 E. Court St., Seguin, TX 78155; (830) 379-5822; gbra.org/conditions/data.aspx. A source for river information.

Seguin Outdoor Learning Center, 1865 US 90 East, Seguin, TX 78155; (830) 379-7652; seguinolc.org. "Our mission is to provide an educational experience for all ages in a natural setting." Hunter's education courses are also offered.

Texas Agricultural Education and Heritage Center, 390 Cordova Rd., Seguin, TX 78155; (830) 379-0933; texagedu.org.

Contact/Outfitter

Austin Canoe & Kayak (ACK), 11604 Stonehollow Dr. #300, Austin, TX 78758; (888) 828-3828; austinkayak.com. Want to rent a boat and take it wherever you decide to go? ACK offers boat rentals from locations in Austin, Houston, San Marcos, San Antonio, and Spring. "Take it anywhere you like," says one ACK representative, "Just bring it back."

Local Events/Attractions

Pecan Fest Heritage Days, Tourist Information Center, 116 North Camp St., Seguin, TX 78155; (800) 580-7322; visitseguin.com. A family event celebrating the area's pecan history and rural heritage.

5 Eagle Loop (Victor Braunig Lake)

On this 5.4-mile, flat-water loop on Victor Braunig Lake, paddlers get a unique opportunity to chase redfish and striped bass or to watch gulls, cormorants, coots, white pelicans, grebes, ibis, osprey, and countless songbirds—maybe even a bald eagle. In calm winds, this trip is suitable for paddlers of any level. When winds are a little higher, fit paddlers can get all the workout they want.

Start: Braunig Lake Park, N29 14.88' / W98 23.63'
End: Braunig Lake Park, N29 14.88' / W98 23.63'
Length: 5.4 miles
Float time: 3–5 hours
Difficulty: Easy to difficult, depending on winds and chop
Rapids: None
River type: Power-plant lake
Current: None
River gradient: Not applicable
River gauge: Not applicable
Land status: Park and private
County: Bexar

Nearest city/town: San Antonio
Boats used: Canoes, kayaks, johnboats, small motorized craft
Season: Year-round. Best when the winds are not strong. Spring and fall offer mildest temperatures.
Fees and permits: Day-use fees are required for adults and children. The boat launch fee is waived for kayaks/canoes.
Maps: TOPO! Texas; USGS Elmendorf TX; DeLorme: Texas Atlas & Gazetteer: page 78
Contact: For information about recreation or water conditions, call Braunig Park at (210) 635-8289.

Put-In and Takeout Information

To put-in/takeout: No shuttle is needed. Put-in and takeout are in the same location. From San Antonio, drive south on I-37 for 3.6 miles. Take exit 125 toward TX 1604 Loop/Anderson Loop for 0.2 mile. Take a right onto the I-37 frontage road for 1.9 miles. Merge right onto I-37 north for 1.3 miles. Take exit 127 toward San Antonio River for 0.1 mile. Veer left onto the I-37 frontage road for 0.4 mile. Turn right onto Donop Road for 0.6 mile. Turn left onto Streich Road for 1.2 miles to Victor Braunig Lake. The boat ramp is on the left, just past the office. (**Tip:** Have exact change for fees.)

Overview

Victor Braunig Lake is part of the San Antonio River basin. It is located on the Calaveras and Chupaderas Creeks, about 17 miles southeast of San Antonio in Bexar County. The 1,350-acre reservoir was impounded in 1964. It reaches depths of 50 feet or more. The reservoir is a source for condenser-cooling water for a steam-electric generating plant for the City of San Antonio. Braunig Lake drains 9 square miles of the surrounding terrain, which is generally flat, loamy, and covered in grass, mesquite,

Braunig Lake, pelicans

cacti, and other flora. The lake is unique in that it offers a chance to catch saltwater red drum (redfish) and hybrid striped bass. The lake hosts Braunig Lake Park, which is owned by CPS Energy and managed by Thousand Trails Management Services, and offers boat ramps and rentals, lighted fishing piers, a fish cleaning station, camp and picnic sites, and restrooms.

Paddle Summary

Stop at the store to pay fees, pick up supplies, and check in on the fishing. The parking lot and boat ramp are on the left when you enter the park. Pull down to the water. The grooved concrete boat ramp offers a gentle slope into a small, protected cove that is lined with marsh grasses. Unload. Park within 100 feet of the launch.

All manner of birds congregate in the cove: gulls, cormorants, coots, white pelicans, grebes, ibis. When I paddled here, an osprey bombed the water and grabbed a wriggling hand-size bluegill. The open lake and tales of recent redfish and striper catches hold promise for anglers. The cove holds fish and most boats race off without fishing it. Note that directly behind the launch is a large metal utility pole and power lines; this will help you navigate back to the launch. Head down the right bank. You will be paddling a counterclockwise loop.

At 0.4 mile, look left to see a water tower and the power plant. On the right, marsh grasses, willows, and young cypress line the banks. Follow the line of white-and-orange "Boats Keep Out" buoys. On the points, bank anglers gather in pickups with rod holders and ice chests and sling surf rods in pursuit of saltwater game fish.

At 0.9 mile, follow the buoys around the point to a grassy, wooded cove. You are still on the right bank of the lake.

At 1.5 miles, Point A on the map, a rocky point and peninsula come into view at point B on the left across the lake. Paddle across open water, pass to the right of Point B, and follow the rock bank. The water shifts in depth from 40 feet to 12 feet. Coots, ducks, pelicans, cormorants, and other birds congregate in the shelter of the leeward bank. On my paddle, a bald eagle landed on a utility pole, hundreds of white pelicans huddled on the water, and some thousand cormorants dotted the banks or craned their serpentine necks from the water as if in a Japanese painting.

Follow the bank to the base of the water tower at mile 2.8. Looking at it with an open mind, the power plant is a beautiful construction in green and tan; it shines with tidy lines and interesting turns that feed a curious mind. Turn around and head back to the rocky Point B. This is the turnaround point of the trip. Pelicans and coots are relatively tolerant so a calm approach can yield a good photograph. Cormorants are less willing to comply.

▶ **Be mindful of the wind direction and speed on Braunig Lake. Wind can pick up quickly here, creating considerable chop and making the paddle back to the put-in a real challenge. If the wind is bad, change your route to paddle with the wind, and you may want to walk back to your vehicle if necessary. If winds are high and the weather cold, use a kayak skirt or another way to protect yourself from the elements.**

After exiting the park, head back toward the interstate. Tom's Burgers & More is on the right, between the Valero gas station and the Days Inn. The cheeseburger combo is something special. It comes with a sho'nuff good cheeseburger, tasty fries, a mini-fried apple pie, and a soft drink. Don't do it everyday; but do it one day. The dress code is camo, Carhartt, or corduroy.

Take a right to round Point B and head to the right. If the wind has picked up, this can be a brutal stretch. The power plant is to the right; head toward it. The water between the plant and the park bank is warmed by a water discharge. Birds here congregate to feed. Fish it. Across from the plant, anglers line the bank with vans, pickups, and PVC rod holders. Turn toward them. Find the utility pole you marked mentally behind the put-in. Follow it back to the launch. Check out the park as you go. It offers picnic tables, camping space, and places to grill, fish from the bank, paddle, or just spend the day.

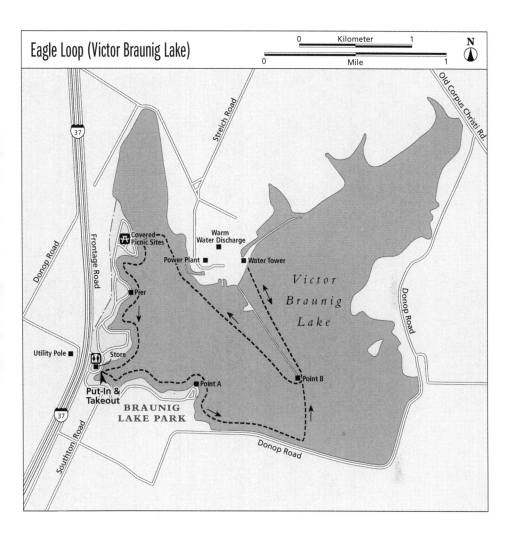

Eagle Loop (Victor Braunig Lake)

(Map labels: 37, Streich Road, Old Corpus Christi Rd, Donop Road, Frontage Road, Covered Picnic Sites, Warm Water Discharge, Power Plant, Water Tower, Pier, Victor Braunig Lake, Utility Pole, Store, Point A, Point B, Put-In & Takeout, BRAUNIG LAKE PARK, 37, Southton Road, Donop Road)

Paddle Information

Organizations

San Antonio River Authority, 100 E. Guenther St., San Antonio, TX 78204; (210) 227-1373; sara-tx.org. This is a great resource for paddlers. The website offers information about water conditions, community activities, and other relevant topics.
Alamo City Rivermen, PO Box 171194, San Antonio, TX 78217; alamocityriver men.org. An open community of paddlers who are "Paddling the fine line between geek and Bubba."

Braunig Lake, kayak angler

Contact / Outfitter

Braunig Lake Park, 17500 Donop Rd., Elmendorf, TX 7811; (210) 635-8289; cpsenergy.com/About_CPS_Energy/Who_We_Are/Lakes/Lake_hours_fees.asp. Call ahead for more information. Open 6 a.m. to 8 p.m.

Austin Canoe & Kayak (ACK), 11604 Stonehollow Dr. #300, Austin, TX 78758; (888) 828-3828; austinkayak.com. Want to rent a boat and take it wherever you decide to go? ACK offers boat rentals from locations in Austin, Houston, San Marcos, San Antonio, and Spring. "Take it anywhere you like," says one ACK representative, "Just bring it back."

Local Events / Attractions

Annual Get Outdoors Event, Mission San Jose, 6701 San Jose Dr., San Antonio, TX 78214; (210) 227-1373; sara-tx.org/events/get_outdoors_event.php. Learn about how your family can get into the great out-of-doors. The event is sponsored by the National Park Service and the San Antonio River Authority.

Hill Country

The Hill Country is the world-famous heart of Texas. Over the years, writers from *Texas Monthly, Southern Living, Canoe & Kayak,* the *New York Times, Fodor, National Geographic,* and many other publications have praised the region for its beauty, culture, wildlife, and food.

The twenty-five-county region features countless springs, rugged limestone hills, granite outcroppings, and swift rivers as cool and clear as you can imagine. They are perfect for a summer day. The region also has more than twenty local and state parks. And, it is home to some of the best post-paddle barbecue in the country.

In this section, you will find floats on the Lower Colorado River, Guadalupe River, South Llano River, and more.

Guadalupe River, fall afternoon

6 Red Bud Isle–Barton Creek Loop (Lower Colorado River)

The Red Bud Isle to Barton Creek loop crawls through natural and constructed scenery, diverse wildlife, and some clear, blue-green water from famed Barton Springs. The lake stays at a nearly constant level and is suitable for all paddlers.

Start: Red Bud Isle, N30 17.484'/W97 47.198'
End: Red Bud Isle, N30 16.05'/W97 44.54'
Length: 6.2 miles
Float time: About 3 hours (more if you are fishing or there are high winds)
Difficulty: Easy
Rapids: None
River type: Reservoir
Current: Often little current, but dependent upon dam release
River gradient: Not applicable
River gauge: Not applicable
Land status: Municipal park and private
County: Travis
Nearest city/town: Austin (aka "Bat City")
Boats used: Canoes, kayaks, johnboats, stand-up paddleboards, rowing boats, inflatable craft
Season: Year-round
Fees and permits: No fees or permits required
Maps: TOPO! Texas; USGS Austin West TX; DeLorme: Texas Atlas & Gazetteer: pages 92–93
Special considerations: Tom Miller Dam, which stands immediately above Red Bud Isle, controls water flows. Release schedules are confidential, but for information about the previous day's scheduled releases and unscheduled releases due to floods, see the Lower Colorado River Association (LCRA) River Report and Flood Summary at http://floodstatus.lcra.org, or call LCRA at (512) 473-3200.

Put-In and Takeout Information

To put-in/takeout: No shuttle required. There is only one location for put-in and takeout. From I-35 southbound in Austin, take exit 234A toward Cesar Chavez/ Holly Streets. Turn right onto 1st/Cesar Chavez Street. Follow Cesar Chavez Street for 2 miles, following signs for Lake Austin Boulevard. Merge onto Lake Austin Boulevard. After 1.7 miles, turn left onto Red Bud Trail. Cross one bridge. At the bottom of the hill, turn left into the parking lot. At the northwest sector of the parking lot, a wide gravel trail leads to the launch.

▶ **Did you know? Texas is home to thirty-three of forty-three species of bats in the United States.**

Overview

Austin's Lady Bird Lake was created in 1960 upon completion of the Longhorn Dam. At 429 feet above sea level, Lady Bird Lake is the last of seven pass-through reservoirs on the Colorado River. At the time of its creation, the lake was known as Town Lake; in 1997, the 468-acre reservoir was renamed in honor of former First Lady Lady Bird Johnson. The reservoir plays an important role in water storage, irrigation,

Lady Bird Lake, Barton Creek stand-up paddle

wildlife habitat, freshwater inflow management for coastal Matagorda Bay, and—in downtown Austin—recreation. Along the length of the lake, paddlers can choose from several access points and several paddling vendors to help get out on the water. The following route will take paddlers around Red Bud Isle, along towering bluffs, downstream to Barton Creek, up to the base of the famed Barton Springs, and back again to Red Bud Isle. (***Note:*** If parking is unavailable at Red Bud Isle, this same route can be approached from several boat rental and river access points.)

Paddle Summary

Red Bud Isle is a popular place for paddlers, anglers, and dog lovers, so arrive early or be prepared to wait for a parking spot. Park smart or earn a fine. At the lot's northwest section, walk the graveled road to the synthetic launch that will not damage a boat. The shallow water here is out of the main current, so launching is simple. From the launch, paddle upstream toward Tom Miller Dam. The route circumnavigates the 13-acre Red Bud Isle. (***Note:*** In high flow, the base of the Tom Miller Dam can present Class II rapids. If going upstream these are easily avoided by hugging the left bank. Or, just turn downstream and enjoy the ride.)

WHY AUSTIN IS KNOWN AS BAT CITY

Austin, Texas, is home to a colony of 1.5 million Mexican free-tailed bats. Most years the colony arrives in March and departs in November for its *vuelta* (return) to Mexico. At about sunset, the bats pour from the belly of the Congress Street Bridge. The hour of flight, or emergence, changes, so check with Bat Conservation International at (512) 327-9721.

If you want a convenient way to watch the emergence, park at the Austin American Statesman parking lot on the river's southern bank. It's free after 6 p.m. An open knoll, ice cream vendors, and an information kiosk dedicated to the bats are along the eastern side of the bridge.

If you're up for more of an adventure, there are canoe and kayak rentals on Lady Bird Lake. For a fee you can paddle into position for a perfect photograph of the flying fox exodus.

The Congress Street Bridge bat experience is unique. Families lounge on blankets. Boat-loads of folks squint into the sunset. Ice cream vendors ring bells. And at dusk, plumes of bats pour across the Austin skyline. There's nothing like it. But, if you prefer a quieter interaction, take a walk on Austin's hike and bike trail system. Many of the bridges you'll encounter are home to bats as well. Here are some telltale signs that bats are under the bridge:

- Strong ammonia odor (you can smell it from atop the bridge, too)
- High-pitched squeaks and chirps
- Dark stripes of accumulated guano on the trail
- Take a look at the concrete seams in the belly of the bridge. Chances are little furry faces will be looking back. (*Tip:* Wear sunglasses when looking up, or else an unwelcome gift may await you.)

Before the dam's orange buoys, the lake opens up to the left into a broad pool where red-eared slider turtles, Texas river cooters, kingfishers, waterfowl, and other wildlife congregate. A pair of bridges marks a swifter current through a stretch of water about 30 yards wide. The grassy eastern edge of the Red Bud Isle park is on the left. Private land is on the right. The stretch runs past the tip of Red Bud Isle and out into the main body of Lady Bird Lake. Aim for the high bluffs on the far bank. The lake opens up to 125 yards, turns east, and offers a crow's flight into downtown Austin.

Any wind in Austin is felt here, so headwinds can be tough. The banks are among the wildest of the paddle. Turtles drop off logs, and periscope their heads and necks. Large bass send baitfish in mirrored sprays. Great blue herons stalk the shallows. Red and yellow flowers grow at the water's edge. Roots dangle like stringy hair.

Hundred-foot bluffs crawl out of the water. Lichen, moss, and scrubby vegetation cling to the craggy high wall, which shines back orange, yellow, black, brown, and

Red Bud Isle–Barton Creek Loop (Lower Colorado River)

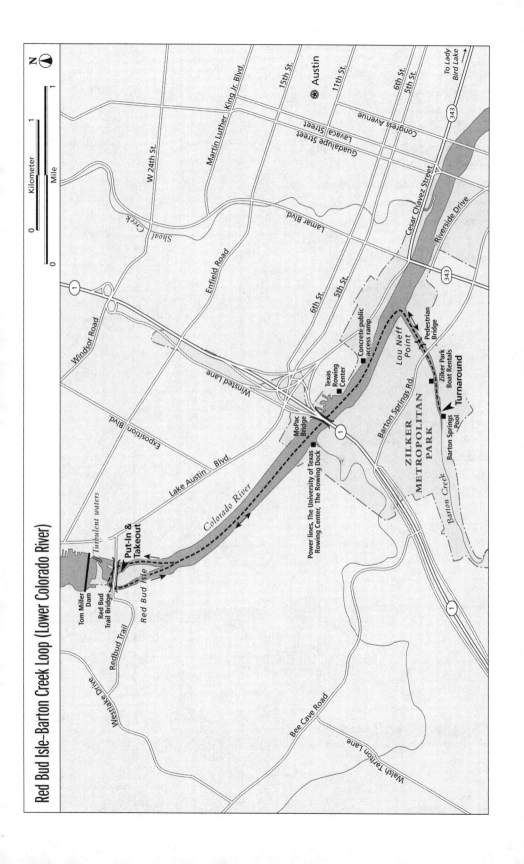

white. On my paddle, a hawk screeched and swept overhead, searching for the birds that hide in the high bank's tangles.

▶ **This urban waterway holds state records for fish caught on a rod and reel: Guadalupe bass (3.06 pounds), common carp (43.75 pounds), American eel (6.45 pounds), northern pike (18.28 pounds), golden redhorse (3.19 pounds), gizzard shad (2.67 pounds), redear sunfish (2.99 pounds), and warmouth (1.30 pounds).**

At 1.7 miles power lines cross the lake. The University of Texas Rowing Center is on the left bank. The Rowing Dock, one of several watercraft outfitters on Lady Bird Lake, is ahead on the right.

At mile 1.9 the MoPac Bridge crosses the lake. In the evenings, nearly year-round, paddlers meet to play kayak rugby under the bridge. Beyond this bridge, a hike-and-bike trail runs along both banks and the paddle changes into more of a community event.

At 2 miles another watercraft outfitter, the Rowing Center, is on the left. The terrain changes. High limestone bluffs shift to lower earthen ridges that trail runners dart along in a blur. Bald cypress line the banks, large enough that four men would likely struggle to link arms around their bases. At some times of year, gulps of cormorants gather on the horizontal limbs at dusk.

A concrete public access ramp enters on the left at 2.3 miles.

Lou Neff Point and Barton Creek enter the lake at 2.6 miles. Enter the creek, which is about 40 yards wide.

Running trails line both banks. People gather to watch rafts of coots, swans, cormorants, teals, grebes, and others. Water in Barton Creek is typically clearer, bluer, and cooler than in the main lake. Ahead, a pair of bridges marks progress toward the turnaround point.

At mile 3.2 Zilker Park Boat Rentals is on the right. Just ahead, at mile 3.3, is the turnaround. This swim hole is a popular—and free—alternative to Barton Springs Pool. This is a great place to go for a swim, to eat, and to recharge before heading back up to Red Bud Isle.

At 6.2 miles arrive back at the put-in.

Paddle Information

Organizations

Colorado River Foundation, PO Box 50029, Austin, TX 78763; (512) 498-1587; coloradoriver.org. Established in 1994, the Colorado River Foundation is the only nonprofit organization dedicated solely to conserving and protecting the Texas Colorado River.

Save Our Springs (S.O.S.) Alliance, PO Box 684881, Austin, TX 78768; (512) 477-2320; sosalliance.org. S.O.S. works to protect Barton Springs, the Edwards Aquifer, and related watersheds.

Contact/Outfitter

Zilker Park Boat Rentals, 2100 Barton Springs Rd., Austin, TX 78746; (512) 478-3852; zilkerboats.com.

Austin Canoe & Kayak (ACK), 11604 Stonehollow Dr. #300, Austin, TX 78758; (888) 828-3828; austinkayak.com. Want to rent a boat and take it wherever you decide to go? ACK offers boat rentals from locations in the cities of Austin, Houston, San Marcos, San Antonio, and Spring. "Take it anywhere you like," says one ACK representative, "Just bring it back."

REI, Austin-Gateway, 9901 N. Capital of Texas Hwy., Suite 200, Austin, TX 78759; (512) 343-5550; rei.com.

Local Events/Attractions

Austin Convention & Visitors Bureau, 209 E. 6th St., Austin; (512) 478-0098; austintexas.org. Find information on hundreds of events in Austin each year.

7 MOC LoCo Float
(Lower Colorado River below Longhorn Dam)

Near downtown Austin, the Colorado River offers a quiet 5.8-mile stretch with easy currents, plentiful wildlife, and some of the best fishing around. Even on weekends, it offers a break from the Lady Bird Lake crowds. Longhorn Dam controls this stretch of the river, which is below Lady Bird Lake. Flows fluctuate and are tied to rainfall and downstream needs, but there is generally enough water for paddlers throughout the year.

Start: MOC Kayaks, N30 15.05'/W97 42.20'
End: Canoe Camp, N30 15.37'/W97 38.06'
Length: 5.8 miles
Float time: 3-4 hours
Difficulty: Easy to moderate, depending upon headwinds, grass, and water levels
Rapids: Class I
River type: Dam-controlled river
Current: Slow to moderate, dependent upon dam release
River gradient: 3.5 feet per mile
River gauge: 80-3,000 cubic feet per second to run river
Land status: Private
County: Travis
Nearest city/town: Austin (aka "Bat City")
Boats used: Canoes, kayaks
Season: Best from Mar to May and Sept to Nov, but enjoyable year-round.

Fees and permits: A water access fee and shuttle fee are charged
Maps: TOPO! Texas; USGS Austin East TX, Montopolis TX; DeLorme: Texas Atlas & Gazetteer: page 69
Contact: MOC Kayaks monitors a river gauge at the launch site and is available at (512) 263-0004 to answer questions about conditions.
Special considerations: Release schedules are confidential, but for information about the previous day's scheduled releases and unscheduled releases due to floods, see the Lower Colorado River Association (LCRA) River Report and Flood Summary at floodstatus.lcra.org, or call LCRA at (512) 473-3200.

Put-In and Takeout Information

To shuttle point/takeout: The takeout and shuttle point are on private land, which is leased by MOC Kayaks. For a fee, the company provides a shuttle service.
To put-in from takeout: From I-35, exit toward Cesar Chavez Street. Turn onto East Cesar Chavez Street and continue for 2 miles. Veer right at Red Bluff Road. MOC Kayaks and the put-in location are on the right, at 4701 Red Bluff Rd.

Overview

The Colorado River is the longest river contained wholly within Texas borders. From its headwaters in Dawson County in western Texas, the river courses some 862

Colorado River below Longhorn Dam, Texas blue and green

miles to the Gulf Coast, where it pours into the briny Matagorda Bay. Along the way it cuts a southeastern route through prairie lands and limestone canyons, juniper-covered hills, and coastal plains.

From its headwaters the river flows unsteadily until its confluence with the Concho River. Some of the best paddling opportunities begin downstream of the confluence in a chain of seven major reservoirs: Lake Buchanan, Inks Lake, Lake LBJ, Lake Marble Falls, Lake Travis, Lake Austin, and Lady Bird Lake. Known as the Highland Lakes system, these reservoirs help meet water needs that range from municipal to industrial, agricultural to recreational. Paddling opportunities continue past the Longhorn Dam, the last in the chain, and through some 290 miles to the coast. Game fish, birds, diverse flora, and a range of wildlife can be found along the way, for the anglers, photographers, and bird watchers of the world.

With its set reservoirs, the Colorado River is not defined by hard-core rapids. However, high water and heat can be dangers. Headwinds, aquatic grass, and low water flows can be hindrances. Before paddling, check with local outfitters about river conditions. The USGS WaterWatch website (waterwatch.usgs.gov) also provides real time stream flow information for the Colorado River and other waterways.

The Lower Colorado River Authority (LCRA) also offers hydrological data at their Hydromet website (hydromet.lcra.org). For information on this stretch of river, choose "Colorado River at Austin" from the pull-down menu.

Paddle Summary

At MOC Kayaks, a boatlift will take your boat to the water while you take the stairs. The put-in is protected from the main current by elephant ears and head-high grasses. Walk the boat downstream to shin-deep waters where hawks hunt overhead, flights of dragonflies drone, and fry dart through grassy shallows.

At the first bend, the river narrows to about 30 yards and picks up the pace to slip past 20-foot cut banks on the right.

At 1 mile an island splits the river. The left route offers Class I rapids and is preferable. The other may not be navigable. Just beyond, bridges for TX 111 and US 183 Montopolis cross at a popular spot for bank anglers. Fallen trees and debris are in the water, but do not obstruct the path and require little effort to navigate. (**Note:** Paddlers interested in a 1-mile trip can exit the river here.) Airplanes from Austin–Bergstrom International Airport pass from the right. Immediately after the bridges, the river splits around a small island and runs under two sets of power lines. The left path is preferable in low water. The river opens up to some 60 yards wide and runs straight and shallow for about 600 yards, offering a nice area for wading.

At 1.9 miles, a concrete form protrudes from the right and sends a 3-foot-diameter pipe across the riverbed. Anglers take note. Then the river deepens and slows. A few bald cypresses join the elms, willows, and sycamores that take turns with sandbars introducing themselves to the water.

At 2.4 miles, metal bulkheads pinch the river to 35 yards but pose no challenges. After a slow bend, the river presents a 0.5-mile straight-away with heavy headwinds.

At 2.6 miles, the white water tower is visible in the distance. This marks the halfway point.

At 2.8 miles, a peninsula and backwater area are on the right. In higher water, this peninsula may become an island. Teal, grebes, and other waterbirds gather here. Texas river cooters, red-eared slider turtles, and spiny soft-shell turtles are here too. Cormorants may dry their wings in a dead tree midriver.

At 3.3 miles, a house is on the left.

At 3.5 miles, a creek enters on the left and creates a broad open area some 200 yards by

▶ Planning to pull your boat through the shallows? Make a towline and handle to save your back and hands. You'll need rope and PVC pipe. Find a 6-foot length of 0.25 inch rope (100 percent nylon kernmantle line is comfortable, strong, and durable, and should be available for a reasonable price per foot). For the handle, get a 4-inch piece of 1-inch-diameter PVC pipe, which may be available at no cost as scrap from a construction site or hardware store. Drill a hole through the pipe. Run the line through the pipe and knot the end. Tie the other end to the bow of your craft.

MOC LoCo Float (Lower Colorado River below Longhorn Dam)

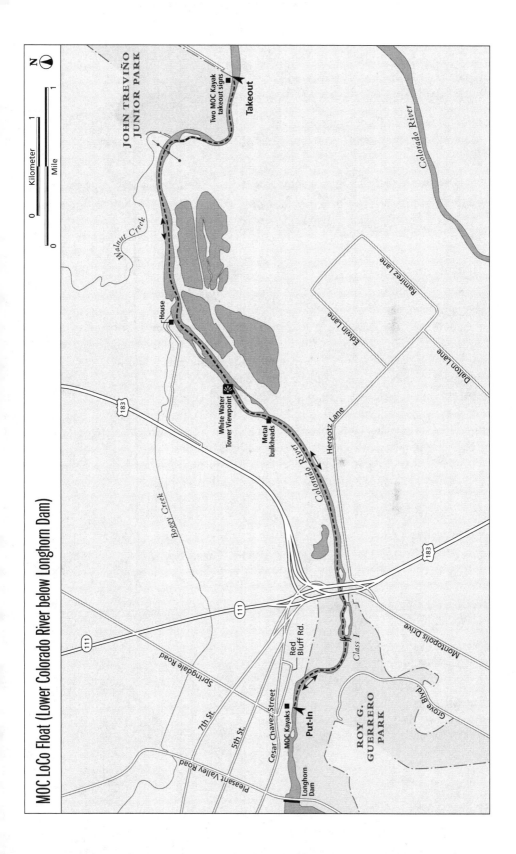

IS AUSTIN HOME TO A MONSTER CARP?

Spend any time talking with people on Lady Bird Lake, just up from the Longhorn Dam, and you might hear tales about Carpy—Austin's Loch Ness Monster. No one has managed to capture it on film, but some credible witnesses—even an Austin mayor—have claimed encounters. *Cyprinus carpio*, the common carp, was introduced to Texas in 1881 as a cheap food source. Common carp are known to live some fifty years and grow to eighty-eight pounds or more. Whether or not Carpy is real, the Lower Colorado River in Austin is now a renowned world-class carp-fishing destination, and the site of a fishy urban legend.

150 yards. Downstream another few yards, the river opens up again. On the far left bank, there is a bulkhead, and water from the treatment facility enters from the pipes. Downstream a hundred yards, thousands of damsel- and dragonflies buzz the water in blurs of metallic blues and greens.

At 4.2 miles, power lines cross the river. When the conditions are right, grass can slow the paddle. Hydrilla grows from the river bottom in light green stalks with star-shaped whorls of darker leaves. The current lays it over in mats at the surface. Sometimes duckweed floats here too. The mats slow the paddle.

At 4.8 miles, a creek enters from the left and is navigable for a short distance. Immediately downstream, an island splits the river. The left navigation moves into a comfortable Class I rapid that stretches a few hundred yards. The right route may not be navigable in low water. Anglers: Fish the cut bank on the right.

At 5.8 miles, two MOC Kayak takeout signs are on the left—one at the water and one in a tree. The number to call for the shuttle is there too. The easy slope is covered in wood chips, which is easy on the footing and on the boat. It will take about 20 minutes for the shuttle to arrive. If you're there in early October, the big pecan tree will have left some treats on the ground for your wait. Feral hogs also enjoy pecans, so pay attention. If you see them coming, make lots of noise.

If you come to a low dam, you've reached the Weir Dam and have passed the takeout by 0.5 a mile.

Paddle Information

Organizations

Colorado River Foundation, PO Box 50029, Austin, TX 78763; (512) 498-1587; coloradoriver.org. Established in 1994, the Colorado River Foundation is the only nonprofit organization dedicated solely to conserving and protecting the Texas Colorado River.

Colorado River below Longhorn Dam, great egret hunting grounds

Contact / Outfitter

MOC Kayaks, 4701 Red Bluff Rd.; (512) 263-0004; mockayaks.com. Trips of 1, 5, and 12 miles available.

Local Events / Attractions

Austin Convention & Visitors Bureau, 209 E. 6th St., Austin, TX 78703; (512) 478-0098; austintexas.org. Find information on hundreds of events in Austin each year.

8 Devil's Waterhole Loop (Inks Lake)

The 2.9-mile flat-water loop through the eastern section of Inks Lake offers access to billion-year-old geological formations, opportunities for fishing and wildlife viewing, and a chance to experience one of the most popular parks in Texas. The lake is kept at a nearly constant level and is suitable for paddlers of all experience levels.

Start: Inks Lake State Park General Store, N30 44.56'/W98 22.03'
End: Inks Lake State Park General Store, N30 44.56'/W98 22.03'
Length: 2.9 miles
Float time: About 2 hours
Difficulty: Easy to moderate, depending on headwinds
Rapids: None
River type: Reservoir
Current: None
River gradient: Not applicable
River gauge: Near constant level (+/- 1 foot); no minimum runnable level
Land status: State park and private
County: Burnet
Nearest city/town: Burnet
Boats used: Canoes, kayaks, johnboats, sailboats, large motorized craft

Season: Year-round. Wildflower viewing is good in March.
Fees and permits: A fee is charged for adults. Children 12 years or younger enter free. Canoes, kayaks, and pedal boats are available for rent by the hour.
Maps: TOPO! Texas; USGS Longhorn Cavern TX; DeLorme: Texas Atlas & Gazetteer: page 69
Special considerations: Buchanan Dam controls water flows into the lake. Water release schedules are confidential, but for information about the previous day's scheduled releases and unscheduled releases due to floods, see the Lower Colorado River Association (LCRA) River Report and Flood Summary at floodstatus.lcra.org, or call LCRA at (512) 473-3200.

Put-In and Takeout Information

To put-in/takeout: No shuttle required. From Burnet, go west 0.3 mile on West Polk Street toward North Water Street. Take TX 29 west for 8.9 miles. Turn left onto Park Road 4 West, and follow it 3.6 miles to Inks Lake State Park at 3630 Park Road 4.

Overview

Inks Lake is the centerpiece in one of the most popular parks in Texas: Inks Lake State Park. At 888 feet above sea level, Inks Lake is the second of seven pass-through reservoirs on the lower Colorado River. At the head of Inks Lake is the 2-mile long Buchanan Dam, which is touted as the longest multiple-arch dam in the United States. At the lake's tail is Inks Dam, which was completed in 1938 as a New Deal flood-control and power-generation project of the LCRA. The lake was named in honor of Roy Inks, an early LCRA leader.

High winds and heavy motorized boat traffic are common on the 831-acre lake. However, several no-wake zones and protected coves will appeal to paddlers, even on the windiest and busiest of days. The following route features the famed Texas swim hole—*Devil's Waterhole*—and takes paddlers through a large, protected, no-wake cove, passes granite outcroppings, and briefly follows the shores of the main lake into a second, more secluded cove, and then back to the launch.

Paddle Summary

Devil's Waterhole may be the most popular paddling destination on Inks Lake, but many of its visitors are late risers. An early morning paddle may be rewarded with a moment of solitude in a uniquely beautiful place.

On the way to the launch, stop at Inks Lake State Park headquarters to pay fees, get a map, and ask questions about lake and weather conditions. The put-in location is on a sandy beach between the busy concrete boat launch and the Inks Lake General Store, which rents watercraft, has a public bathroom, and sells everything from guidebooks to gum. It even has a giant checkers board on the back porch.

A concrete driveway leads to the beach. Unload there and park on the hill near the gazebo. From the launch, scoot out on the leeward side of a peninsula into a no-wake zone that is some 620 yards wide at its broadest. Keep the bank on the right for all but the last stretch of the paddle. Bear right to explore the wind-protected inlet that stretches some 300 yards into the campground and offers views of waterfowl and multicolored tents. In the early morning, a few campers will be

Inks Lake, Devil's Waterhole

casting from the bank, working to pull largemouth bass from the grass line.

At about 0.3 mile, a pier stands on the right. Out of respect for the anglers, stay 100 feet or so from the pier. Continue following the bank toward Spring Creek. On this stretch, couples sit in lawn chairs, drinking coffee and fishing from the bank. Be sure to say, "Morning."

At 0.7 mile, the lake narrows to 100 yards and continues to taper for the approach to Devil's Waterhole, where the lake ends and Spring Creek begins. On the bank, the campground gives way to wilder areas, where multicolored granite shines from outcrops and bluffs.

Mark the heart of Devil's Waterhole at 1 mile. This uniquely beautiful place has a history that stretches back some billion years to the creation of the surrounding gneiss formations. It's easy to imagine the rock's liquid lineage. In places, the rock seems to flow like freshly poured cake batter. A red vein runs through the surrounding smooth dark stone. Elsewhere the rock is pink, pocked, lipped, cracked, or bubbly-burnt like the cheese on school cafeteria pizza.

▶ **Interested in discounted state park access? The annual Texas State Parks Pass allows the cardholder and guests unlimited visits to more than ninety state parks. The pass is available at any Texas state park or by calling the Texas Parks & Wildlife customer service center at (512) 389-8900.**

On the north bank, Chicken Rock and Jump Rock tower over the water, awaiting the next batch of leaping swimmers who come here to cool from the Texas heat, though signs reading "Swim at Own Risk" and "Danger Underwater Hazards" warn against the idea. These granite formations are also worth exploring on foot. Near sunrise, the perches give a quiet and beautifully lit look at an ancient place. Later they may offer a chance to watch the morning awaken the park, as the shine of one yellow kayak becomes the multicolored glow of a flotilla of kayaks, canoes, pedal boats, rainbow-sailed sailboats, and 20-foot craft flying American flags.

After exploring Devil's Waterhole, and perhaps walking down the dry Spring Creek, continue the loop. Hug the right bank to avoid the lines of bank anglers on the left. Mind the granite outcrops on the right. Grebes, kingfishers, coots, great blue herons, and other waterbirds gather here. Follow the shore through a series of inlets on the way toward the main lake. These grassy, tree-lined banks host no campers, so things are quieter, wilder. But headwinds may slow the paddle and speed the need for lunch, especially with smells of burgers coming across the bow. Along the way, downed trees and granite outcrops dot the shore. Head to the mouth of the no-wake zone, where the inlet meets the main lake.

At 1.9 miles, the no-wake zone meets the main lake in a bend that is some 600 yards by 1,400 yards. Winds can be strong here, and boats of 20 feet or more zip around, so hug the bank and bear right to follow the shoreline to the next no-wake inlet, just 300 yards away. Keep watch on the bank for white-tailed deer and other wildlife. The inlet runs about 300 yards back.

At the back of the inlet, beyond the remnants of a barbed-wire fence, wood ducks and other waterfowl gather. After exploring the inlet, turn around, put the bank on

Inks Lake (Devil's Waterhole Loop)

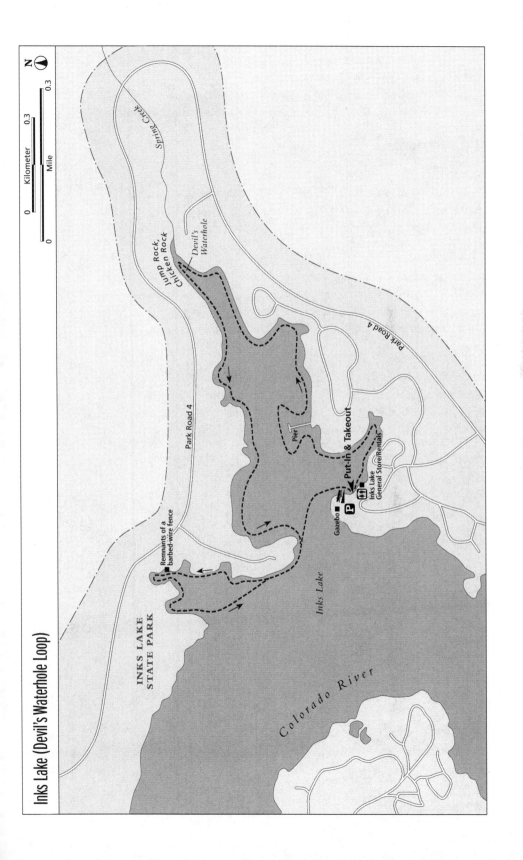

Kilometer 0 — 0.3 — 0.3

Mile 0 — 0.3

N

Spring Creek

Jump Rock, Chicken Rock

Devil's Waterhole

Park Road 4

Park Road 4

Pier

Put-in & Takeout

Inks Lake General Store/Rentals

P

Gazebo

Remnants of a barbed-wire fence

INKS LAKE STATE PARK

Inks Lake

Colorado River

your left shoulder, look for the gazebo near the launch, and head back to the put-in. Arrive back at the put-in at 2.9 miles.

Note: When winds are high, whitecaps can jump up on the main lake and the water can crash over the bow of a kayak, so don't take the lake lightly.

Paddle Information

Organizations

Lake Buchanan–Inks Lake Chamber of Commerce, PO Box 282, 19611 E. TX 29, Buchanan Dam, Texas 78609; (512) 793-2803; buchanan-inks.com. This site offers helpful information for visitors.

Contact / Outfitter

Inks Lake State Park, 3630 Park Road 4 West, Burnet, TX 78611; (800) 792-1112 or (512) 793-4689; tpwd.state.tx.us/state-parks/inks-lake. Canoes and paddleboats are available from the park. Call for more information. Ask about the canoe and kayak basics course, which includes a paddle to Devil's Waterhole.

Local Information

Painted Sky Inn, 1400 CR 128, Burnet, TX 78611; (512) 715-9896; paintedskyinn .com. This great waterfront lodge is about a half-hour's drive from Inks Lake.
Ray's Striper Fishing Guide Service, 319 Lakewood Dr., Burnet, TX 78611; (512) 825-8746; raysstriperguideservice.com. A friendly and skilled Inks Lake guide.

Inks Lake, old anglers in the making

9 Schumacher's Crossing (Guadalupe River)

"This is a beginner's trip because the trip is short. It's also an angler's trip because the fishing is good," says second-generation river guide Corey Miller. The trip is also rugged, so whoever runs it—and everyone should—should prepare for a day that includes flat, calm water, countless beginner-friendly runs, and rugged moonscape drops that are best portaged. Anglers take note: The fishing is great.

Start: Schumacher Crossing, N30 04.13'/W99 19.35'
End: Boat ramp for Ingram Lake, N30 04.40'/W99 15.85'
Length: 3.9 miles
Float time: 3–6 hours, depending on river level and desire
Difficulty: Moderate due to portages and rapids
Rapids: Countless Class I; one Class II, one Class III
River type: Dam-controlled river
Current: Moderate, with swift stretches
River gradient: 16.4 feet per mile
River gauge: 100–1,000 cubic feet per second to run

Land status: Private
County: Kerr
Nearest city/town: Hunt
Boats used: Canoes, kayaks, johnboats in some areas
Season: Year-round. Fall and spring offer mild temperatures.
Fees and permits: None
Maps: TOPO! Texas; USGS Hunt TX; DeLorme: Texas Atlas & Gazetteer: page 68
Contact: For information about river conditions and for help planning your trip, call Corey Miller at (830) 459-2122.

Put-In and Takeout Information

To shuttle point/takeout: From I-10 at Kerrville, take exit 508 for TX 16 toward Kerrville for 0.3 mile. Turn right onto TX 16 for 2.3 miles. Turn right onto TX 27 West/Main Street and follow it for 6.3 miles. Continue onto TX 39 west for 1.6 miles. The Ingram Lake boat ramp is at the bottom of a public driveway, and a parking area is on the left.

To put-in from takeout: From Ingram Lake boat ramp, turn left to go west on TX 39 for 1.7 miles. A stone gateway for Canyon Springs Ranch is on the right. On the left, green-and-white signs mark the Guadalupe River and Schumacher Crossing. Follow the concrete path on the downstream side of the bridge.

River Overview

Guadalupe River is one of the most scenic in Texas. It is also a river of a forked origin. Its north fork emerges about 4 miles from the Kerr County–Real County line, and flows some 20 miles toward the town of Hunt. The south fork of the Guadalupe River begins near the intersection of TX 39 and Farm Road 187, and runs some 20 miles northward. The confluence of the north and south forks is near Hunt. The

▶ **Want to learn more about the river? Check out Wayne H. McAlister's** *Paddling the Guadalupe,* **a river guidebook, sponsored by The Meadows Center for Water and the Environment.**

Guadalupe River continues another 230 miles to its mouth on San Antonio Bay. Along the way, it drains 6,000 square miles, and runs from the high limestone bluffs of the Edwards Plateau to the low coastal plains. The path of the Guadalupe River is home to a single major reservoir (Canyon Reservoir) and a succession of smaller ones. The river offers great opportunities for paddling, fishing, wildlife viewing, photography, tubing, and other activities. The river is also home to 1,900-acre Guadalupe River State Park in Kendall and Comal Counties.

Paddle Summary

Schumacher's Crossing—which has been called one of the top ten swim holes in Texas Hill Country—marks the beginning of this scenic river trip. Park on the concrete drive alongside the access road. Carry the boat to the bridge to launch. The water is as clear as water can be. It's about 6 feet deep and cold. Near the bank, an eddy makes for an easy, step-in launch. Turn downstream and ride the current along banks of manicured greenery and cypress trees so big that three adults would struggle to reach around them.

At 0.3 mile, a phone line crosses the river, and there is an inlet on the right bank. Along the river are many sets of stairs, rope swings, and floating docks. The trees are mostly cypress the girth of 50-gallon drums, and some pecan trees.

At 0.6 mile, a phone line crosses the river. The river is 100 yards wide and the wind is heavy. At least four types of aquatic grasses harass the water's surface. Large bass swim through.

At 0.7 mile, a Class II rapid bends through for 75–100 yards. The river narrows into a small stream running between tightly placed cedars. Limestone rocks rise through the shallow water. The water accelerates enough to

Guadalupe River, carved by water

pin a misguided boat to a rock. Two 18-inch pipes are in the river. The river splits. Going left is not navigable. Consider portaging to the right. If not, scout it and run the swift, narrow, bending path to the right. After a hard right, the river bends hard to the left, drops, and crosses a concrete slab that stretches mostly across the narrow stream. Portage or paddle along the left bank.

At 0.9 mile, the river splits. Follow swifter water through a 6-foot gap to the left to enter a stretch that is about 3 yards wide, shallow, and some 100 yards long. The banks are covered in baseball-size rocks that are perfect for throwing. The bottom of the stream is grassy again.

At 1 mile, the river drops some 4 feet over a 30-yard stretch.

At 1.1 miles, a concrete slab is on the left. Ahead, a beautiful stretch of river drops and curls and bends and churns through a moonscape of river rock. This 100-yard stretch should not be attempted by novice paddlers. As a Class III rapid, this is the most dangerous stretch on this paddle and should be respected as such. Line or portage this section. These rocks are slick, so you'll need water shoes with sticky soles. After this drop, the water turns slow, deep, and calm.

At 1.2 miles, water enters from the right.

At 1.9 miles, pass under power lines.

At 2 miles, Kelly Creek Road crosses the river. Approach the bridge from the right. Pull up and walk across the road to find the shortest portage, which should be some 30 yards. On the other side of the bridge is a series of low dams of stacked rock, which may require a short portage. Sheets of limestone that are some 3 feet thick, 4 feet across, and 6 feet long, lay on the banks.

▶ **Low water levels reveal the river's rocky bottom and uncover obstacles and drops for the paddler. To learn more, talk to Corey Miller of Kerrville Kayak and Canoe when planning your trip.**

At 3.1 miles, the river runs across Rio Vista Road. If the river levels require portaging over the road, expect a slippery path. Approach the road from the left. A power line runs overhead.

At 3.5 miles, water enters from the right. Bear left. (*Note:* If you instead bear right, you'll overshoot the takeout.)

At 3.9 miles, the takeout is on the left. A driveway runs from the road to the river. A knee-high fence of green pipe separates public and private land. A wooden dock with a metal surface is on the left. Take out here.

Paddle Information

Organizations

Guadalupe–Blanco River Authority, General Office, 933 E. Court St., Seguin, TX 78155; (830) 379-5822; gbra.org/conditions/data.aspx. A source for river information.

Schumacher's Crossing (Guadalupe River)

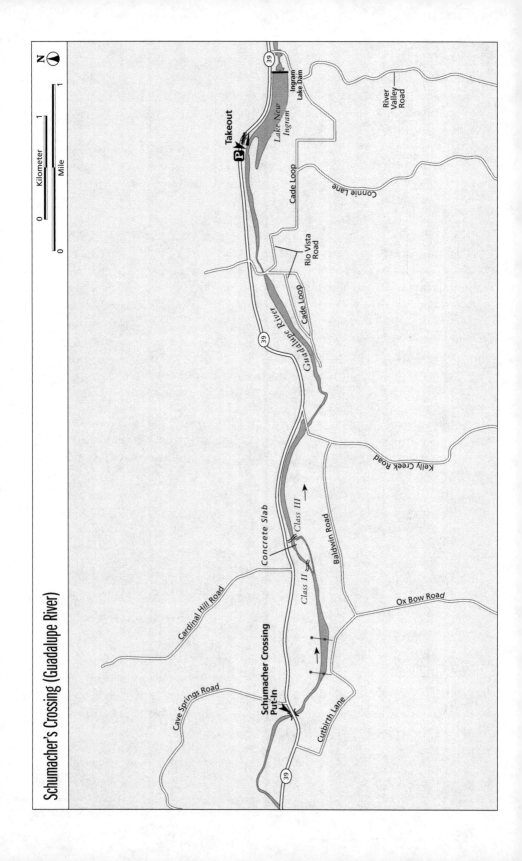

Guadalupe River, easy portage

Contact / Outfitter

Corey Miller, Kerrville Kayak and Canoe, 130 W. Main St., Kerrville, TX 78028; (830) 459-2122; paddlekerrville.com. This company has been in business for two generations. Call ahead to ask Corey about water levels and safety.

Local Events / Attractions

Kerrville Folk Festival, Quiet Valley Ranch, 3876 Medina Hwy., Kerrville, TX 78028; (830) 257-3600; kerrville-music.com. Held for eighteen days in May and June each year, this festival is said to be "the longest continuously running music festival of its kind in North America."

Kerrville Wine & Music Festival (aka "Little Folk"), Quiet Valley Ranch, 3876 Medina Hwy., Kerrville, TX 78028; (830) 257-3600; kerrville-music.com. This three-day event is held on Labor Day weekend each year.

10 South Llano River State Park "700 Springs" Run (South Llano River)

This 7-mile stretch of river likely offers as close to a drought-proof river paddle in Texas Hill Country as you will find. The water runs at a nice clip, and the fishing is fantastic. Bird watchers, photographers, and wildlife lovers will find plenty to keep them busy. Toe-dippers, too, will appreciate the cold water of "700 Springs" on the 100-degree Texas days.

Start: South Llano River State Park, N30 27.01′/W99 48.76′
End: Kimble County River Park, N30 29.21′/W99 45.65′
Length: 7.1 miles
Float time: 3-5 hours
Difficulty: Easy due to length and current. Do pay attention to limbs reaching out from the banks in the outside bends.
Rapids: Countless Class I; one Class I/II
River type: Spring-fed, dam-controlled river
Current: Moderate and swift
River gradient: 4.57 feet per mile
River gauge: 70-700 cubic feet per second to run river

Land status: State park and private
County: Kimble
Nearest city/town: Junction
Boats used: Canoes, kayaks
Season: Year-round. Fishing is very good in October.
Fees and permits: A state park fee is charged; entrance is free with a Texas State Parks Pass
Maps: TOPO! Texas; USGS Junction TX; DeLorme: Texas Atlas & Gazetteer: page 67
Contact: Contact South Llano River State Park, (325) 446-3994, for information about river conditions and details about recreation.

Put-In and Takeout Information

To shuttle point/takeout: From Junction, take TX 481 across the South Llano River. Turn left onto Farm Road 2169. Take the first left on a dirt road that leads into the Kimble County River Park. Drive toward the bridge. The launch is on the right.
To put-in from takeout: From Kimble County River Park, turn right onto Farm Road 2169. Turn right onto TX 481 Loop West for 0.7 miles. Turn left onto US 377/11th Street for 4.3 miles. The entrance to the state park is on the left and marked with a large white sign that reads "South Llano Farms, Pecan & River Co. Groceries Pecan Products Drinks ★ Snacks ★ Ice" and a brown-and-yellow sign that reads "South Llano River State Park Texas Park and Wildlife Department." Turn in and bear left. Note a concrete

▶ The South Llano River is home to the Oktoberfisch fly-fishing festival. For more information see fredericksburgflyfishers.com, write oktober fisch@hotmail.com, or call (830) 998-2477.

South Llano, Shane in shallow water

pad to the left as you approach the river. This is the launch where you may load your boat. Turn left onto State Park Road 73 for 0.3 mile to the park headquarters to check in.

Overview

"We have 700 springs here," outfitter Dan Meacham says. "That's what makes this place special."

The South Llano River carves through the limestone cap of the Edwards Plateau. Springs spill from the coulee walls to feed the river. The woodland is home to walnut, persimmon, hackberry, and oaks, kingfishers, phoebes, wild turkeys, and finches. And, even in the driest times, the South Llano River flows through miles of Hill Country to its confluence with the North Llano River in Kimble County, where it forms the Llano River. The Llano River then flows eastward for some 100 miles to join the Colorado River. The 524-acre South Llano River State Park is located on the South Llano River in Kimble County, southwest of Junction.

Paddle Summary

Visit the park headquarters to pay fees, get information, and buy provisions. The South Llano River Information map is helpful. Ask about the deer, feral hogs, hawks, Rio Grande turkeys, and other wildlife and fish species in the area.

Drive back toward the entrance. Cross the river, then reach the concrete pad on the right. Slip the boat into a small pocket of calm water. Park in the lot across the river.

One stroke puts the bow in fast water. From this point forward, the trip is a river equivalent of Chutes & Ladders, where shallow water zips through bends and slower, wider, deeper, straights give a slower pace.

Paddlers will find lots of shallow water. Some notes on finding the deep path through it:

- Inside bends present the shortest distance, but they can also present shallow water. Stick to the deeper water on the outside bend for the fastest progress and the fewest portages.

- Even when the banks run straight, the deep water may not. Look at limbs, rocks, and other objects in the water, follow the meandering channel.

- Water often jams into the outside bank and runs swiftly along it; beware of brush, limbs, and other protrusions. Be mindful of fishing rods and other objects as you move along.

At 0.5 mile, the river splits around a small island gravel bar. Veer right.

At 0.6 mile, a creek enters from the left. Less than 0.1 mile beyond, the river forks. Veer right.

At 1.2 miles, the river splits around a gravel island. Veer right.

At 1.5 miles, a mobile home is on the left bank.

At 1.6 miles, the river splits around a gravel island. Veer right.

▶ When fishing on the South Llano River, find a lure that won't hang in the rocks on the bottom. Guide Dan Meacham says pink flies, white flies, and brightly colored Road Runner jigs work well.

At 2 miles, an octagonal State Park Boundary sign is on the right bank. Less than 0.1 mile beyond, water enters from the left. Beyond that, power lines cross the river.

At 2.3 miles, water enters from the left.

At 2.7 miles, reach a logjam. Take the 3-foot passage that has been cut to the left. Just beyond is a gravel island. Veer right.

At 3.3 miles, veer right around a gravel island.

At 3.4 miles, water enters from the right.

At 3.7 miles, utility poles are on the left, and power lines overhead.

At 3.9 miles, veer right at a logjam.

At 4.1 miles, veer left at a gravel island.

At 4.9 miles, reach a logjam with a path cut through the middle.

South Llano River State Park "700 Springs" Run (South Llano River)

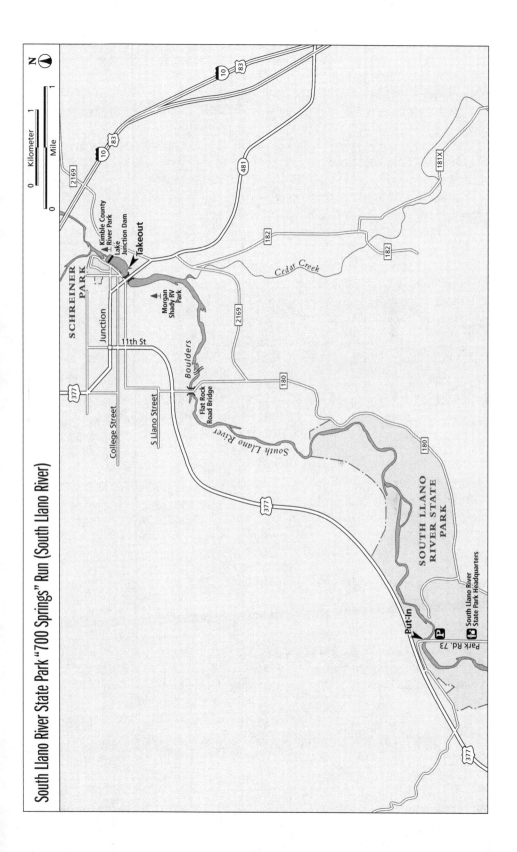

At 5 miles, concrete steps and a private property sign are on the left.

At 5.3 miles, reach Flat Rock Road Bridge. Hug the right bank to pass underneath. A series of limestone tabletops create a Class I/II rapid just below the bridge. Veer right.

At 5.6 miles, a utility pole is on the left, and three communications towers are ahead.

At 5.9 miles, reach a 1-acre bed of brown-stemmed aquatic vegetation. Veer right, watching for deep water. Cut back to the left.

At 6.2 miles, power lines cross the river near a boat dock.

At 6.4 miles, Morgan Shady RV park is on the left. Water enters from the foot of a butte on the right. The river splits around head-high grass ahead. Veer left.

At 6.8 miles, water enters from the right, and the white "Junction" tower is on the left.

At 7 miles, the TX 481 bridge crosses the river. Schreiner Park is on the left. Kimble County River Park is on the right. Ahead is a long drop over a dam. Get to right bank immediately after the bridge.

The takeout is at 7.1 miles, at a concrete boat ramp in the protected slip.

Paddle Information

Organizations

Fredericksburg Fly Fishers, PO Box 3002, Fredericksburg, TX 78624; (830) 456-3593; fredericksburgflyfishers.com. This organization is dedicated to promoting fly fishing, conserving local natural resources, and educating the public about both.

Contact/Outfitter

Meacham Rentals (Dan Meacham), 1214 Main S., Junction, TX 76849; (432) 288-3656; meachamrentals@gmail.com.

South Llano River Canoes & Kayaks (Curtis Thomas), 519 Odessa Road, US 377, Junction, TX 76849; (325) 446-2220; facebook.com/SouthLlanoRiverCanoes.

Local Information

Morgan Shady Park, 600 S. 6th St., Junction, TX 76849; (325) 446-2071; morgan shadypark.com.

Local Events/Attractions

South Llano River State Park, 1927 Park Road 73, Junction, TX 76849; (325) 446-3994, tpwd.state.tx.us/state-parks/south-llano-river.

Annual Kimble County Wild Game Dinner, Coke Stevenson Memorial Center, 440 N. US 83 Hwy 83. Junction, TX 76849; (325) 446-3190. Proceeds of a raffle go to the Kimble County Chamber of Commerce and Junction Volunteer Fire Department.

11 Limestone Loop (Lake Georgetown)

This 7.3-mile float takes paddlers along a fish-laden dam, past rocky points and rugged Hill Country parklands, along limestone bluffs and heavily wooded banks, past boulders the size of cabanas, and back again. The long, narrow lake is a popular weekend boating destination, so it's a great weekday paddle. And, if the wind picks up, there are plenty of protected nooks and tucked-away coves to explore. This paddle gives a taste of a good-size lake and an opportunity for as much of a paddle as you want.

Start: Cedar Breaks Park boat ramp, N30 40.37'/W97 44.08'
End: Cedar Breaks Park boat ramp, N30 40.37'/W97 44.08'
Length: 7.3 miles
Float time: 3-5 hours
Difficulty: Easy to difficult, depending on the wind, boat traffic, and chop
Rapids: None
River type: Reservoir
Current: None
River gradient: Not applicable
River gauge: Not applicable
Land status: Corps of Engineers

County: Williamson
Nearest city/town: Georgetown
Boats used: Canoes, kayaks, johnboats, small motorized craft
Season: Spring, summer, and fall
Fees and permits: Small fee for launching
Maps: TOPO! Texas; USGS Georgetown TX; DeLorme: Texas Atlas & Gazetteer: page 69
Contact: For information about Lake Georgetown's water conditions or recreational opportunities, contact US Army Corps of Engineers at 500 Lake Overlook Dr., Georgetown, TX 78628-4901; (512) 930-5253.

Put-In and Takeout Information

To put-in/takeout: No shuttle is required. There is only one location for put-in and takeout. From I-35 in Georgetown, take TX 29 West/West University Avenue for 1.2 miles. Turn right onto D. B. Wood Road and follow it for 1.9 miles. Turn left onto Cedar Breaks Road for 1.4 miles. Turn left onto Cedar Breaks Park Road. Stop at the security booth to pay the fee. Continue straight for 0.4 mile to the boat ramp.

Overview

Lake Georgetown is located some 4 miles northwest of Georgetown on the north fork of the San Gabriel River. It is part of the Brazos River basin. The US Army Corps of Engineers built the 7,000-foot rock dam in 1978 to control flood waters, to offer recreational opportunities, and to supply water to the surrounding area. The lake, which has a surface area of about 8 square miles, drains some 250 square miles of the surrounding countryside.

Lake Georgetown, Lake Georgetown dam

Paddle Summary

On the way to the launch, stop at Cedar Breaks Park Corps of Engineers booth to pay fees and ask questions about the lake and weather conditions. The put-in location is at the bottom of a steep, 100-foot concrete boat ramp near Dry Creek. Launch to the right of the ramp from a bank of rock and sand. Unload on the bank and park on the hill in the heart of the park.

From the launch, scoot out into a no-wake zone that is protected from the wind by 20-foot limestone banks. Keep the bank on the right for the remainder of the paddle.

At 0.4 mile, a cove is on the right that is some 100 yards wide. Just ahead are twelve large pipes on the right. Maintain 200 feet distance from the Keep Out buoy and sign.

At 0.5 mile, reach the dam's right edge. Turn left and follow the dam across the lake. Look for fish working the surface. At the end of the levee, turn left and continue following the lakeshore. People walk the trails there. Banks are covered in scrub.

At 0.7 mile, an 8-foot limestone bluff begins on the right bank.

Limestone Loop (Lake Georgetown)

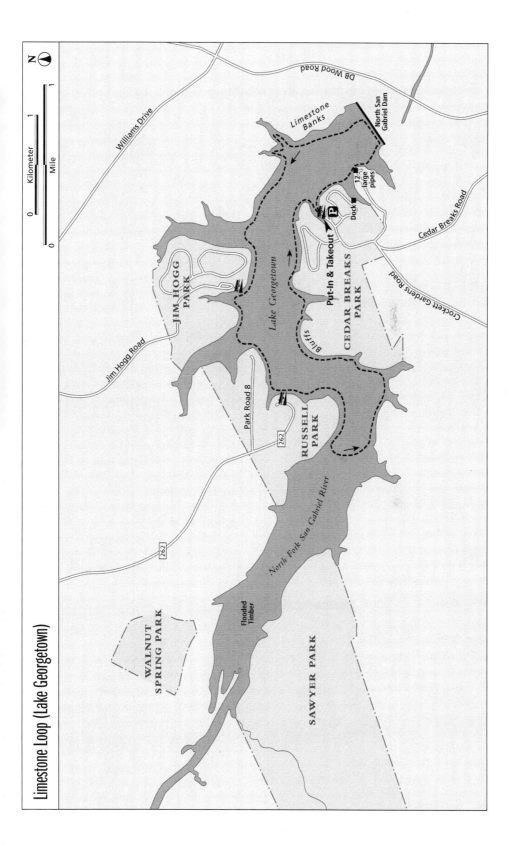

At 1 mile, a point reaches out before a cove on the right. The cove is covered in flooded timber. Bank anglers, birds, and boats gather here to catch fish. The right bank grows to 30 feet. Great blue herons stand guard in dead trees and along banks. Bass boats race past.

At 1.3 miles, No Wake buoys mark a cove on the right, in front of Jim Hogg Park. Boulders the size of cabanas shine white across the lake. Two docks stand on the right.

At 1.6 miles, houses are visible to the right, at the back of a cove.

▶ Georgetown is said to have "the most beautiful town square in Texas." The best time to see the Victorian architecture for yourself may be during the annual Red Poppy Festival.

At 1.7 miles, car-size boulders are on the right. Across the lake on the left are 50-foot limestone bluffs.

At 1.8 miles, a concrete boat ramp stands on the right, at Russell Park.

At 2.4 miles, a long straightaway leads toward the narrower river stretch, stands of flooded timber, and the wildlife management area. The wind can quickly pick up here, which raises a chop and can turn the paddle into a grind. Either push through or cross the lake to the far bank and head back.

At 2.7 miles, a cove is on the right. On my paddle, an osprey flew over, with a fish turned into the wind. Turn left to paddle due south to the far side of lake.

At 3.2 miles, reach the south bank. Turn left to put the bank on your right shoulder and head back toward the put-in.

At 4.2 miles, 50-foot sheer limestone bluffs make the right bank. They are best viewed in the afternoon in full light.

At 4.8 mile, a cove stretches well back. Continue following the bank back toward the put-in.

At 7.3 miles, No Wake buoys and covered picnic tables mark your approach to the put-in/takeout location. Turn right into the cove. Take out at the ramp on the left.

Paddle Information

Contact/Outfitter

US Army Corps of Engineers, Lake Georgetown Project Office, 500 Lake Overlook Dr., Georgetown, TX 78633; (512) 930-5253; swf-wc.usace.army.mil/georgetown

Austin Canoe & Kayak (ACK), 11604 Stonehollow Dr. #300, Austin, TX 78758; (888) 828-3828; austinkayak.com. Want to rent a boat and take it wherever you decide to go? ACK offers boat rentals from locations in the cities of Austin, Houston, San Marcos, San Antonio, and Spring. "Take it anywhere you like," says one ACK representative, "Just bring it back."

REI, Austin-Gateway, 9901 N. Capital of Texas Hwy. Suite 200, Austin, TX 78759; (512) 343-5550; rei.com

Lake Georgetown, flooded treetops

Local Events/Attractions

Georgetown Convention & Visitors Bureau, 101 W. 7th St. Georgetown, TX 78626; (800) 436-8696; visit.georgetown.org.

Inner Space Caverns, 4200 S. I-35, Georgetown; (512) 931-CAVE (2283), myinnerspacecavern.com. One of the best preserved caves in Texas.

Berry Springs Park and Preserve, 1801 County Road 152, Georgetown, TX 78626, (512) 943-1920, parks.wilco.org/Home/Parks/BerrySpringsParkandPreserve/tabid/2466/Default.aspx—Voted "Best Kept Secret" in "The Best of Georgetown" contest.

12 Sandy Creek's Paddle Hard Loop (Lake Travis)

This stretch of Austin's best-known leisure lake is good for paddlers looking to dig in for a good workout, search for the lost treasures of weekend merrymakers, or add a little floating to a day that includes Sandy Creek Park and several other nearby attractions.

Start: Sandy Creek Park boat ramp, N30 28.27'/W97 54.48'
End: Sandy Creek Park boat ramp, N30 28.27'/W97 54.48'
Length: 3.5 miles
Float time: 3–7 hours
Difficulty: Easy to difficult, depending on wind, boat traffic, and chop
Rapids: None
River type: Reservoir
Current: None
River gradient: Not applicable

River gauge: Not applicable
Land status: Municipal park and private
County: Travis
Nearest city/town: Volente
Boats used: Canoes, kayaks, johnboats, small motorized craft, jet skis
Season: Spring, summer, and fall; summer will have more boat traffic.
Fees and permits: Park usage fee
Maps: TOPO! Texas; USGS Mansfield Dam TX; DeLorme: Texas Atlas & Gazetteer: page 69

Put-In and Takeout Information

To put-in/takeout: No shuttle is required. There is only one location for put-in and takeout. From Austin, travel north on US 83 until you reach Anderson Mill Road. Go west on Anderson Mill Road for 5.9 miles. Turn left onto Lime Creek Road for 4.8 miles. Turn into Sandy Creek Park at the sign reading "Welcome Sandy Creek A Travis County Park." Stop at the guardhouse. Turn left and follow signs to the boat ramp.

Overview

Lake Travis was formed upon completion of the Marshall Ford Dam in 1939, and reformed in 1942 with the completion of the larger Mansfield Dam. The 65-mile-long lake is the penultimate pass-through reservoir on the Colorado River. The reservoir drains some 38,000 square miles of countryside and plays an important role in water storage, irrigation, wildlife habitat, freshwater inflow management for coastal Matagorda Bay, and recreation. High winds and heavy traffic from motorized craft, skiers, bass fishermen, and leisure boaters can make the lake a challenge to paddle.

With its set reservoirs, the Colorado River is not defined by hard-core rapids. However, high water, boat traffic, and heat can be dangers. Headwinds and low water flows can be hindrances. Before paddling, check with local outfitters. The USGS WaterWatch website (waterwatch.usgs.gov) also provides real time stream flow information for the Colorado River and other waterways. The Lower Colorado River

Lake Travis, sailboat at the launch

Authority (LCRA) also offers hydrological data at its Hydromet website (hydromet
.lcra.org/full.aspx).

Paddle Summary

On the way to the boat ramp, stop at Sandy Creek Park guardhouse to pay fees and
ask about lake conditions. Follow the signs to the boat ramp at the edge of Sandy
Creek Park, which offers 25 acres of public space for swimming, nature walks, birding,
camping, and fishing. Drive to the bottom of the steep 100-foot concrete boat ramp.
Unload the boat. Drive up to the parking area and follow the footpath back to the
boat. Launch from a sandy and rocky bank into a protected cove. The cove continues
to the right and ends in a dry creek. Ahead, on the far hill, is a house that looks like
a lighthouse. Turn to the left and follow the water out to the finger of the lake. On
the right is a limestone point that stands 25 feet high, with the limestone stacked like
pancakes. Turn right to follow the finger of the lake.

Bluff-top estates line the 100-foot banks. Stairs lead from the houses to the water's
edge. Houseboats and boat docks line the banks. The hills are juniper green and the
limestone white and yellow.

At 0.5 mile Jones Harbor Marina is on the left. Behind it is a line of luxury hillside condos. The water ends ahead, turn around there. Tiny shorebirds explore the seemingly barren limestone banks, shelves, and cracks.

At 1.2 miles, a cove and creek enter the lake on the left near a series of three roofed barges with pumping gear. Signs demand boaters maintain a 200-foot distance. On my paddle, I noted that four great blue herons had disregarded the warning and nested on the roofs. Across the river, a section of submerged stumps stands before a large cobble beach.

At 1.5 miles, two rows of boathouses signal the approach to the Sandy Creek Yacht Club & Marina on the left. The boathouses, which are filled with yachts, speedboats, sailboats, etc., take up most of the river. Paddle to the right of the boat houses. Be mindful of boat traffic here. Sandy Creek Store sits at the end of the boathouse and offers snacks, beverages, tackle, and so on.

At 1.6 miles, a cove and dry creek are on the right. The homes grow up out of the hill country and the water gives the perfect view.

At 2.1 miles, the lake turns. The headwinds can pick up significantly here, adding resistance to the paddle. Whitecaps can kick up quickly and can throw water over the bow. A blue water tower is visible ahead on the horizon. To the right, on the far bank, a yellow house stands alone on the limestone bluff. When the wind is out of the south and pushing at 15 miles per hour or more, this is a good place to work on kayak sprints. Paddle hard into the wind. Ride the wind back. Repeat. Do as many sprints as you like, then turn around and head back to the put-in.

At 3.4 miles, see the cove near your put-in/takeout location on the right.

At 3.5 miles, arrive at the boat ramp. (Distance depends on the number of sprints.)

Option: Adventurous paddlers may choose to continue ahead to Starnes Island, which is a popular summer day party destination.

Adding the Starnes Island leg will add 3–4 miles to the trip (a total of about 7.5 miles). The water is likely to be rougher. The wind may be stronger and the waves bigger. And, the water will likely be busier with bass boats, party barges, ski boats, and so on. If you want to do this stretch, paddling on cool days, in the early mornings, and on weekdays are likely best. Be really careful with the boat traffic.

Paddle Information

Organizations

Colorado River Foundation, PO Box 50029, Austin, TX 78763; (512) 498-1587; coloradoriver.org. Established in 1994, the Colorado River Foundation is the only nonprofit organization dedicated solely to conserving and protecting the Texas Colorado River.

Save Our Springs (S.O.S.) Alliance, PO Box 684881, Austin, TX 78768; (512) 477-2320; sosalliance.org. S.O.S. works to protect Barton Springs, the Edwards Aquifer, and related watersheds.

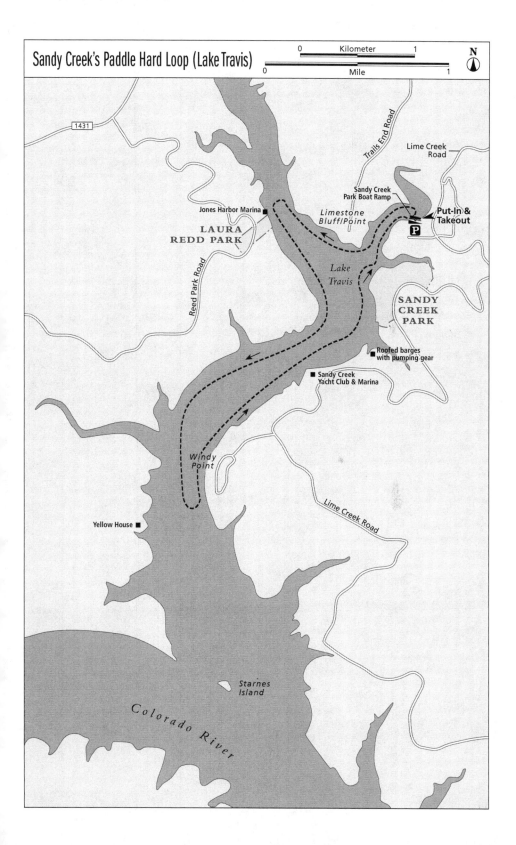

Sandy Creek's Paddle Hard Loop (Lake Travis)

0 Kilometer 1

0 Mile 1

N

1431

Trails End Road

Lime Creek Road

Sandy Creek Park Boat Ramp

Put-In & Takeout

Jones Harbor Marina

Limestone Bluff/Point

LAURA REDD PARK

P

Lake Travis

SANDY CREEK PARK

Reed Park Road

Roofed barges with pumping gear

Sandy Creek Yacht Club & Marina

Windy Point

Lime Creek Road

Yellow House

Starnes Island

Colorado River

Contact / Outfitter

Austin Canoe & Kayak (ACK), 11604 Stonehollow Dr. #300, Austin, TX 78758; (888) 828-3828, austinkayak.com. Want to rent a boat and take it wherever you decide to go? ACK offers boat rentals from locations in the cities of Austin, Houston, San Marcos, San Antonio, and Spring. "Take it anywhere you like," says one ACK representative, "Just bring it back."

REI, Austin-Gateway, 9901 N. Capital of Texas Hwy. Suite 200, Austin, TX 78759; (512) 343-5550; rei.com.

Local Events / Attractions

Austin Convention & Visitors Bureau, 209 E. 6th St., Austin, TX 78701; (512) 478-0098; austintexas.org. Find information on hundreds of events in Austin each year.

Hippie Hollow Park, 7000 Comanche Trail, Austin, TX 78732; hippiehollow.com. The only public clothing-optional park in Texas.

Anderson Mill Museum and Grist Mill, 13974 Farm Rd. 2769 (Volente Road), Volente, TX 78641; (512) 258-2613; austintexas.org. This little-known mill museum is dedicated to the history of Volente and the practice of flour milling.

Prairies & Lakes

The Prairies & Lakes region meanders along between the Hill Country and the eastern Piney Woods, and northward through Dallas to the Texas–Oklahoma border. Though it's home to Dallas–Ft. Worth (one of the largest metroplexes in the United States), the 45,000-square-mile region is defined by ranchland, lazy hills, prairies, and stand of forest. The Prairies & Lakes region is home to more than thirty local and state parks, three major rivers—the Trinity River, the Red River, and the Brazos River—and some of the best freshwater fishing in the state.

In this section, you will find floats along the Bosque, Brazos, Navasota, Leon, Lampasas, Lower Colorado, San Marcos, and Trinity Rivers, and more.

Runaway Bay, Canada geese

13 Luling-Zedler Mill Paddling Trail (San Marcos River)

In 1962, Bill George and Frank Brown paddled from San Marcos to Corpus Christi. The 260-mile Texas Water Safari was born in 1963, and it has run the San Marcos River ever since. Few of us are paddle-mad enough to take on "the world's toughest canoe race." Still, the San Marcos River above Zedler Mill gives bird watchers, anglers, and lazy floaters a great day on the water. The upper stretch runs fast and clear. The lower crawls dark and shady. Guadalupe and largemouth bass, catfish, and sunfish are abundant. Deer, wild turkeys, feral hogs, and countless bird species are common companions along the rural corridor.

Start: River Trail Park, N29 40.06' / W97 41.98'
End: Luling Southside Park, N29 40.00' / W97 39.14'
Length: 6.5 miles
Float time: 4-6 hours
Difficulty: Easy to moderate
Rapids: Many Class I within the first several miles, depending upon water levels
River type: Spring-fed, dammed river
Current: Swift to minimal
River gradient: 1.14 feet per mile
River gauge: 100-1,000 cubic feet per second to run river

Land status: Municipal park and private
County: Caldwell
Nearest city/town: Luling
Boats used: Canoes, kayaks
Season: Year-round
Fees and permits: None
Maps: TOPO! Texas; USGS Luling TX; DeLorme: Texas Atlas & Gazetteer: page 69
Contact: For information on river conditions, call the Guadalupe-Blanco River Authority at (830) 379-5822.

Put-In and Takeout Information

To shuttle point/takeout: From Luling, take TX 80 south/South Magnolia Street for 1.1 miles across the river bridge. Turn right onto a dirt road at the blue Texas Paddling Trails sign. (If you cross a second bridge, you've gone too far.) Cross the cattle gap and drive through the gate. When the road splits bear left, away from the bridge. Continue to the boat launch at the water's edge. Bear left at the covered picnic tables and park.

▶ You can scuba dive at Spring Lake! To learn more, contact The Meadows Center for Water and the Environment at meadowscenter.txstate.edu, or call (512) 245-9200.

To put-in from takeout: From Luling City Park, turn left out of the park to head north on TX 80 for 1.1 miles. Turn left onto US 90 west for 3.5 miles. Before the San Marcos River bridge, on the left, is large brown sign with yellow letters that reads "City of Luling River Trail Park Luling Paddling Trail." Turn left into the driveway. Follow the road and pass under

Zedler Mill, unloading at the put-in

the bridge, then veer left. Pass under the bridge again and follow the loop down to the river's edge.

Overview

The San Marcos River rises at the heart of the Texas State University's San Marcos campus, at the San Marcos Springs, which flow from the Edwards Aquifer. Just beyond the boundaries of the protected springs, the river hosts tubers and swimmers throughout much of the year. Texas Parks & Wildlife called the San Marcos "one of the most popular recreational rivers in Texas." A few miles beyond campus, the Blanco River joins the San Marcos. The San Marcos continues flowing to the southeast for some 75 miles to its confluence with the Guadalupe River near Gonzales. Increasing water demands and potential aquifer depletion endanger the San Marcos River, which is the sole habitat for several plant and animal species, including Texas wild rice and the Texas blind salamander.

▶ The nearby town of Lockhart is known as the "Barbecue Capital of Texas." The town's four barbecue restaurants—Black's, Chisholm Trail, Kreuz, and Smitty's—feed an estimated 5,000 people each week.

Paddle Summary

The gravel road in the River Trail Park loops within 20 feet of the river, just down from the US 90 bridge. Unload here. Park in the lot nearby. Carry the boat down the gradual, gravel bank. Scoot out into the pleasantly swift water of the narrow river. Willows and oaks host songbirds along the banks, and a cloud of gnats may rise and fall like a jig. Turn the bow downstream and steer as the river accelerates through the first bend. The water remains mostly swift—catching its breath occasionally—until about 1.3 miles, when it slows for some time.

At 1.9 miles, the water again accelerates.

At 2.4 miles, on the banks of a pecan plantation on the left, stands a blue-and-yellow sign that reads "Zedler Mill 4 miles For emergency call 911."

At 2.7 miles, a dry creek enters on the right.

At 3.6 miles, pass a sign labeled "Zedler Mill 3 miles."

At 4.1 miles, a creek enters from the right, near a set of stairs and a No Trespassing sign.

At 4.5 miles, on the left, stands a sign labeled "Zedler Mill 2 Miles."

At 5.5 miles, on the left, stands a sign labeled "Zedler Mill 1 Mile."

At 5.9 miles, a telephone line crosses the river. The river here bears little resemblance to the swift, snaking stretch at the launch site. Here it is 30 yards wide and offers no noticeable current. Leaves hold their positions as if they were in a bathtub.

At 6.2 miles, a metal wall is on the left bank of the river. As soon as you see this wall, paddle to the right side of the river. Two houses on the left signal your approach to the takeout at Luling City Park. Bank anglers will be fishing on the right bank.

▶ **Want to learn more about the river? Check out Jim Kimmel's book *The San Marcos—A River's Story*. It was sponsored by The Meadows Center for Water and the Environment.**

Spot the historic Zedler Mill on the left. Listen for the sounds of the highway and falling water. Ahead, beyond the mill and the waterfall, the TX 80 bridge crosses the river. On the left is a concrete boat ramp and covered picnic tables.

At 6.5 miles, a metal-and-concrete boat launch is on the right. This is the takeout. Do not paddle past this. Paddle alongside the boat ramp. Step up out of the boat. Pull the car down; use the emergency brake and chock a tire if you can.

Paddle Information

Organizations

Guadalupe–Blanco River Authority, 933 E. Court St., Seguin, TX 78155; (830) 379-5822; gbra.org. The authority provides information about water conditions, community services, events, and recreation.

Luling-Zedler Mill Paddling Trail (San Marcos River)

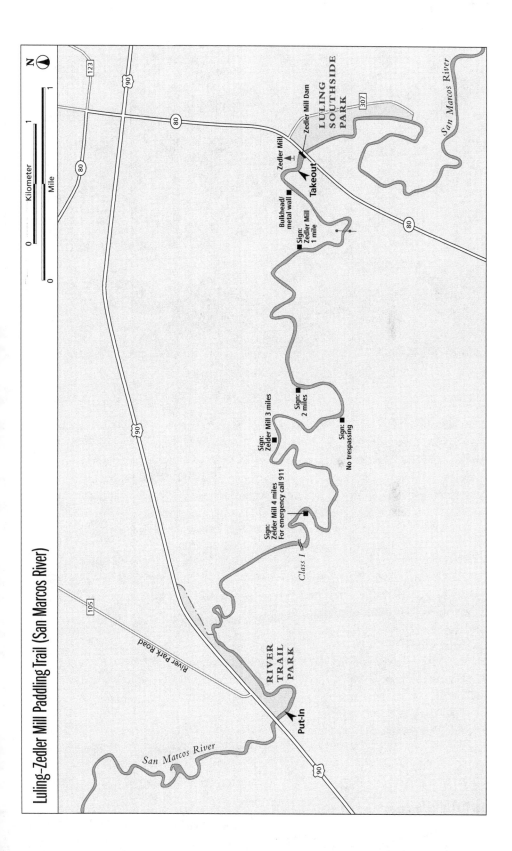

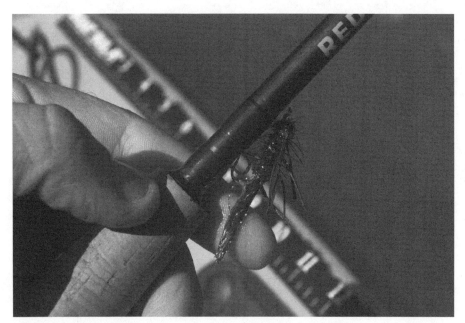

Zedler Mill, the deadly wooly bugger

The Meadows Center for Water and the Environment at Texas State University, 601 University Dr., San Marcos, TX 78666; (512) 245-9200; meadowscenter .txstate.edu. This organization is committed to helping protect and conserve water resources while promoting economic development and social well-being. Contact the center to learn about opportunities for scuba diving, citizen science, outdoor learning, on-site events, Spring Lake glass-bottom boat tours, glass-bottom kayak tours, guided hiking tours on the 251-acre Spring Lake Natural Area, and more.

Contact / Outfitter

City of Luling Parks Department, 509 E. Crockett St., Luling, TX 78648; (512) 227-1724; cityofluling.net. A shuttle service is available for a fee. Canoes and kayaks rentals are also available. Call a day ahead.

Local Events / Attractions

Zedler Mill Classic Canoe Race, Zedler Mill Park, Luling, TX 78648; (830) 875-3214; zedlermill.com. Canoe races, food, a pie contest and auction, and music are offered on the San Marcos River to raise money for the Zedler Mill Foundation & Paddling Trail.

Black's Barbecue, 215 N. Main St., Lockhart TX 78644; (512) 398-2712; blacks bbq.com. Established in 1932, this is one of the oldest barbecue joints in Texas to be continuously owned and operated by one family.

14 Chupacabra Point Loop (Trinity River at Lake Bridgeport)

This paddle offers a little bit of creek and a whole lot of lake. Kingfishers, hawks, shorebirds, waterfowl, and countless other birds are common companions along this loop. Labyrinths of stumps and stobs offer great fishing for crappie. The hybrid striped bass fishing is excellent. The wind can whip up pretty quickly, so be ready for that. And, don't overlook this paddle in winter. It's quite an experience to paddle through an icy creek at sunrise, troll for big striped bass, and finish the cold morning with a cup of hot coffee and a famous chupacabra burger from the 1Stop of Texas.

Start: Chupacabra Point, N33 09.49'/W97 52.32'
End: Chupacabra Point, N33 09.49'/W97 52.32'
Length: 4.8 miles
Float time: 2-4 hours
Difficulty: Easy due to flat water
Rapids: None
River type: Reservoir
Current: None
River gradient: Not applicable
River gauge: Not applicable
Land status: Municipal park and private
County: Wise

Nearest city/town: Runaway Bay
Boats used: Canoes, kayaks, johnboats, small motorized craft
Season: Fall and spring
Fees and permits: None
Maps: TOPO! Texas; USGS Wizard Wells TX and Bridgeport West TX; DeLorme: Texas Atlas & Gazetteer: page 45
Contact: For info on conditions and recreation at Lake Bridgeport, contact the Tarrant Regional Water Authority, 1710 Farm Rd. 1658, Bridgeport, TX 76426; (817) 335-2491 or (940) 683-2349; trwd.com.

Put-In and Takeout Information

To put-in/takeout: No shuttle is needed; put-in and takeout are at the same location. From Runaway Bridge on the west side of the TX 114/US 380 bridge continue for 0.5 mile. Turn left onto Port O Call Drive for 0.4 mile. Turn left onto Lanai Drive for 0.2 mile. Turn left onto Blue Fathom Drive for 0.2 mile. At the corner of Marco Polo Drive, look right to a parking lot with a Chupacabra Point sign.

Overview

The Trinity River has four forks originating in separate places: East Fork (Grayson County), Elm Fork (Montague County), West Fork (Archer County), and Clear Fork (Parker County). The confluence of Elm Fork and West Fork in Dallas creates the mainstream. From its origins to the coastal Trinity Bay, the river meanders some 550 miles. Along its path, the river runs through three reservoirs: Lake Worth, Eagle Mountain, and Lake Bridgeport. Lake Bridgeport is located on the West Fork Trinity

River in Wise County. The reservoir was created with the completion of the Bridge-port Dam in 1931. Tarrant Regional Water District owns the lake and uses it for flood control, water storage, and recreation. The 12,000-acre lake drains some 1,111 square miles of the surrounding countryside.

Paddle Summary

Park in a gravel lot at the corner of Marco Drive and Blue Fathom Drive. Carry your boat some 100 yards past the red Chupacabra sign to get to the water. Launch down a 6-foot embankment of sand and mud into a narrow creek. In the winter, this will ice over.

Note the off-white home and its boathouse near the launch. It'll help you find your takeout spot later since it will not be marked. Also look for the foot-prints and other clues that will show you where you launched.

Turn left and head along the narrow, winding creek toward the lake. Lost angling gear and other artifacts from higher water litter the banks. Drift-wood reclaims its terrestrial life. Trotlines run from one piece of driftwood to another on oppo-site banks.

At 0.7 mile, the creek forks around a mud island. A maze of stobs stands on the left, creating good cover for fish in higher water and an easily navigable obstacle in low water. Go left.

Runaway Bay, icy waters

The stobs continue down the left bank all the way toward the lake homes on the distant bank.

At 0.8 mile, a set of stobs on the right guards the entrance to the main lake. Pass through these.

As you turn put the bank on your left shoulder. Note the floating green boat-house on the left. It will help in navigation later. Ahead, in the distance, are two large Y-shaped utility poles and a bridge. Pass through a deep narrow channel.

At 0.9 mile, reach a white No Wake buoy. Here the lake opens a bit. Follow the left bank toward the bridge.

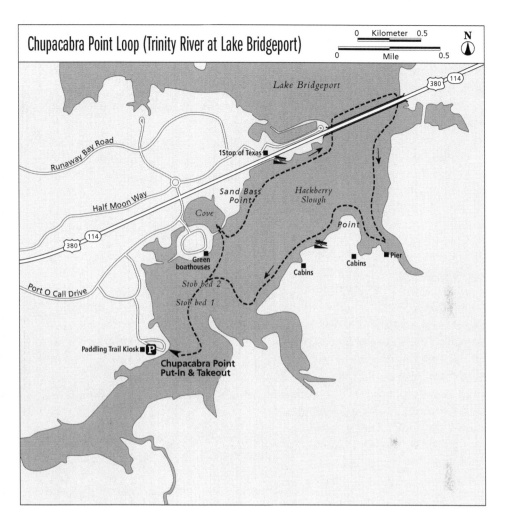

Chupacabra Point Loop (Trinity River at Lake Bridgeport)

At 1.1 miles, the entrance to a cove is on the left. Enter through a narrow pass to explore. Continue down the bank toward the bridge.

At 1.4 miles, a Sand Bass Point sign is posted in a yard on the left.

At 1.5 miles, a boat ramp is on the left just behind 1Stop of Texas. Stop in for coffee?

Continue along the left bank. Pass a blue sign for the City of Runaway Bay. Heavy agricultural equipment moves along on the highway, hinting at the local livelihood.

A concrete boat ramp stands at 1.8 miles.

Pass under the TX 114 bridge at 2.1 miles. A Runaway Bay sign is on the left bank. Ahead is open lake. Paddle down through the bridge pilings.

At 2.7 miles, turn right to follow the bank. Ahead is a set of lights like those found at a sports complex. Head toward those.

At 2.9 miles, enter a cove on the left. Follow the water toward the creek, past cabins and a picnic pavilion.

At 3 miles, reach a power line and a pier. Turn around here and head back toward the main lake. Keep the bank on the left.

At 3.4 miles, beneath the oaks, is a large point. Watch for deer and other wildlife. Turn left to follow the left bank.

At 3.5 miles, four steep-roofed cabins peek from behind a line of trees on the ledge.

At 3.7 miles, a boat ramp is on the left. Follow the shoreline and watch for wildlife.

Starting at 3.9 miles, you will see a red rooftop straight ahead in the distance. Look at the 2 o'clock position to see the green boathouse from earlier, which marks your path back to the creek.

Near the boathouse, pass through the stobs. Turn left to enter the creek from which you launched. Look for the off-white colored house and your launch spot on the right at 4.8 miles.

Paddle Information

Contact / Outfitter

Paddle Bound River Outfitters, 505 Leta Ln., Colleyville, TX 76034; (817) 282-3135; paddlebound.com. The outfitter offers sales, classes, rentals, and events focused on paddling.

Mountain Sports, 2025 W. Pioneer Pkwy., Arlington, TX 76013-6005; (817) 461-4503; mountainsports.com. The company carries a large selection of gear for camping, kayaking, and other outdoor pursuits.

Austin Canoe & Kayak (ACK), 11604 Stonehollow Dr. #300, Austin, TX 78758; (888) 828-3828; austinkayak.com. Want to rent a boat and take it wherever you decide to go? ACK offers boat rentals from locations in the cities of Austin, Houston,

▶ You'll paddle past the 1Stop of Texas at mile 1.5. After the paddle, stop in and look for a lady in a furry Chupacabra hat. That's the owner, Linda. She'll fix you a chupacabra burger. Some call it the "strangest burger in Texas." It's certainly a tasty beast worth trying, but don't be afraid to share it with friends.

Runaway Bay, the famous Chupacabra burger

San Marcos, San Antonio, and Spring. "Take it anywhere you like," says one ACK representative, "Just bring it back."

Local Information

Rural Texas Tourism Center, 812 A Halsell St., Bridgeport, TX 76426; (940) 683-2076; ruraltexastourism.org. This tourism promotion program supports economic preservation for rural communities across Texas. Call the number above for information about Bridgeport; see the website anytime you're headed out through rural Texas.

Local Events/Attractions

Caddo/LBJ National Grasslands, 1400 US 81/287 (PO Box 507), Decatur, TX 76234; (940) 627-5475; fs.usda.gov/detail/texas/about-forest/districts/?cid=fswdev3_008440. This site offers opportunities for hiking, camping, fishing, hunting, horseback riding, mountain biking, wildlife viewing, and photography.

Wise County Park on Lake Bridgeport, 372 CR 1638, Chico, TX 76431; (940) 644-1910. The park offers public restrooms, showers, boat ramps, piers, picnic tables, a playground, and opportunities for camping, swimming, and fishing.

15 LBJ Grasslands Loop (Black Creek Reservoir)

This place is out of the way. It's secluded. At times, it is absolutely empty. It's a great little float in a great place to camp, paddle, hike, bike, and explore the Caddo–LBJ National Grasslands. The 2-mile loop passes through pines, juniper, oaks, and willows, and offers a chance to see deer, wild turkeys, gulls, grebes, and countless other birds and wildlife.

Start: Black Creek Lake boat ramp, N33 20.70'/W97 35.77'
End: Black Creek Lake boat ramp, N33 20.70'/W97 35.77'
Length: 2 miles
Float time: 1-2 hours
Difficulty: Easy due to flat, protected water
Rapids: None
River type: Reservoir
Current: None
River gradient: Not applicable
River gauge: Not applicable
County: Wise

Land status: Public
Nearest city/town: Decatur
Boats used: Canoe, kayaks, johnboats
Season: Year-round
Fees and permits: Day-use fee
Maps: TOPO! Texas; USGS Pecan Creek TX; DeLorme: Texas Atlas & Gazetteer: page 45
Contact: Caddo-LBJ National Grasslands district office, 1400 US 81/287 (PO Box 507), Decatur, TX 76234; (940) 627-5475; fs.usda.gov/detail/texas/about-forest/districts/?cid=fswdev3_008440

Put-In and Takeout Information

To put-in/takeout: No shuttle is needed; put-in and takeout are in the same location. From US 380 in Decatur, take the Farm Road 730 exit and follow Farm Road 730 for 0.3 mile. Turn left onto Farm Road 730 north/North Trinity Street and follow Farm Road 730 north for 3.1 miles. Veer left onto CR 2360 for 2.1 miles. Turn left to stay on CR 2360 for an additional 1.4 miles. Turn left onto CR 2372 for 0.3 mile. Take the first right onto CR 2461, and continue 0.5 mile. Take the first left onto FS 902. Watch for Black Creek Lake signs along the way. Arrive in 0.4 mile. As you enter the park, on the right are signs announcing the "Black Creek Recreation Area" and the "Black Creek–Cotton Wood Hiking Trail 901." On the left, before the public restrooms, is a tower built for chimney swifts in 2005 by the Tallgrass Prairie Audubon Society. Bear left here toward the ramp. Park in the gravel area above the concrete boat ramp.

Overview

Black Creek Reservoir is one of the lesser-known lakes in Texas. The small, secluded lake offers a quiet paddle in the 20,250-acre Lyndon B. Johnson National Grasslands. Along the banks of the 35-acre Black Creek Reservoir are picnic areas, a boat launch, restrooms, hiking trails, and walk-in camping sites. (***Note:*** No drinking water

Black Creek, at the put-in

is available.) The lake also offers access to a series of hiking trails that are marked and maintained.

Paddle Summary

The put-in location is about 30 yards to the right of the boat ramp, on the right side of the small peninsula. From the sandy bank here, launch into a protected cove about 25 yards across. Behind the launch is a playground, ecofriendly bathrooms, picnic tables, and fire pits. Across the lake are 100-foot pines.

A creek stretches off into the woods on the right. For this paddle, turn left into the main lake and follow the bank. This is a clockwise loop. Park benches overlook the water. Dogs hunt down the creek. Hardwoods and high grasses stand on top of 10-foot sandy banks. Enter the lake within 25 yards. Follow the bank on the left. Because the lake is small and the area is heavily wooded, the winds are not usually an issue.

At 0.25 mile, reach a concrete structure in the water and a 20-foot levee.

At 0.3 mile, enter the creek on the left. Search the bank of sand and loam for tracks of raccoons, herons, and other animals. Watch the pines for birds and deer and turkeys. Explore the creek as far as you like and as the water allows.

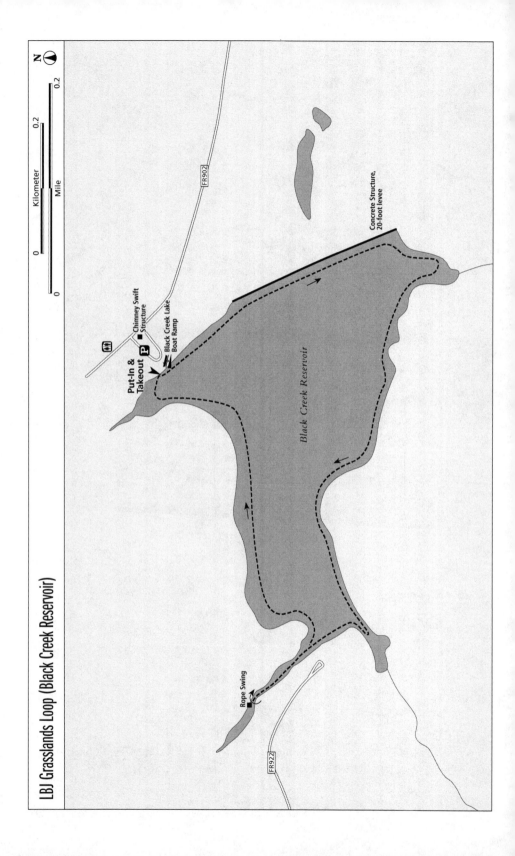

LBJ Grasslands Loop (Black Creek Reservoir)

At 0.75 mile, enter the creek to the left. Pines become hardwoods. Felled trees in water give cover for fish. Game trails lead to the water. Squirrels slip through the hardwood knuckles, knees, and knobs. Once you've explored enough, head back out toward the reservoir. The banks are soft, dark earth capped with a layer of golden grass.

Round the peninsula on the left as you enter the lake.

At 1.1 miles, enter a creek. Follow it through the hardwood bottom. Note the rope swing on the right. Explore creek as desire and water allow.

For this trip, turn around at N33 20.67'/W97 36.16', at 1.45 miles. Head back toward the reservoir and the launch.

At 2 miles enter the creek from which you launched. Explore it and return to the launch.

Paddle Information

Contact / Outfitter

Caddo/LBJ National Grasslands, 1400 US 81/TX 287 (PO Box 507), Decatur, TX 76234; (940) 627-5475; fs.usda.gov/detail/texas/about-forest/districts/?cid=fswdev3_008440. Call for more information about Black Creek Lake. The LBJ Grasslands offer opportunities for hiking, camping, fishing, hunting, horseback riding, mountain biking, wildlife viewing, and photography.

Paddle Bound River Outfitters, 505 Leta Ln., Colleyville, TX 76034; (817) 282-3135, paddlebound.com. The outfitter offers sales, classes, rentals, and events focused on paddling.

Mountain Sports, 2025 W. Pioneer Pkwy., Arlington, TX 76013-6005; (817) 461-4503; mountainsports.com. The company carries a large selection of gear for camping, kayaking, and other outdoor pursuits.

Austin Canoe & Kayak (ACK), 11604 Stonehollow Dr. #300, Austin, TX 78758; (888) 828-3828; austinkayak.com. Want to rent a boat and take it wherever you decide to go? ACK offers boat rentals from locations in the cities of Austin, Houston, San Marcos, San Antonio, and Spring. "Take it anywhere you like," says one ACK representative, "Just bring it back."

Local Events / Attractions

Decatur Baptist College and Heritage Museum, 1602 S. Trinity St., Decatur, TX 76234; (940) 627-5586; wisehistory.com/baptistcollege.html. Built in 1892, the building later housed the first junior college in the country and is now home to the Wise County Heritage Museum.

16 Bosque Bluffs Loop (Bosque River)

This loop in the middle of Waco is easy for most anyone, and jam-packed with things to see and do. It leads from near the River Stage, along the famed Bosque Bluffs, through two popular public parks, and down the Bosque and Brazos Rivers. Spend the day on the water here, and add a little paddling to your Waco visit.

Start: McLennan Community College boat ramp, N31 35.57'/W97 10.15'
End: McLennan Community College boat ramp, N31 35.57'/W97 10.15'
Length: 2 miles
Float time: 1–2 hours
Difficulty: Easy due to calm, protected water
Rapids: None
River type: Dam-controlled river
Current: Mild
River gradient: Not applicable

River gauge: 125–700 cubic feet per second to run
Land status: Municipal park and private
County: McLennan
Nearest city/town: Waco
Boats used: Canoes, kayaks
Season: Year-round
Fees and permits: None
Maps: TOPO! Texas; USGS Waco TX; DeLorme: Texas Atlas & Gazetteer, page 58

Put-In and Takeout Information

To put-in/takeout: No shuttle is needed; put-in and takeout are in the same location. In Waco, leave I-35 on exit 334 toward US 77 South/17th and 18th Streets. Merge onto the US 77 south/north I-35 frontage road for 0.2 mile. Turn right onto South 17th Street and drive 1.8 miles. Continue onto Homan Avenue. Turn right onto North 18th Street for 0.4 mile. Keep left at the fork, for 1.2 miles. Veer left onto North 18th Street and continue 0.1 mile. Watch for Bosque River Stage signs. Continue onto North 19th Street for 1.5 miles. Turn right into McLennan Community College at Lake Shore Drive. Take the first left onto Cameron Road. Pass the baseball fields on the left. Veer left into the parking lot that serves the college, the Bosque River Stage, and the paddling trail. The boat ramp is straight ahead.

Overview

The Bosque River begins in Erath County and flows some 115 miles through hills, post oaks, and junipers to the southeast. It has four main forks: the East, North, Middle, and South. The mouth of the Bosque River is at its confluence with the Brazos River, at Cameron Park in the city of Waco. The Bosque helps form Lake Waco in McLennan County. Bosque is the Spanish word for "forest." At the time of Spain's first encounter with the river, the banks would likely have been forested. Some have found a way to see past this coincidence and have credited the river's naming to French fur trader Juan Bosquet.

Paddle Summary

Drive down the long, steep, concrete boat ramp toward the floating dock at the water's edge. Unload and prepare to launch to the left of the floating dock. Drive back up to the hill some 40 yards away and park near the Texas Paddling Trails sign in the parking area labeled as "Parking J Students & Visitors."

Step into the boat and slide into the slow river, which is some 50 yards wide. Many songbirds sing. At sunrise, fog slips across water between you and banks of hardwoods hanging with vines. Many felled trees line the banks. Joggers and dog walkers pass the launch.

Turn left out of the ramp for just a few yards to see the Bosque River Stage, which is a beautiful facility on the riverbank where outdoor events are held. Then turn downstream and start paddling into the rising sun.

At 0.25 mile, a wooden pedestrian bridge is on the left bank. Follow the 3-foot riverbank on the right. Joggers and walkers move along the riverside

Bosque, put-in at dawn

trail. Behind them, some few feet from the river, a shear ledge of 100 feet stands. Stone blocks the size of small cars line the bank.

At 0.4 mile, 100-foot chalky limestone bluffs can be seen on the right. These are Lover's Leap and Emmons Cliff.

At 0.5 mile, a stand of bamboo nearly glows green and yellow from atop the bluff. On the left, the bank is low and covered in hardwoods. Young junipers cling to the shear walls on the right. Small birds flutter into the underside of limestone lips and ledges. The bluffs are somewhat in the shade in the sunrise, but likely shine high later in the day.

At 0.8 mile, a boat slip made of concrete sacks is on the left.

The point at 0.9 mile marks the confluence of the Bosque and Brazos Rivers. On the right is Cameron Park. On the left is Brazos Park East. A power line crosses the

Bosque Bluffs Loop (Bosque River)

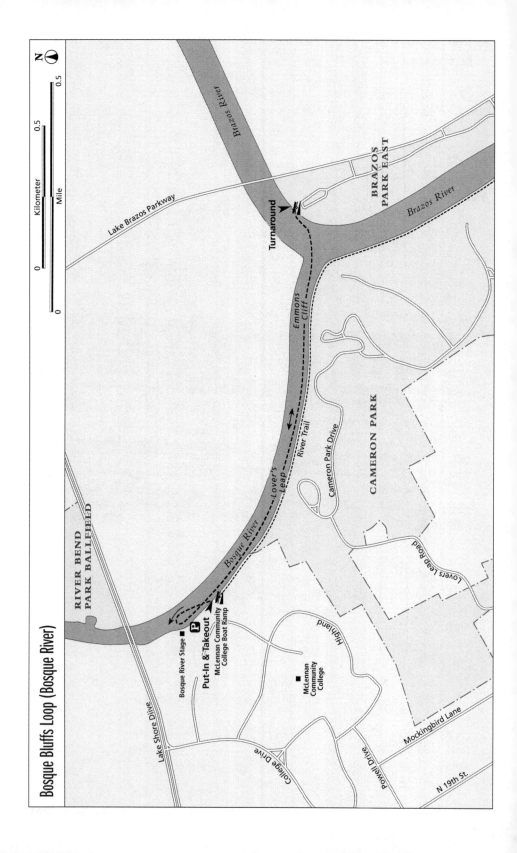

river. Downstream to the right is a power line, several bridges, and many large build-ings. To the left (upstream) is the Lake Brazos Parkway Bridge. Veer left toward the bridge. Paddle to the blue roof, rocky bank, and concrete boat ramp on the far side of the river at Brazos Park East.

At 1 mile, arrive at the boat ramp. This is a good place to get out for a bit and enjoy the park. After, turn around and head back to the put-in.

At 2 miles, the put-in/takeout location is on the left.

Paddle Information

Contact / Outfitter

City of Waco Parks and Recreation Department, 300 Austin Ave. (PO Box 2570), Waco, TX 76702; (254) 750-5980; waco-texas.com. Call about river condi-tions, outfitters, etc.

Geared Canoe & Kayak, 4227 N. 19th St., Waco, TX 76708; (254) 537-3697; geared.shutterfly.com. Learn about rentals, events, and more. Call a few days ahead of your trip.

Austin Canoe & Kayak (ACK), 11604 Stonehollow Dr. #300, Austin, TX 78758; (888) 828-3828; austinkayak.com. Want to rent a boat and take it wherever you decide to go? ACK offers boat rentals from locations in the cities of Austin, Houston, San Marcos, San Antonio, and Spring. "Take it anywhere you like," says one ACK representative, "Just bring it back."

Local Events / Attractions

Texas Ranger Hall of Fame and Museum, 100 Texas Ranger Trail, Waco, TX 76706; (254) 750-8631; texasranger.org. Commemorates the Texas Rangers law enforcement agency.

Waco Mammoth Site, 6220 Steinbeck Bend, Waco, TX 76702; (254) 750-7946); wacomammoth.org. Exhibits and tours. "The nation's first and only recorded discov-ery of a nursery herd of Pleistocene mammoths."

Balcones Distilling, 212 S. 17th St., Waco, TX 76706; (254) 755-6003; balcones distilling.com. Try signature blue corn whisky at Texas's only whisky distillery—well, maybe the only legal one.

Downtown Farmers Market, 400 S. University Parks Dr., Waco, TX 76706; wacodowntownfarmersmarket.com. Open every Saturday from 9 a.m. to 1 p.m., year-round.

Bosque River Stage, 1400 College Dr., Waco, TX 76706; (254) 299-8200; mclen nan.edu/brs. A 530-seat amphitheater on the Bosque River.

17 Brazos Bridges Loop (Brazos River)

This 5-mile stretch at the heart of Waco offers paddlers just a taste of marshy backwaters, miles of the broad Brazos, and opportunities to fish, watch birds or people, or study the famed Brazos Bridges. Turn this float into a full day's paddle or use it as an excuse to explore Brazos Park East and the rest of what Waco has to offer.

Start: Brazos Park East kayak launch, N31 35.27' / W97 09.20'
End: Brazos Park East kayak launch, N31 35.27' / W97 09.20'
Length: 5 miles
Float time: 2–5 hours
Difficulty: Easy to moderate, depending on the wind
Rapids: None
River type: Dam-controlled river
Current: Mild
River gradient: Not applicable
River gauge: 300–4,000 cubic feet per second to run

Land status: Municipal park and private
County: McLennan
Nearest city/town: Waco
Boats used: Canoes, kayaks
Season: Year-round
Fees and permits: None
Maps: TOPO! Texas; USGS Waco TX; DeLorme: Texas Atlas & Gazetteer: page 58
Contact: For information on river conditions, contact the Brazos River Authority at PO Box 7555, Waco, TX 76714; (254) 761-3100.

Put-In and Takeout Information

To put-in/takeout: No shuttle is required; the put-in and takeout are in the same location. In Waco, leave I-35 via exit 335C toward Martin Luther King Jr. Boulevard/ Lake Brazos Parkway. Merge onto the I-35 frontage road. Turn left onto South Lake Brazos Parkway/North Martin Luther King Jr. Boulevard for 2.2 miles. Cameron Park's Brazos Park East is on the right. You will see the Brazos Park East sign immediately before the turn into the park on the right, at blue gateway sign.

Overview

The Brazos River is the longest river in Texas. It begins in Stonewall County and flows 840 miles to its mouth near Freeport, in Brazoria County. The Brazos River is made up of seven main tributaries: the Salt Fork, the Double Mountain Fork, the Clear Fork, the Bosque River, the Little River, the Navasota River, and Yegua Creek. The main river begins at the confluence of the Double Mountain and Salt Forks in Stonewall County. The river creates a 1,000-mile watershed that runs through canyons, plains, hills, and coastal areas along its path from New Mexico to the Gulf. The river runs through sandy loams and clays, oaks, grasses, junipers, and farmland. Before the Civil War, 250 miles of the river were navigable, from the Gulf of Mexico to Washington-on-the-Brazos, the "Birthplace of Texas"—so called because it

Brazos, calm river

was the site of the Convention of 1836 and the signing of the Texas Declaration of Independence.

Paddle Summary

Great 100-foot limestone bluffs are the first thing you see. The Texas Parks & Wildlife information kiosk and launch are straight ahead, but closer. A concrete ramp leads to the kayak launch site. Unload the boat and drive some 75 yards to the top of the hill to parallel park. Launch into a calm area that sits off the main river. It is covered with aquatic grasses and willows, and is full of birds and wildlife.

At the 12 o'clock position from the launch is a narrow strip of water that passes through a reed and grass bed. Follow that some 50 feet to the Brazos River. Hawks call, songbirds sing, and frogs chirp from the cattails.

Turn left to head downstream. On the right, across the river, note the gazebo. This will mark your turn on the return. Power lines cross the river, from atop 100-foot white bluffs on the far bank to a low grassy area in the park on the left. Along the far bank, cyclists streak by as blurs of red, yellow, and green along the park trail.

At 0.4 mile, a white-and-orange sign reading "Circle Point" is on the right bank, across from the bathrooms on the left bank. Grebes hide in the tangles of branches and roots hanging in the water on the right bank.

At 0.6 mile, on the left bank, pass a concrete boat ramp and a manicured park dotted with hardwood trees. On the right, the bluffs undulate along, trading peaks for hollows. High junipers run the hills. Hardwoods rule the bottoms. They reconcile at the river. There are many felled trees along banks, but the bulk of the river's surface is free of obstruction.

▶ In *Goodbye to a River* (1960), John Graves recounts his canoe trip down the Brazos River in the 1950s.

At 0.9 mile, the manicured park appears on the right.

At 1.2 miles, a creek is on the left. The Herring Avenue Bridge is overhead. If you're fishing, be mindful that beneath the surface, wood, trees, flotsam, and jetsam gather into great clogs. They hold fish and steal lures.

At 1.5 miles, a stone staircase on the right runs to the water.

At 1.6 miles, on the right, pass a popular place for bank anglers. Just beyond, pass a culvert on the left.

At 1.7 miles, pass a cove on the left, at the back of which is a culvert large enough to drive a vehicle through, it seems. Not far beyond, a stone structure with a tin roof is on the left.

At 1.8 miles, pass under a power line. Ahead, a tall brick building dominates the skyline to the right.

At 2.2 miles, the Waco Drive Bridge and the Bledsoe-Miller Recreation Center are on the left. After passing under the bridge, look at the 2 o'clock position to see the largest building on the skyline. It is labeled "ALICO" in large, red letters.

At 2.5 miles, a creek is on right. On the left are a large tan building, a boat ramp, picnic tables, and a playground. On the right is the ALICO building. Ahead is a set of the Bosque Bridges. Turn around here, and head back toward the put-in.

Look for the power lines, gazebo, and point you noted at your entry to the river. Turn right to the launch at 5 miles.

Paddle Information

Contact/Outfitter

City of Waco Parks and Recreation Department, 300 Austin Ave. (PO Box 2570), Waco, TX 76702; (254) 750-5980; waco-texas.com. Call about river conditions, outfitters, etc.

Geared Canoe & Kayak, 4227 N. 19th St., Waco, TX 76708; (254) 537-3697; geared.shutterfly.com. Providers of rentals, events, and more. Call a few days ahead of your trip.

Austin Canoe & Kayak (ACK), 11604 Stonehollow Dr. #300, Austin, TX 78758; (888) 828-3828; austinkayak.com. Want to rent a boat and take it wherever you decide to go? ACK offers boat rentals from locations in the cities of Austin, Houston,

Brazos Bridges Loop (Brazos River)

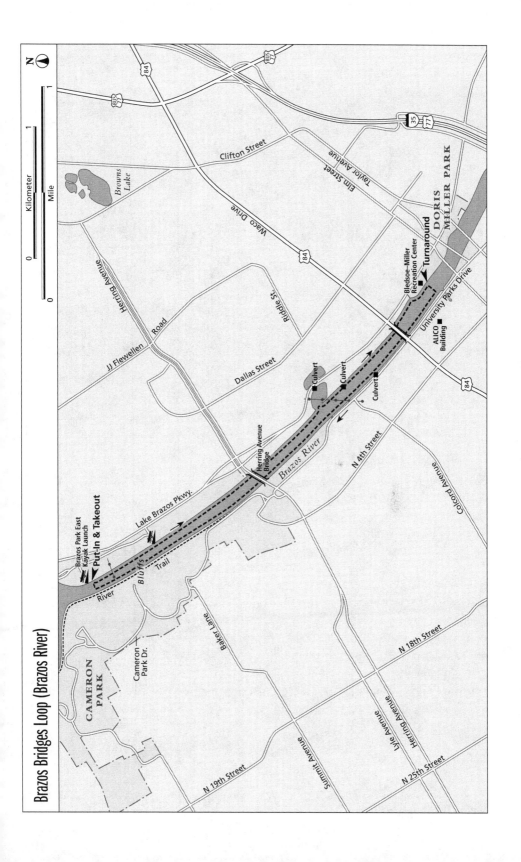

Brazos, put-in at Brazos Park East

San Marcos, San Antonio, and Spring. "Take it anywhere you like," says one ACK representative, "Just bring it back."

Local Events / Attractions

Texas Ranger Hall of Fame and Museum, 100 Texas Ranger Trail, Waco, TX 76706; (254) 750-8631; texasranger.org. Commemorates the Texas Rangers law enforcement agency.

Waco Mammoth Site, 6220 Steinbeck Bend, Waco, TX 76706; (254) 750-7946; wacomammoth.org. The facility offers tours of what they claim is "the nation's first and only recorded discovery of a nursery herd of Pleistocene mammoths."

Balcones Distilling, 212 S. 17th St., Waco, TX 76706; (254) 755-6003; balconesdis tilling.com. Try signature blue corn whisky at Texas's only whisky distillery—well, maybe the only legal one.

Downtown Farmers Market, 400 S. University Parks Dr., Waco, TX 76706; wacodowntownfarmersmarket.com/. Open every Saturday from 9 a.m. to 1 p.m., year-round.

Bosque River Stage, 1400 College Dr., Waco, TX 76706; (254) 299-8200; mclennan.edu/brs. This 530-seat amphitheater is on the Bosque River.

18 Limestone Bluffs Trail (Navasota River)

This 5.5-mile lazy float takes paddlers from rugged, limestone-layered country down to the swampy bottoms of Fort Parker Lake. Whether you're into fishing, watching birds and wildlife, or adding a little paddling to a day at the tourist destinations that bookend the trip, there is plenty worth seeing.

Start: Confederate Reunion Grounds State Historic Site, N31 37.99' / W96 33.72'
End: Fort Parker State Park, N31 35.77' / W96 32.13'
Length: 5.5 miles
Float time: 2–5 hours
Difficulty: Easy due to slow, protected waters.
Rapids: None
River type: Dam-controlled river
Current: Mild
River gradient: Not applicable
River gauge: Not applicable
Land status: Historical site, state park, and private

County: Limestone
Nearest city/town: Mexia
Boats used: Canoes, kayaks, johnboats, small motorized craft
Season: Year-round
Fees and permits: Day-use fee for Confederate Reunion Grounds; day-use for Fort Parker State Park; free with Texas State Parks Pass
Maps: TOPO! Texas; USGS Groesbeck TX; DeLorme: Texas Atlas & Gazetteer: page 58
Contact: Fort Parker State Park, 194 Park Road 28, Mexia, TX 76667; (254) 562-5751; tpwd.state.tx.us/state-parks/fort-parker

Put-In and Takeout Information

To shuttle point/takeout: From US 84 in Mexia, head south on TX 14 for 6.6 miles. Turn right onto Park Road 28 at the Fort Parker State Park sign. Park headquarters is on the right. A self-pay station for late arrivals is on the left.

To put-in from takeout: From Fort Parker State Park, take Park Road 28 for 1.4 miles. Turn left onto TX 14 for 1.7 miles. Turn left onto Farm Road 2705 and continue 2.4 miles. Follow Farm Road 2705/Farm Road 1633 for 0.3 mile. Turn right onto Farm Road 2705 for 300 feet. (*Note:* Follow the Confederate Reunion Grounds State Historic Site signs along Farm Roads 2705 and 1633, and on the gate of the park on the left.) The put-in is at a Texas Parks & Wildlife Paddling Trail kiosk near a set of stairs and a canoe trolley system.

Overview

The Navasota River rises northeast of the town of Mount Calm in Hill County, and flows some 125 miles south to its confluence with the Brazos River in Grimes County. Along its course, the narrow river runs through forests of oak, hickory, elm, pecan, and other trees. Big Creek, Little Cedar Creek, Sand Creek, and Panther Creek are among its tributaries. The Navasota River is dammed to create several reservoirs along its length: Lake Mexia, Joe Echols Lake, Lake Groesbeck, Lake Limestone, Mar-

Navasota, low dams at the put-in

tin Lake, and Springfield Lake—which is also known as Fort Parker Lake. The 700-acre lake is the centerpiece of the 1,500-acre Fort Parker State Park, near Mexia in Limestone County.

Paddle Summary

As you enter the Confederate Reunion Grounds State Historic Site, the office will be on the right. Stop here to pay fees. (***Note:*** The gates close at 5 p.m., so plan for parking accordingly.) Ask for directions to the kayak/canoe launch.

Park and unload near the Texas Parks & Wildlife Paddling Trail sign. A canoe/kayak trolley system is set up there to help move boats to the riverside; but it may be easier just to carry your boat down the stairs. At the river's edge, the steps enter the water behind a low concrete dam, which creates a calm place to launch. Set the boat in, load it, step in, and begin the float through a hardwood bottom. The river is some 10 yards wide here, and slow.

▶ **If you plan to park at the Confederate Reunion Grounds, park outside the gate. Gates close at 5 p.m.**

Kingfishers, crows, ducks, great blue herons, woodpeckers, and countless turtles share the waterway. The paths of deer and other game are obvious on the riverbanks. Felled trees lie along the river and make good homes for fish. The banks are covered in root tangles.

At 0.6 mile, a small creek enters on the left.

At 0.9 mile, a 25-foot limestone bluff is on the right. The limestone is stacked in layered crags and ledges. It's covered in lichen and alive. Just beyond, a house is on the right. Cormorant, crows, and hawks gather there.

At 1 mile, an old outdoor fireplace and abandoned cabin are on the left. This begins series of cabins, floating docks, platforms, fishing lights, and old johnboats. Stop paddling here and chances are you'll hear no human sounds.

At 1.4 miles, the river is 40 yards wide. A concrete dam reaches across the river; but a hole some 20 yards wide allows easy passage. The river is full of trees and limbs and tangles and they steal fishing lures. Try lures that float or are weedless.

▶ At Fort Parker State Park, the Civilian Conservation Corps built the dam and other park structures in the 1930s.

At 1.7 miles, a creek is on the left, with four rusty metal pilings, the Farm Road 1633 bridge, and power lines. You might also hear the wind chimes of a house on the left.

At 1.9 miles, pass a power line and No Trespassing sign on the left. Beyond, a large outcropping/point of limestone is on the left.

At 2 miles, a creek is on the right. The woods change along here. Beyond this point, the trees are a bit larger, and there are more small hardwoods. The topography mellows too, dropping and leveling out.

At 2.4 miles, a creek is on the right.

At 2.9 miles, a creek is on the right and "Petroleum Pipeline 2" is on a white-and-red sign and a white-and-yellow post.

At 3.1 miles, an old phone pole with the brown porcelain pieces is on the right.

At 3.3 miles, stone steps and a No Trespassing sign are on the left.

At 3.7 miles, a creek is on the right and a public boat ramp on the left. By this point the limestone bluffs are no more. This is a swampy hardwood bottomland with low mud banks.

At 4.3 miles, the river enters the state park lake. At 10 o'clock position, you'll see the campground and a tower on the far bank. At the 12 o'clock position is a line of small grass islands, with a wooded ridge on the far bank. Work along the grass islands, where white pelicans may gather. After passing the grass islands, turn left and paddle toward the tower and campground.

Near shore, pass the orange buoys at the swim area and head to the marsh-grass–covered point. Round it to the left, and enter the protected cove. Continue to the floating dock on the left.

At 5.5 miles, arrive at the takeout at the concrete boat ramp on the left, just past the dock.

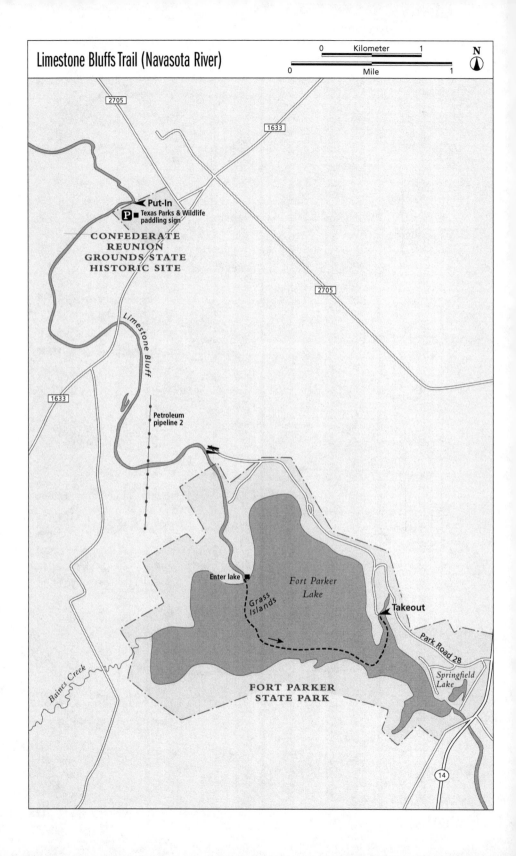

Limestone Bluffs Trail (Navasota River)

0   Kilometer   1
0   Mile   1

N

2705

1633

Put-In
P ■ Texas Parks & Wildlife
paddling sign

CONFEDERATE
REUNION
GROUNDS STATE
HISTORIC SITE

Limestone Bluff

2705

1633

Petroleum
pipeline 2

Enter lake ■

*Grass
Islands*

*Fort Parker
Lake*

Takeout

Park Road 28

FORT PARKER
STATE PARK

*Springfield
Lake*

Baines Creek

14

Paddle Information

Contact / Outfitter

Fort Parker State Park, 194 Park Road 28, Mexia, TX 76667; (254) 562-5751; tpwd.state.tx.us/state-parks/fort-parker. The park hosts opportunities for paddling, camping, picnicking, swimming, fishing, birding, hiking, cycling, nature study, and baseball. Call about water conditions.

Austin Canoe & Kayak (ACK), 11604 Stonehollow Dr. #300, Austin, TX 78758; (888) 828-3828; austinkayak.com. Want to rent a boat and take it wherever you decide to go? ACK offers boat rentals from locations in the cities of Austin, Houston, San Marcos, San Antonio, and Spring. "Take it anywhere you like," says one ACK representative, "Just bring it back."

Local Information

Confederate Reunion Grounds State Historic Site, 1738 Farm Rd. 2705, Mexia, TX 76667; (254) 472-0959; visitconfederatereuniongrounds.com. This Texas Historical Commission site preserves and interprets three periods of Texas history: prehistoric cultures, the late nineteenth-century reunion movement, and the early twentieth-century Mexia oil boom.

Local Events / Attractions

Limestone County Fair, PO Box 965, Groesbeck, TX 76642; (254) 729-3293; cityofgroesbeck.com. Call for dates and details. There may well be greased pigs, bucking bulls, meats on sticks, rides, and games at the fair.

Southwest Fiddle Championships, Groesbeck City Park Pavilion, TX 164 west/West Yeagua Street, Groesbeck, TX 76642; (254) 729-3293; cityofgroesbeck.com. Call for details on this year's sawing rendition of a long-standing tradition.

19 New Life Loop (Bastrop State Park Lake)

This is the littlest paddle, but it's an important one. Arguably a mile long if you hug the banks, this trip puts paddlers up close and personal with a rarely appreciated part of nature: Wildfire. The surrounding woods and wildlife are recovering from a devastating fire in 2011, and that recovery is a beautiful thing. A paddle here offers both a chance to learn about and support the recovery and the new life it's bringing to the park's forest. Call Bastrop State Park to learn about all there is to do while you're at the park.

Start: Bastrop State Park Lake, N30 06.78'/W97 16.59'
End: Bastrop State Park Lake, N30 06.78'/W97 16.59'
Length: 1 mile
Float time: Less than 1 hour
Difficulty: Easy due to flat, protected water
Rapids: None
River type: Lake
Current: None
River gradient: Not applicable
River gauge: Not applicable

Land status: Public
County: Bastrop
Nearest city/town: Bastrop
Boats used: Canoes, kayaks
Season: Year-round
Fees and permits: A day-use fee is charged; free for everyone in a vehicle with a Texas State Parks Pass
Maps: TOPO! Texas; USGS Bastrop TX; DeLorme: Texas Atlas & Gazetteer: page 70
Contact: Contact Bastrop State Park for more information at (512) 321-2101.

Put-In and Takeout Information

To put-in/takeout: No shuttle is necessary; the put-in and takeout are in the same location. From Bastrop, exit TX 71 by turning left onto TX 21 east/TX 95 north. Go 0.3 mile and turn right onto TX 21 east/Chestnut Street for 0.9 mile. Turn right onto Park Road 1 for 0.3 mile. Veer right to stay on Park Road 1, and continue 0.3 mile. Veer left onto Park Road 1A for 0.5 mile, then continue onto Park Road 1B for 0.6 mile to Bastrop State Park Lake. The lake is on the left, in a curve in a pine bottom.

Overview

You're not likely to read about Bastrop State Park Lake—well, anywhere else really. It's only about three drips past a pond. But it is tucked away, and is quiet and beautiful. If you are near Bastrop and begging for a paddling quickie, check it out. You can also easily do this and nearby Buescher Lake in the same day. Buescher State Park and Bastrop State Park are separated by only about 5 miles. These two parks lie in what is known as the "Lost Pines," which are the westernmost stand of loblolly pines in the United States. In September 2011, fire destroyed much of the

▶ **If you're looking for two nice, short paddles in a day, paddle Bastrop State Park and Buescher State Park.**

forest in this area. Now the small lake offers a chance to take a close look, a quiet look, and the time to notice the rebirth after the fire. Come paddle the lake to watch the pine forest recover. Pileated woodpeckers, white-tailed deer, rabbits, squirrels, opossums, armadillos, and perhaps the endangered Houston toad, will be nearby. *Note:* While the fire hit Bastrop State Park hard, Buescher State Park was spared, so there's an opportunity to see the beauty of the pines before the fire, as well as the harsh beauty of them as they recover.

Paddle Summary

Stop in at the Bastrop State Park headquarters to pay fees, learn about all the park has to offer, and get directions to the lake. Park at the designated spot along Park Road 1B on the far side of the lake. Unload here. The put-in location is situated at the bottom of a slow-sloping staircase made of sand and wood. Launch along the rocks to the left of the stairs. Turn left and begin following the shoreline around the entire lake.

There is no current. The water offers little visibility. The banks of the lake are covered in pine forest, which was hit hard by the fire of 2011. The park is again busy with people who camp, golf, paddle, and hike, and in the burned forest green emerges, trumpeting the royal recovery to come.

At 0.1 mile, a cove and creek are on the left. Turn in to explore the area. On the right bank there is a brown cabin on the hill. The water extends back into forest. The gradual banks of gravel and sand hold many pines, some burned completely, others charred red and black, and others still new and fresh green. Explore the high pines and follow the water as far as the depth allows.

At 0.2 mile, a metal pipe runs overhead across the creek. When the creek ends, turn back in and take a left along the bank and continue the shoreline exploration.

At 0.4 mile, a group of stone and wooden cabins on a hill overlooks the cove on the left. Felled trees and flooded willows line the banks.

Bastrop, at the put-in

GET KIDS OUTDOORS: FOLLOW THE WATER

"We're genetically hardwired to be hunter-gatherers, and to be outside," said environmentalist Richard Louv in a June 2007 interview with *Field & Stream*. "You can't replace that with an Xbox and not see consequences."

Louv's best-selling *Last Child in the Woods* introduced nature deficit disorder into our lexicon. He showed that the outdoors is essential to physical, emotional, and spiritual childhood development, and is a potent therapy for depression, obesity, and attention deficit disorder. In doing so, Louv inspired much social introspection and a national movement to get kids into the great out-of-doors.

Because 80 percent of Americans now live in urban areas and are, in essence, landless, public lands are the primary way for children to access the outdoors. In Texas, though, 98 percent of the state's 171-million-acre outdoors is privately owned. The good news: The public body runs a network of 15 major rivers, 3,700 named streams, and 3,300 miles of tidal shoreline. That network is public.

If you want to get kids outdoors in Texas, follow the water. And along the way, watch birds, photograph wildlife, camp, fish, hunt, study geology, or just get a little exercise.

Here are some resources for getting kids outdoors:

· Texas Outdoor Family Program: tpwd.state.tx.us/outdoor-learning/texas-outdoor -family
· Kids Outdoor Zone: KidsOutdoorZone.com
· Expedition School: expeditionschool.com
· Texas Junior Naturalists: tpwd.state.tx.us/learning/junior_naturalists
· 4-H Youth Shooting Sports: texas4-h.tamu.edu/shootingsports
· Texas Parks & Wildlife Kids Page: tpwd.state.tx.us/kids
· Children & Nature Network: childrenandnature.org
· Outdoor Nation: outdoornation.org
· Boy Scouts of America: scouting.org
· Girl Scouts: girlscouts.org

At 0.5 mile, a cove reaches the earthen levee. Just beyond, a finger reaches deeper into the pine forest. Follow the water as far as the depth allows. Look for deer, ducks, and other birds and wildlife.

At 0.7 mile, a cove on the left is filled with felled trees and willows. Mallards and other ducks follow the creek into the high pines and 60-foot hills. Return to the main lake and continue down the bank toward the launch.

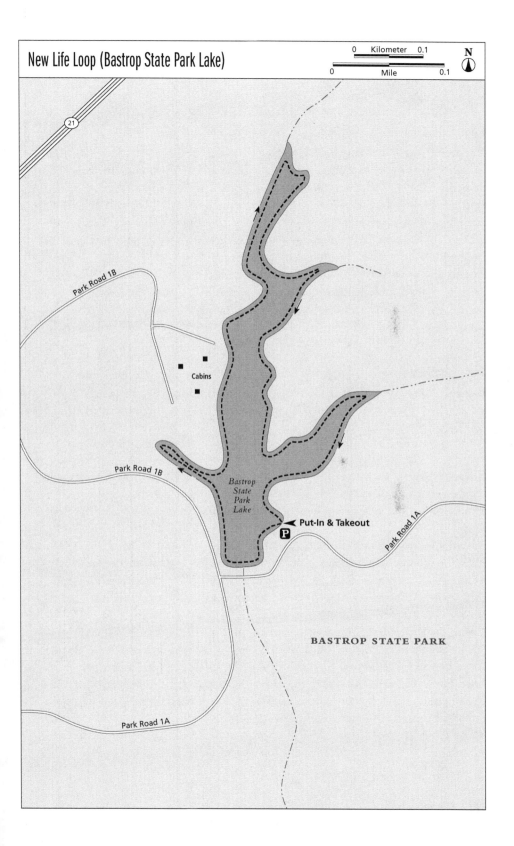

New Life Loop (Bastrop State Park Lake)

21

Park Road 1B

Cabins

Park Road 1B

Bastrop
State
Park
Lake

Put-In & Takeout

P

Park Road 1A

BASTROP STATE PARK

Park Road 1A

N

0   Kilometer   0.1

0   Mile   0.1

At 1 mile, the put-in/takeout is on the left. After loading the boat, look across the road. Signs mark a hiking trail. Lace up and head out.

Paddle Information

Contact/Outfitter

Bastrop River Company, 601 Chestnut St., Bastrop, TX 78602; (512) 988-1154; bastroprivercompany.com. "Paddle trips, gear, and shuttles around Bastrop," says owner Lee Harle. "That's what we do."

Bastrop State Park, 3005 TX 21 East, Bastrop, TX 78602; (512) 321-2101; tpwd .state.tx.us/state-parks/bastrop. Call about water conditions. The park offers opportunities for camping, picnicking, canoeing (rental canoes available), golfing, wildlife viewing, hiking, and participation in interpretive programs.

Austin Canoe & Kayak (ACK), 11604 Stonehollow Dr. #300, Austin, TX 78758; (888) 828-3828; austinkayak.com. Want to rent a boat and take it wherever you decide to go? ACK offers boat rentals from locations in the cities of Austin, Houston, San Marcos, San Antonio, and Spring. "Take it anywhere you like," says one ACK representative, "Just bring it back."

Local Information

Bastrop Museum & Visitor Center, 904 Main St., Bastrop, TX 78602; (512) 303-0904; visitbastroptx.com. Bastrop is happening. Poke around. You'll be surprised what you find.

Local Events/Attractions

Buescher State Park, PO Box 75, Smithville, TX 78957; (512) 237-2241; tpwd .state.tx.us/state-parks/buescher. Activities include paddling (rental canoes available), fishing, nature study, hiking, geocaching, cycling, and participation in interpretive tours.

Bastrop Homecoming & Rodeo, PO Box 215, Bastrop, TX 78602; (512) 303-0558; On the first weekend in August, Bastrop throws its biggest annual party.

Yesterfest, Downtown Business Alliance, 906 Main St. #123, Bastrop, TX 78602; (512) 657-4275; bastropdba.org/yesterfest. Come celebrate Bastrop's pioneer heritage and reconnect with your own.

Colorado River 100, 7825 Beauregard Circle 20B, Austin, TX 78745; (512) 970-8703; coloradoriver100.com. One of the biggest canoe races in Texas, the Colorado River 100 begins in Bastrop and ends at Howell Canoe Livery in Columbus.

Lost Pines Artisans Alliance, 301 Burleson, Smithville, TX 78957; (512) 237-9299; lostpinesartisansalliance.org. Located at the Mary Nichols Art Center, classes, a gallery, and events are open to the public.

20 Bass Hog Loop (Buescher Lake)

Buescher State Park Lake is quiet, small, unassuming, and absolutely wonderful. Pop in to float laps while you chase monster bass. Use paddling as an excuse for a weekend of cabin or tent camping at the state park, or paddle this and Bastrop State Park Lake in a single day. There's no going wrong with this paddle-perfect lake.

Start: Buescher Lake, N30 02.47'/W97 09.61'
End: Buescher Lake, N30 02.47'/W97 09.61'
Length: 1.4 miles
Float time: 1-2 hours
Difficulty: Easy due to flat, protected water
Rapids: None
River type: Lake
Current: None
River gradient: Not applicable
River gauge: Not applicable
Land status: Public

County: Bastrop
Nearest city/town: Smithville
Boats used: Canoes, kayaks
Season: Year-round
Fees and permits: A day-use fee is charged; free for everyone in a vehicle with a Texas State Parks Pass
Maps: TOPO! Texas; USGS Smithville TX; DeLorme: Texas Atlas & Gazetteer: page 70
Contact: For information call Buescher State Park at (512) 237-2241.

Put-In and Takeout Information

To put-in/takeout: No shuttle is necessary; the put-in and takeout are in the same location. From Smithville, leave TX 71 by taking the TX 95 south/TX 230 Loop exit. Go 0.4 mile on TX 95/230. Turn right onto Farm Road 153 for 0.4 mile. Turn left onto Park Road 1C. Veer left at the park headquarters. The lake is on the right.

Overview

The 15-acre lake is the centerpiece of Buescher State Park, which is located near Bastrop and Smithville. Buescher State Park and Bastrop State Park are separated by only about 5 miles. Non-motorized boating is allowed on the lake. There is no boat ramp.

The lake is a bit bigger than neighboring Bastrop State Park Lake. But it too is tucked away, quiet, and beautiful. You can fish here all day, or paddle this and nearby Bastrop State Park Lake in the same day. These two state park lakes lie in what is known as the "Lost Pines," which are the westernmost stand of loblolly pines in the United States. In September 2011, fire destroyed much of the forest in the area. While Bastrop State Park was devastated, Buescher State Park was spared. In these two parks, there's an

▶ **Buescher Lake produces monster largemouth bass. Many of these hogs have topped 13 pounds. According to the rangers, a 10-pounder may drop a rod tip, but it hardly raises an eyebrow anymore.**

Buescher, morning paddle

opportunity to see the beauty of the pines before fire and the harsh beauty of them as they recover.

Paddle Summary

Stop by the Buescher State Park headquarters to pay fees and ask about the water conditions and latest fishing reports. The headquarters also offers a modest selection of provisions, books, and other items for sale.

Buescher State Park Lake has no boat ramp. Park in the designated parking area near the brown building labeled with the Canoe Rental sign. Unload and head down the easy, grassy slope to the waters edge in the corner of the lake, near the levee. Scoot into the water. Ahead is the open lake. On the left is a point that is popular with anglers. On the right is a levee. Put the bank on your right shoulder, where it will remain for the duration of the float.

At 0.1 mile, pass a shallow cove and a concrete spillway. Turn left and continue following the bank past another great fishing spot.

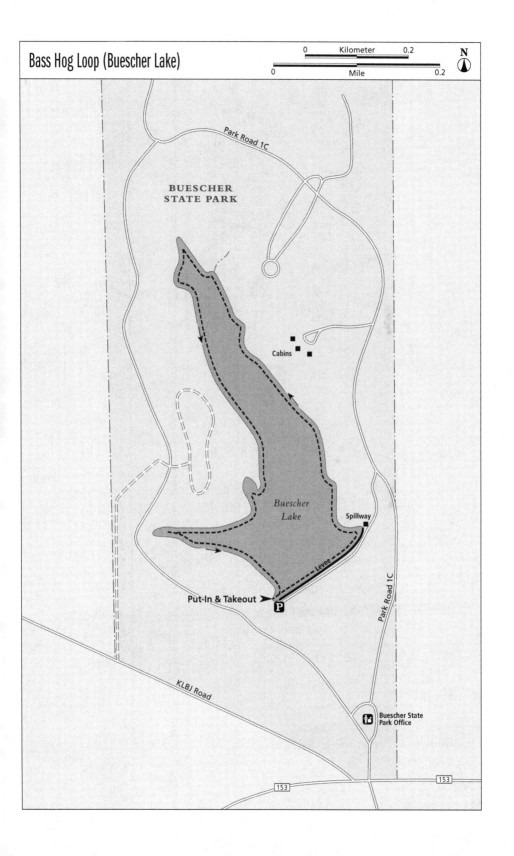

Bass Hog Loop (Buescher Lake)

Kilometer
0   0.2

Mile
0   0.2

N

Park Road 1C

BUESCHER
STATE PARK

Cabins

Buescher
Lake

Spillway

Levee

Put-In & Takeout
P

Park Road 1C

KLBJ Road

Buescher State
Park Office

153   153

Buescher, father and son

At 0.2 mile, a large, hollow concrete column is at the edge of the lake. It is thought to have been a Civilian Conservation Corps-era depth gauge. Cabins peak through the woods for the next 0.1 mile or so.

At 0.4 mile, a creek is on the right. Beavers work here, cutting small trees and logs. Follow the creek as far as the water will allow. Then return to the main lake, turn right, and continue to follow the bank around as the water narrows and reaches back.

At 0.5 mile, a footpath from the water's edge stretches through a hardwood stand and leads to a pavilion in the distance. The cove here is full of felled trees, flooded grasses, and willows. Continue following the bank around.

Brown wooden cabins stand at 0.7 mile.

At 1 mile, a mossy oak on the right reaches out from a point into the lake. Follow the bank to the right, into a finger that stretches back into the woods. Paddle through felled trees. Continue in and out of the cove, and then paddle back toward the put-in. Round the point near the launch.

At 1.4 miles, the put-in/takeout is on the right.

Paddle Information

Contact/Outfitter

Buescher State Park, PO Box 75, Smithville, TX 78957; (512) 237-2241; tpwd .state.tx.us/state-parks/buescher. Activities include paddling (rental canoes available), fishing, nature study, hiking, geo-caching, cycling, and participation in interpretive tours.

Bastrop River Company, 601 Chestnut St., Bastrop, TX 78602; (512) 988-1154; bastroprivercompany.com. "Paddle trips, gear, and shuttles around Bastrop," says owner Lee Harle. "That's what we do."

Austin Canoe & Kayak (ACK), 11604 Stonehollow Dr. #300, Austin, TX 78758; (888) 828-3828; austinkayak.com. Want to rent a boat and take it wherever you decide to go? ACK offers boat rentals from locations in the cities of Austin, Houston, San Marcos, San Antonio, and Spring. "Take it anywhere you like," says one ACK representative, "Just bring it back."

Local Events/Attractions

Bastrop State Park, 3005 TX 21 East, Bastrop, TX 78602; (512) 321-2101; tpwd .state.tx.us/state-parks/bastrop. Call about water conditions. The park offers opportunities for camping, picnicking, canoeing (rental canoes available), golfing, wildlife viewing, hiking, and participation in interpretive programs.

Bastrop Homecoming & Rodeo, PO Box 215, Bastrop, TX 78602; (512) 303-0558. On the first weekend in August, Bastrop throws its biggest annual party.

Lost Pines Artisans Alliance, 301 Burleson, Smithville, TX 78957; (512) 237-9299; lostpinesartisansalliance.org. Located at the Mary Nichols Art Center, classes, a gallery, and events are open to the public.

Yesterfest, Downtown Business Alliance, 906 Main St. #123, Bastrop, TX 78602; (512) 657-4275; bastropdba.org/yesterfest. Come celebrate Bastrop's pioneer heritage and reconnect with your own.

Colorado River 100, 7825 Beauregard Circle 20B, Austin, TX 78745; (512) 970-8703; coloradoriver100.com. One of the biggest canoe races in Texas, the Colorado River 100 begins in Bastrop and ends at Howell Canoe Livery in Columbus.

21 El Camino Real Paddling Trail (Lower Colorado River)

This scenic river float takes paddlers from the heart of Bastrop, "The Most Historic Small Town in Texas," to the Lost Pines Recreational Trails some 6.5 miles downstream. It's as lazy a float as you want it to be. Paddle fast and you can power through it pretty quickly. But, if you lay back and let the river do the work, you'll get there . . . in time.

Start: Bastrop River Company, N30 06.56' / W97 19.31'
End: Lost Pines Recreational Trails, N30 04.40' / W97 18.58'
Length: 6.5 miles
Float time: 3–6 hours
Difficulty: Easy due to river flow
Rapids: Many Class I, depending on water levels
River type: Dam-controlled river
Current: Moderate
River gradient: 1.69 feet per mile
River gauge: 250–2,000 cubic feet per second to run
Land status: Municipal park and private
County: Bastrop
Nearest city/town: Bastrop

Boats used: Canoes, kayaks, johnboats, tubes
Season: Year-round
Fees and permits: Put-in fees included in rental and shuttles. Put in for free at Fisherman's Park, 2 blocks upstream at the corner of Willow and Farm Streets.
Maps: TOPO! Texas; USGS Bastrop TX; DeLorme: Texas Atlas & Gazetteer: page 70
Contact: Call the Bastrop River Company ahead of time to make a reservation and discuss water conditions. Water-release schedules are confidential, but for information about the previous day's scheduled releases and unscheduled releases due to floods, see the Lower Colorado River Association (LCRA) River Report and Flood Summary, or call LCRA at (512) 473-3200.

Put-In and Takeout Information

To shuttle point/takeout: From Bastrop, exit TX 71 by turning south onto Tahitian Drive for 2.2 miles. Turn right onto Riverside Drive. In 1.7 miles turn left at the Texas Parks & Wildlife Paddling Trail sign. Follow the dirt driveway into the riverside park. At the entrance to the parking area, there is a blue Texas Paddling Trails sign. Near the takeout, there is another Texas Paddling Trails sign.

To put-in from takeout: From the takeout, drive east on Riverside Drive for 1.7 miles. Turn left onto Tahitian Drive for 2.2 miles. Turn left onto TX 71 West for 1.4 miles. Turn right onto TX 21 east/TX 95 north for 0.4 mile. Turn left onto Chestnut Street, and go 0.8 mile. Bastrop River Company, at 601 Chestnut St., is on the left.

Overview

The Colorado River is the longest river contained wholly within Texas borders. From its headwaters in Dawson County in western Texas, the river courses some 862 miles to the Gulf Coast, where it pours into the briny Matagorda Bay. Along the

way it cuts a southeastern route
through prairie lands and limestone canyons, juniper-covered
hills, and coastal plains.

From its headwaters the river
flows unsteadily to its confluence
with the Concho River. Some
of the best paddling opportunities begin downstream in a
chain of seven major reservoirs:
Lake Buchanan, Inks Lake, Lake
LBJ, Lake Marble Falls, Lake Travis, Lake Austin, and Lady Bird
Lake. Known as the Highland
Lakes system, these reservoirs
help meet water needs that range
from municipal to industrial,
agricultural to recreational. Paddling opportunities continue
past the Longhorn Dam, the last
in the chain, and through some
290 miles to the coast. Game
fish, birds, diverse flora, and a
range of wildlife can be found
along the way, for the anglers,
photographers, and bird watchers of the world.

Lower Colorado River near Bastrop, all clear

With its set of reservoirs, the Colorado River is not defined by hard-core rapids.
However, high water and heat can be dangers. Headwinds, aquatic grass, and low
water flows can be hindrances. Before paddling, check with local outfitters about
river conditions. The USGS WaterWatch website (waterwatch.usgs.gov) also provides real time stream flow information for the Colorado River and other waterways.
The Lower Colorado River Authority (LCRA) also offers hydrological data at its
Hydromet website (hydromet.lcra.org). For information on this stretch of river, see
the Colorado River at Austin in the pull-down menu.

Paddle Summary

Call the Bastrop River Company ahead of time, at (512) 988-1154, to make a reservation and discuss water conditions.

The put-in location is at a private dock directly behind Bastrop River Company,
just below the TX 71 Bridge. It takes two people to get a boat comfortably down the
wooden stairs and to the water. The water here is calm and deep. The river is 50 yards
wide and offers no protection from the sun.

At 0.4 mile, pass the TX 150 Bridge and power lines.

At 0.5 mile, pass under power lines. Sandy banks range from 10 to 30 feet. Just beyond, a culvert is on the left.

At 0.6 mile, a creek is on the left.

At 0.7 mile, the river splits around a small island at a power line. Go left. The water quickens and narrows.

At 0.8 mile, pass power lines.

At 1 mile, a creek is on the right.

By 1.2 miles, the sounds of Bastrop are replaced with those of tractors.

At 1.4 miles, a 50-yard stretch of big rocks is in the river. They are easy to navigate.

▶ **If you need neither boat nor shuttle, launch at Fisherman's Park, just a few hundred yards upstream from the Bastrop River Company at 1200 Willow St. There are no fees to launch there.**

At 2 miles, power lines cross the river. Less than 0.1 mile beyond, the river splits into three. Take the main river path, through the middle.

At 2.1 miles, a creek is to the right.

At 2.4 miles, a gravel island splits the river. Go right.

At 2.6 miles, a creek is on the right.

At 2.9 miles, a tan metal building stands on the hill to the right.

At 3.1 miles, a creek is on the right.

At 3.5 miles, a creek is on the right.

At 4.2 miles, a 60-foot limestone bluff is on the right.

At 4.4 miles, many houses stand on the left.

At 5.5 miles, a creek is on the left.

At 5.7 miles, near power lines, the river splits around an island. Go right.

At 5.75 miles, reach a train trestle and many felled trees. It is easy to navigate here, but you must pay attention.

At 5.8 miles, a wooden pedestrian bridge is on the left. Ahead is a communications tower.

At 6.1 miles, a "three rope-swing tree" is on the right.

At 6.4 miles, picnic tables and garbage cans are on the left.

At 6.5 miles, the takeout is on the left. It is marked with yellow posts and a tree that has been painted orange, green, and blue. Take out on the bar of sand and gravel.

Paddle Information

Contact/Outfitter

Bastrop River Company, 601 Chestnut St., Bastrop, TX 78602; (512) 988-1154; bastroprivercompany.com. "Paddle trips, gear, and shuttles around Bastrop," says owner Lee Harle. "That's what we do." Be sure to call about river conditions before your trip.

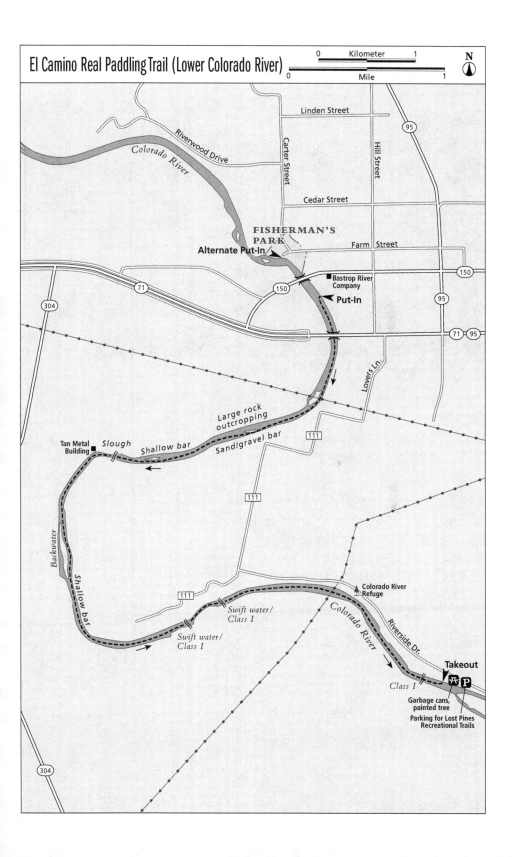

El Camino Real Paddling Trail (Lower Colorado River)

LoCo Bastrop, where the sky begins

Local Information

Bastrop Museum & Visitor Center, 904 Main St., Bastrop, TX 78602; (512) 303-0904; visitbastroptx.com. Bastrop is happening. Poke around. You'll be surprised what you find.

Local Events/Attractions

Bastrop Homecoming & Rodeo, PO Box 215, Bastrop, TX 78602; (512) 303-0558. On the first weekend in August, Bastrop throws its biggest annual party.

Yesterfest, Downtown Business Alliance, 906 Main St. #123, Bastrop, TX 78602; (512) 657-4275; bastropdba.org/yesterfest. Come celebrate Bastrop's pioneer heritage and reconnect with your own.

Colorado River 100, 7825 Beauregard Circle 20B, Austin, TX 78745; (512) 970-8703; coloradoriver100.com. One of the biggest canoe races in Texas, the Colorado River 100 begins in Bastrop and ends at Howell Canoe Livery in Columbus.

22　Columbus Trail (Lower Colorado River)

This 6.9-mile trip gives paddlers a chance to spot a bald eagle, watch hundreds of ducks floating in rafts, catch Guadalupe bass on ultralight gear, or just paddle and float. Be aware that the tailwind at the beginning of the paddle will become a headwind by mile 3. These winds can be very strong, so call Howell Canoe Livery ahead of time to check on wind and water conditions.

Start: Howell Canoe Livery, N29 42.76'/W96 32.73'
End: Beason's Park on the Colorado, N29 42.31'/W96 32.12'
Length: 6.9 miles
Float time: 3–5 hours
Difficulty: Moderate to difficult, depending upon the wind
Rapids: Many Class I; strainers to avoid, depending on river conditions, but always one at the 0.3-mile mark
River type: Dam-controlled river
Current: Moderate to difficult, depending upon the wind
River gradient: 2.46 feet per mile
River gauge: 200–2,000 cubic feet per second to run
Land status: Municipal park and private
County: Colorado
Nearest city/town: Columbus

Boats used: Canoes, kayaks, johnboats, small motorized craft
Season: Year-round
Fees and permits: Put-in fee included in costs for rentals and shuttles. Launch at no cost at TX Business 71/North River Bridge, some 200 yards upstream from the Howell Canoe Livery launch.
Maps: TOPO! Texas; USGS Columbus TX; DeLorme: Texas Atlas & Gazetteer: page 70
Contact: Howell Canoe Livery, 804 Robson St., Columbus, TX 78934; (979) 732-3816; howellcanoe.com
Special considerations: Water-release schedules are confidential, but for information about the previous day's scheduled releases and unscheduled releases due to floods, see the Lower Colorado River Association (LCRA) River Report and Flood Summary, or call LCRA at (512) 473-3200.

Put-In and Takeout Information

To shuttle point/takeout: From Columbus, drive east on US 90/Walnut Street. Cross the Colorado River bridge. Take the first left, just past the Colorado River Trail sign. Turn right into a driveway toward the river near the sign that reads "Beason's Park on the Colorado River, Colorado River Trail."

To put-in from takeout: From Beason's Park, drive west on US 90 west/Walnut Street toward Front Street for 0.7 mile. Turn right onto Prairie Street for 0.4 mile. Turn left onto Robson Street. Howell Canoe Livery is on the right. It is a tan building with racks of colorful canoes. The sign is hand-painted in red letters on a sheet of tin and attached to a wire fence. The put-in location is directly below the livery at a private dock.

Columbus, put-in

Overview

The Colorado River is the longest river contained wholly within Texas borders. From its headwaters in Dawson County in western Texas, the river courses some 862 miles to the Gulf Coast, where it pours into the briny Matagorda Bay. Along the way it cuts a southeastern route through prairie lands and limestone canyons, juniper-covered hills, and coastal plains.

From its headwaters, the river flows unsteadily to its confluence with the Concho River. Some of the best paddling opportunities begin downstream in a chain of seven major reservoirs: Lake Buchanan, Inks Lake, Lake LBJ, Lake Marble Falls, Lake Travis, Lake Austin, and Lady Bird Lake. Known as the Highland Lakes system, these reservoirs help meet water needs that range from municipal to industrial, agricultural to recreational. Paddling opportunities continue past the Longhorn Dam, the last in the chain, and through some 290 miles to the coast. Game fish, birds, diverse flora, and a range of wildlife can be found along the way, for the anglers, photographers, and bird watchers of the world.

The Colorado River is defined by a string of reservoirs, so hard-core rapids are not really a danger. But high water and heat are. Headwinds, aquatic grass, and low water flows can be hindrances. The Lower Colorado River Authority (LCRA) offers hydrological data at its Hydromet website (hydromet.lcra.org). The USGS Water-Watch website (waterwatch.usgs.gov) also provides real time stream flow information for the Colorado River and other waterways. Check these resources and contact local outfitters before paddling.

Paddle Summary

Call ahead to make arrangements with Howell Canoe Livery. After you pay your fees, you'll get a great orientation. The river guides' best advice? "The rule for this stretch of river is to stay right, when in doubt."

A private road leads to the river. Drive down and unload. Carry the boat down a set of steps. Park as directed. Launch from a sand bank into a pocket of shallow, protected water. One stroke of the paddle, and the bow is in current. The river is some 60 yards wide here. The 20-foot grassy banks are lined with pecans and other hardwoods.

At 0.3 mile, a culvert is on the right. Just beyond, many rocks and large pieces of concrete are on both sides of the river. The river splits around an island. The current picks up into Class 1. Go right. The left path has a strainer of rocks and felled trees. Avoid this. The left bank is covered with grass and trees. The edge is a sheer, low, limestone wall. A 40-foot bluff makes the right bank.

At 0.8 mile, a sandy beach is on the left, with grills and covered picnic tables. This is privately owned.

At 0.9 mile, an island stands in the middle of the river. Go right.

At 1.2 miles, a stand of willows 100 yards long leans out over the river.

At 1.3 miles, a creek on the left stands in a hardwood bottom.

At 1.6 miles, the river splits around an island. Go right, through a 20-yard wide pass over gravel and aquatic grasses.

At 1.8 miles, water joins from the left. Beyond that, a gravel bar island splits the river into three paths. Take the center path.

At 2.1 miles, water joins on the left near a house.

At 2.2 miles, a gravel bar island splits the river. Go right, through a broad shallow area. Water reconnects from the left at speed, and makes a swift area that stretches another 200 yards.

At 3.1 miles, a gravel bar island is at the right edge. Go left.

At 3.6 miles, the water speeds up, and the wind picks up and puts whitecaps on the water.

At 3.8 miles, Cummins Creek enters on the left.

At 4.4 miles, a high bluff is on the left.

At 4.6 miles, a 100-yard stretch of sticks and snags is on the right. Stay left.

At 5.2 miles, there are houses on the right.

At 6.3 miles, a long stretch of wooden pilings, planks, and metal pieces is on the

0   Kilometer   1

0   Mile   1

N

109

G Miller Road

Class I

High Bluff

Dry Creek

109

Burford Street

Cummins Creek

Private Beach

71

Rocks   *Class I*

Colorado River

Alternate Launch   ■ Howell Canoe Livery

Put-In

Debris area, planks

Train Trestle Metal Pylons ■   Wooden Wall

90

90

71   52

Beason's Park

Takeout

90

10

90

left. They've collected trees and other matter that has washed down the river. Stay right to stay out of this area. The current is slow here, and easy to navigate. It is protected from the wind as well.

At 6.3 miles, reach the "Wooden Wall," which starts on the bank, runs into the water, and crumbles over a long stretch, leaving only debris. (*Note:* The wall looks like it could give out at any time; so don't get under it.) Do, however, cast a small spinner bait or a Rapala lure along the way as you pass.

At 6.7 miles, a row of posts and stobs stick up from the water at the train trestle. Stay left. After the train trestle, the headwind returns.

At 6.8 miles, a power line crosses the river between the train trestle and the TX 71 Business bridge.

At 6.9 miles, immediately after the bridge, "Beasons" is hand-painted on one of a pair of old metal pilings. Take out here, on a sandy bank. Carry the boat up the bank to the edge of the road. Drive down and load.

Paddle Information

Contact / Outfitter

Howell Canoe Livery, 804 Robson St., Columbus, TX 78934; (979) 732-3816; howellcanoe.com. They know the river.

Local Information

Columbus Chamber of Commerce, 425 Spring St., Columbus, TX 78934; (979) 732-8385; columbustexas.org.

Local Events / Attractions

Texas Independence Relay, texasindependencerelay.com. A 200-mile footrace consisting of 40 relay legs takes participants along Texas's path to independence. Columbus is just one stop along the way.

Colorado River 100, 7825 Beauregard Circle 20B, Austin, TX 78745; (512) 970-8703; coloradoriver100.com. One of the biggest canoe races in Texas, the Colorado River 100 begins in Bastrop and ends at Howell Canoe Livery in Columbus.

23 Oak Park Loop (Navarro Mills Lake)

This 4.9-mile float takes paddlers from a narrow creek to big water and back again. Wood ducks, gulls, white pelicans, and cormorants are common companions along the way. Launch in Oak Park. Lunch and swim across the lake in Liberty Hill Park. This paddle gives a taste of the big lake, and an opportunity for as much of a paddle as you want.

Start: Oak Park, N31 57.96'/W96 41.79'
End: Oak Park, N31 57.96'/W96 41.79'
Length: 4.9 miles
Float time: 2–4 hours
Difficulty: Moderate due to winds and boat traffic
Rapids: None
River type: Reservoir
Current: None
River gradient: Not applicable
River gauge: Not applicable
Land status: Corps of Engineers Park and private

County: Navarro
Nearest city/town: Corsicana
Boats used: Canoes, kayaks, johnboats, small motorized craft, bass boats, speed boats
Season: Year-round
Fees and permits: Day-use fee
Maps: TOPO! Texas; USGS Dawson TX; DeLorme: Texas Atlas & Gazetteer: page 58
Contact: For information about recreation or lake conditions call the Fort Worth District of the US Army Corps of Engineers at (254) 578-1431.

Put-In and Takeout Information

To put-in/takeout: No shuttle is required. There is only one location for put-in and takeout. From I-45 in Corsicana, head west on Martin Luther King Jr. Boulevard for 1.3 miles. Continue onto TX 31 West, and follow for 16 miles. Turn right onto Farm Road 667 for 1.4 miles. After you pass the Navarro Mills Project Office on the left, start looking for the turn. Turn left at a brown sign on the left that reads "Oak Park U.S. Corps of Engineers Navarro Mills Lake." It's across from RD's RV Park and Storage on the right. Stop at the park entrance and ask about water conditions. The boat launch is straight ahead and well marked.

Overview

Navarro Mills Lake is located about 15 miles west of Corsicana in Navarro County. The 5,060-acre US Army Corps of Engineers reservoir drains some 320 square miles of Richland Creek in Navarro and Hill Counties. The dam construction began in 1960, with the purposes of controlling floodwaters and providing a water supply. The 7,700-foot dam rises some 80 feet above the streambed, and contains six 40- by 30-foot gates to control the release of water. The Corps of Engineers offers four areas along the 38-mile shoreline where the public can access the lake, which is a recre-

Navarro, welcome to Oak Park

ational center for the area. Anglers take note: This lake yielded a 4.56-pound white crappie, which is the Texas state record. Relatively flat terrain, clay and sandy loam soils, hardwoods, and wild grasses surround the lake.

Paddle Summary

Stop at the Corps of Engineers' Oak Park Navarro Mills Lake guard station to pay fees and check on water conditions. The put-in location is between a concrete boat ramp and dock. Drive to the bottom of the long boat ramp. Unload. Drive some 75 yards to the top of the hill to park near the showers.

Scoot out into the protected cove. The far bank is 100 yards across the water and is covered in small hardwoods. The main lake is to the left.

Turn right toward the creek where crappie anglers fish from the bank, pier, and boats. The creek/lake is less than 50 yards wide.

At 0.1 mile, reach the fishing pier. (*Note:* If people are fishing from the pier, it may be best to paddle under the walkway instead of messing up their lines.) Continue up the creek as far as you can or would like. Squirrels play, buzzards roost, downed timber crowds the narrow 15-foot-wide creek that runs the hardwood bottom.

At 0.3 mile, turn around and head back out toward the main lake.

At 0.5 mile, the creek reaches the body of the lake. The wind picks up. Bear right and follow the bank.

At 0.7 mile, follow the bank in and out of a long cove. (**Note:** If the wind is bad, just stay in these coves and out of the main lake. Or, if you're up for the chop and paddle challenge, take it on.)

At 1.1 miles, a house stands on the right bank; it is the first in a string of lakeside homes.

At 1.6 miles, the bank on the right comes to a wooded point and retreats several hundred yards into a cove. As you paddle along the bank, look to the 11 o'clock position, on the far left bank, to a communications tower on top of a green field. Paddle toward the park and boat launch there. This is a mile-long paddle across open water. It can be windy and rough. Commit only if you're comfortable with the conditions.

As you near the bank, a levee is on the left and a boat ramp, fishing docks, a pavilion, and covered picnic areas are ahead. A 25-foot sand bank welcomes you to the swimming area of Liberty Hill Park.

At 2.5 miles, a playground, garbage cans, covered areas, boat ramps, and screened units are on the right. Pull in here for a picnic and a swim before paddling back. Then turn toward the levee.

TEXAS HIGHWAYS BIGGEST HITS: FAUNAL MISFORTUNES

Some 300,000 miles of road run through Texas, which means two things: Texas has more road miles than any other state, and Texas is home to lots of road kill. Why's that important? If you're Texas paddling, you're driving plenty.

Deer collisions have gotten a lot of attention in the media lately, and rightly so. According to insurance industry statistics, in the United States every year, deer collisions are said to cause 200 deaths and cost $4 billion. Watch out for deer. If you see them, slow down.

Deer, though, are not the only animals to look out for while on the Texas highways. Here's a list of the five animals that most often lose the battle of the bumper. (Before you swerve to avoid one, ask yourself if it's worth driving into oncoming traffic.)

#5: Rabbits: eastern cottontail, swamp rabbit, and California jackrabbit (really a hare)

#4: Common raccoons and ringtails

#3: Nine-banded armadillos

#2: Virginia opossums (the only marsupial in Texas)

#1: Skunks: Texas has five species—the hooded skunk, spotted skunk, striped skunk, and two species of hog-nosed skunk.

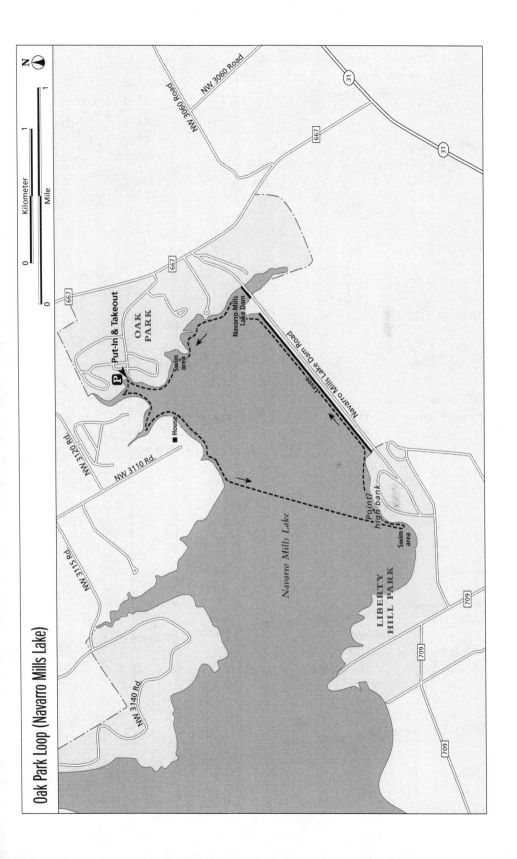

Oak Park Loop (Navarro Mills Lake)

N

| 0 | 1 | Kilometer |
| 0 | 1 | Mile |

NW 3060 Road

NW 3060 Road

31

667

31

667

667

OAK
PARK

Put-In & Takeout

P

Swim
area

Navarro Mills
Lake Dam

NW 3120 Rd.

House

NW 3110 Rd.

NW 3115 Rd.

NW 3140 Rd.

Navarro Mills Lake

Navarro Mills Lake Dam Road
(levee)

point/
high bank

Swim
area

LIBERTY
HILL PARK

709

709

709

At 3 miles, the levee begins on the right. For about 1 mile, follow the levee. There may be a headwind the whole way. You'll earn your progress and you may well get wet from the chop.

At 3.8 miles, arrive at the Navarro Mills Lake Dam. Go left at the rocky bank.

At 4.2 miles, a peninsula is on the right near a parking area. Follow the bank toward the put-in/takeout location. Bass Tracker boats, yellow-and-white minnow buckets, unmanned rods and reels, and temporarily empty lawn chairs are all staked out before RVs. The seductive scent of bacon hangs like a mist among 50-foot hardwoods.

At 4.9 miles, the put-in/takeout is on the right. A patch of bluebonnet blooms here in season to welcome you.

▶ Navarro Mills Lake is home to the Texas state record for the largest white crappie. C. G. Woodson's 4.68-pound fish—a behemoth crappie—has held the state record since 1968.

Paddle Information

Contact/Outfitter

US Army Corps of Engineers, Navarro Mills Lake Office, 1175 Farm Rd. 667, Purdon, TX 76679; (254) 578-1431; swf-wc.usace.army.mil/navarro. Call for information on the lake, events, and fishing.

Austin Canoe & Kayak (ACK), 11604 Stonehollow Dr. #300, Austin, TX 78758; (888) 828-3828; austinkayak.com. Want to rent a boat and take it wherever you decide to go? ACK offers boat rentals from locations in the cities of Austin, Houston, San Marcos, San Antonio, and Spring. "Take it anywhere you like," says one ACK representative, "Just bring it back."

Navarro Mills Lake Marina, Liberty Hill Park, 1800 Farm Rd. 709 North, Dawson, TX 76639; (254) 578-1131; navarromillslake.com.

Local Information

Corsicana & Navarro County Chamber of Commerce, 120 N. 12th St., Corsicana, TX 75110; (903) 874-4731; corsicana.org. Contact the chamber for a schedule of events.

Local Events/Attractions

North American Wood Ape Conservancy, PO Box 866621, Plano, TX 75086-6621; woodape.org. This Texas nonprofit organization is dedicated to proving the existence of Bigfoot. Yes, Bigfoot.

24 ShareLunker Loop (Purtis Creek Lake)

"The best little fishing lake in Texas," some folks call it, which makes sense since Purtis Creek Lake was designed for anglers. The best way to fish the lake is by canoe or kayak. This 5.4-mile route takes paddlers on a course through coves, flooded timber, and open water, where anglers have a real chance at catching limits of crappie, big channel catfish, or sunfish. And the lake is full of trophy largemouth bass. As of 2013, it has produced four 13-pound largemouth bass for the ShareLunker Program. Not interested in fish? No worries. This is beautiful water with plenty to see with paddle in hand.

Start: Next to the boat ramp, N32 21.44'/W95 59.67'
End: Next to the boat ramp, N32 21.44'/W95 59.67'
Length: 5.4 miles
Float time: 2–5 hours
Difficulty: Easy
Rapids: None
River type: Reservoir
Current: None
River gradient: Not applicable
River gauge: Not applicable
Land status: Public

County: Henderson and Van Zandt
Nearest city/town: Eustace
Boats used: Canoes, kayaks, johnboats, small motorized craft
Season: Year-round
Fees and permits: An entrance fee; free with the Texas State Parks Pass
Maps: TOPO! Texas; USGS Stockard TX; DeLorme: Texas Atlas & Gazetteer: page 47
Contact: For information about recreational uses or water conditions, call Purtis Creek State Park at (903) 425-2332.

Put-In and Takeout Information

To put-in/takeout: No shuttle is required. There is only one location for put-in and takeout. From TX 175 in Eustace, turn left onto Farm Road 316 north for 3.4 miles. When you see the Purtis Creek State Park sign turn left onto the park road. Stop at the headquarters to pay entrance fees. Continue straight for 0.3 mile. Bear left toward the boat ramp. The put-in is to the right of the concrete boat ramp, near the kayak rental house.

Overview

The lake at Purtis Creek State Park, where largemouth bass fishing is limited to catch-and-release only, was designed specifically for recreational angling. The 350-acre reservoir near Athens was impounded in 1985 and has a maximum depth of about 30 feet. Game fish include largemouth bass, crappie, catfish, sunfish, and white bass. The banks of the lake are covered with vegetation and trees, and much of the lake is populated with stands of flooded timber. This lake is particularly good for paddlers because it is a no-wake lake, and only 50 motorized boats are allowed on the lake at any one time.

Paddle Summary

Before heading to the launch, stop by the Purtis Creek State Park headquarters to pay fees and check on water conditions and other information.

Park and unload within 100 feet of the put-in location, which is situated to the right of the concrete boat ramp on a grassy slope near a collection of canoes, kayaks, and pedal boats.

Scoot into a small, wind-protected cove. To the right, the campground is dotted with hardwoods. Bear right to follow the bank around the cove, past a swimming area, and out toward the main lake.

At 0.4 mile, the cove meets the main lake. Turn right and follow the bank through flooded timber and along a series of coves. The banks are grassy. The woods are composed of small hardwoods.

Follow the coves along the shoreline in and out, weaving through stumps and aquatic grasses, watching the banks for birds and wildlife. Work your way toward the back section of the lake, where the giant carp bully through the shallows.

At 1.9 miles, a small grass-and-scrub island is at the back of the lake. Just the tops of the trees show above the shallow water. The lake narrows into a dense stand of trees. Explore these shallows. Then turn around, work through long stretches of flooded timber, and head back up the bank opposite the one you came in on.

At 2.7 miles, continue past the island on the left.

At 4.2 miles, bank anglers cast from a fishing pier on the right.

At 4.25 miles, another set of anglers cast from a second pier.

At 4.6 miles, an information kiosk stands on the right. Kayaks may launch from the grass banks here. Just beyond, arrive at the levee. Turn left to follow the levee and a walking trail. Note the information stands along the way. Pass a cove on the right. Note the fish cleaning station near the parking lot.

At 5.3 miles, pass another pier. The boat ramp is ahead on the right.

At 5.4 miles, arrive at the put-in/takeout location, which is on the right.

Paddle Information

Organizations

Tyler Audubon Society, PO Box 132926, Tyler, TX 75713; (903) 714-7889; tyler audubon.org. One of twenty Audubon chapters in Texas dedicated to conserving and restoring natural ecosystems, this organization focuses on birds, other wildlife, and their habitats for the benefit of humanity and the earth's biological diversity.

ShareLunker Loop (Purtis Creek Lake)

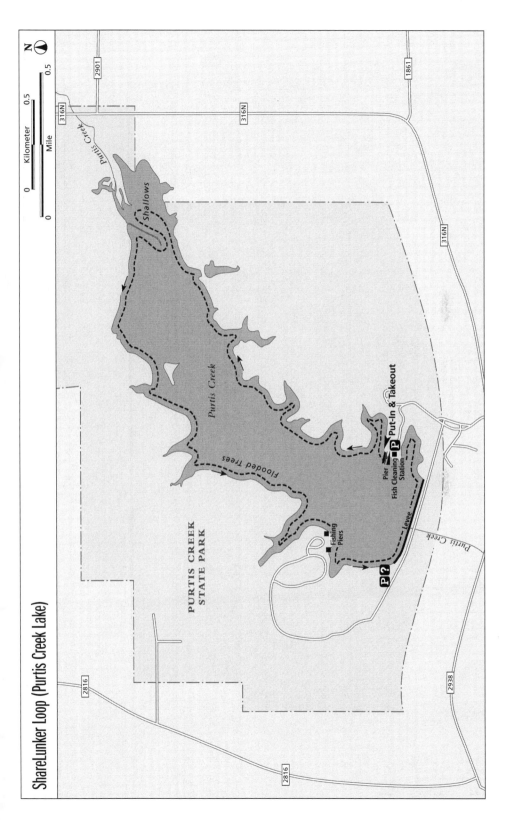

Contact / Outfitter

Purtis Creek State Park, 14225 Farm Rd. 316, Eustace, TX 75124; (903) 425-2332; tpwd.state.tx.us/state-parks/purtis-creek. Call for details on water, weather, and fishing. Canoes, kayaks, paddleboats, and a rowboat are available for rent. The park participates in the Texas Parks & Wildlife Angler Education Tackle Loaner Program.

Local Events / Attractions

Texas Freshwater Fisheries Center, 5550 Farm Rd. 2495, Athens, TX 75752; (903) 676-2277; tpwd.state.tx.us/spdest/visitorcenters/tffc. The Edwin L. Cox Jr. Texas Freshwater Fisheries Center provides an educational, entertaining visitor experience that promotes freshwater sport fishing and the enhancement, conservation, and stewardship of aquatic resources in Texas.

City of Athens Department of Tourism, 201 W. Corsicana St., Athens, TX 75752; (903) 677-0775; athenstx.org. Reach out to the department for ideas on activities, eats, and places to stay.

25 Calamity Jane Loop (Belton Lake on the Leon River)

This 3.2-mile paddle gives just a taste of the water Belton Lake has to offer. It begins in a calm cove where deer gather, runs across bigger water to a series of high-bluffed coves and a grassy isle, continues to a secluded stretch of water where fox have been spotted on the rocky shores, then back to the put-in at a popular local marina. Depending on a paddler's fitness, preparedness, and desire, this lake can give you as much paddle as you want. Call ahead to ask about the wind and water conditions.

Start: Morgan's Point Resort Marina, N31 08.73'/W97 28.33'
End: Morgan's Point Resort Marina, N31 08.73'/W97 28.33'
Length: 3.2 miles
Float time: 1–3 hours
Difficulty: Easy to difficult, depending on the wind and waves
Rapids: None
River type: Reservoir
Current: None
River gradient: Not applicable
River gauge: Not applicable

Land status: Corps of Engineers and private
County: Harris
Nearest city/town: Morgan's Point Resort
Boats used: Canoes, kayaks, johnboats, small motorized craft, jet skis
Season: Spring, summer, and fall
Fees and permits: None
Maps: TOPO! Texas; USGS Moffat TX; DeLorme: Texas Atlas & Gazetteer: page 57
Contact: For information about recreation or water conditions, contact the US Army Corps of Engineers at Belton/Stillhouse Hollow Lake; (254) 939-2461.

Put-In and Takeout Information

To put-in/takeout: No shuttle is required. There is only one location for put-in and takeout. From I-35 in Temple, take exit 301, then follow TX 53 west for 0.2 mile. Turn left onto TX 53 west/West Adams Avenue for 0.1 mile. Veer right onto Airport Road, and go 5.6 miles. Veer right to merge onto TX 317 south for 1.6 miles. Turn right onto Farm Road 2483. Follow Farm Road 2483 for 1.5 miles. Turn right onto Morgan's Point Road for 0.4 mile. Turn left onto Cheyenne Trail for 0.3 mile. Turn left onto Calamity Jane Drive; your destination will be on the right after 0.2 mile. Pull down the hill. Launch to the left or right of the Private Boat Ramp sign, where there's rock instead of concrete.

Overview

The Leon River begins in Eastland County as three forks: the north, middle, and south. From the confluence of these arms, the main river flows some 185 miles to the southeast, where it joins the Lampasas River and, ultimately, helps form the Little River. Near the city of Belton in Bell County, the US Army Corps of Engineers built a dam in 1954 to create the reservoir known as Belton Lake. The spillway and earth-fill dam are some 5,500 feet long. The 12,300-acre lake drains more than 3,600 square miles of the surrounding countryside, and provides storage for flood control. It also provides a water supply, fish and wildlife habitat, and opportunities for public recreation.

Paddle Summary

Unload near the concrete boat ramp at the marina, which consists of four boathouses, an office, and a dock for sailboats. The walk down to the put-in can be a little treacherous while carrying a boat, so take your time. If parking near the ramp is unavailable, there is additional parking on top of the hill.

Take a right from the bank and another left within 100 feet to work your way out of the marina and toward the main lake. This is a popular place for bank anglers. The marina can be busy, so expect company unless you're there early in the morning, during the week, or in cooler weather. As you near the main lake, you may see a herd of deer perusing the 60-foot limestone bank on the right.

The water is green and clear. Even in 30-degree weather, turtles poke around—just slowly.

Morgans Point, clear water and shining bluffs

At 0.2 mile, the cove meets the main lake. Great blue herons hunt along the shores. Songbirds sing and you may hear a loon call from the water. Gulls may gather. There is plenty of water to paddle to the left and to the right, but for this paddle, head straight across. Note the grass island on your right as you go. Straight across the lake, at the nearest point, there are high banks and a series of wind-protected coves. The rising sun sends warmth once you're in the main body of the lake and free from the cove's shadows.

At 0.4 mile, arrive at the point. Continue right along the bank. Ahead are many coves to explore.

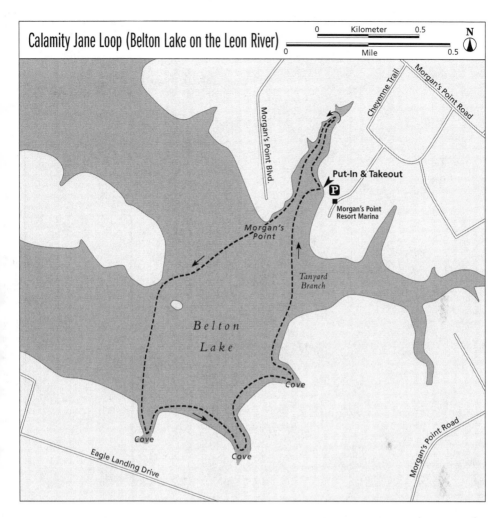

At 0.6 mile, enter the first cove on the left. Sixty-foot limestone bluffs shield much of the cove from the rising sun. Even in the shade, these cool coves boast yellows and whites and greys, and many other colors. The bluffs jut straight up out of the lake and are lined with scrub and juniper and other pioneering plants. The water's edge is lined in felled trees. A few long walkways run from homes to the water. Limestone shelves jut out some 20 feet. Follow the bank out of the cove.

At 1 mile, a cove is on the left. Explore it. There are no houses on this one. The banks are like stone monuments. At the back of the cove is a large limestone overhang where an aspiring central Texas Romeo has painted "Hey Maggie, I like you." Continue following the bank out of the cove. At the point, take a left and follow the bank. Ahead, at the 12 o'clock position, a white boathouse is on the horizon.

At 1.4 miles, enter the cove on the left.

From the point at 1.7 miles, turn toward the put-in and head to the grass island you passed on the way over.

At 2 miles, paddle through a narrow 100-yard pass that runs along the left side of the island. The marina is at the 2 o'clock position. (This island may not be visible in higher water.) Many flooded trees are in the shallows to the left. Birds gather here. Stop and explore the island. There's sign of a stone fire ring and beds of beautiful rocks on the shoreline.

Leave the island and head back toward the marina.

At 2.5 miles, pass the marina. Continue down the narrowing cove. Deer hide under the shade of low scrub on the left bank. When I paddled here, two groups of small birds flew back and forth in shifts from the top of a tree to the water's edge, as if one group was standing lookout and the other bathing and drinking. The cove narrows and banks lower to 30 feet.

At 2.8 miles, a house is on the left. The cove narrows to 30 yards wide.

At 2.9 miles, turn around and head back to the put-in.

At 3.2 miles, arrive at the put-in/takeout on the left.

Paddle Information

Organizations

Central Texas Audubon Society, 1308 Circlewood Dr., Waco, TX 76712; (254) 776-3385; centexaudubon.org.

Contact/Outfitter

Morgan's Point Resort Marina, 16 Calamity Jane Dr., Morgan's Point Resort, TX 76513; (254) 780-1334; morganspointresorttx.com. Call about water conditions.
Austin Canoe & Kayak (ACK), 11604 Stonehollow Dr. #300, Austin, TX 78758; (888) 828-3828; austinkayak.com. Want to rent a boat and take it wherever you decide to go? ACK offers boat rentals from locations in the cities of Austin, Houston, San Marcos, San Antonio, and Spring. "Take it anywhere you like," says one ACK representative, "Just bring it back."
REI Austin-Gateway, 9901 N. Capital of Texas Hwy. Suite 200, Austin, TX 78759; (512) 343-5550; rei.com.
REI Dallas, 4515 LBJ Freeway, Dallas, TX 75244; (972) 490-5989; rei.com.
US Army Corps of Engineers, Belton/Stillhouse Hollow Lake, 3740 Farm Rd. 1670, Belton, TX 76513; (254) 939-2461; swf-wc.usace.army.mil/belton/index.asp.

Local Events/Attractions

Experience Belton Convention & Visitors Bureau, 412 E. Central Ave. (PO Box 659), Belton, TX 76513; (254) 939-3551; seebelton.com. Belton has rodeos, arts and craft shows, museums, golf, shopping, fine arts, and dining. You can find all the information here.
Texas Ranger Hall of Fame, 100 Texas Ranger Trail, Waco, TX 76706; (254) 750-8631; texasranger.org. Commemorates the Texas Rangers law enforcement agency.

Morgans Point, sunrise marina

Waco Mammoth Site, 6220 Steinbeck Bend, Waco, TX 76708; (254) 750-7946; wacomammoth.org. See fossils and take tours through what the organizers call, "The nation's first and only recorded discovery of a nursery herd of Pleistocene mammoths." **Balcones Distilling,** 212 S. 17th St., Waco, TX 76701; (254) 755-6003; balcones distilling.com. Try the signature blue corn whisky at Texas's only whisky distillery—well, maybe the only legal one.

26 Comanche Gap Loop (Lampasas River at Stillhouse Hollow Lake)

This 9.9-mile loop offers paddlers flat water enough to fill the day. Bird watchers will enjoy the osprey, loons, cormorants, and gulls. Anglers will enjoy the pursuit of white bass, largemouth bass, and crappie. And all will enjoy a hillside landscape reminiscent of the Philippines' renowned Chocolate Hills. The wind can be tough and chop can hop up quickly, so call ahead, know your abilities, and plan your paddle accordingly.

Start: Dana Peak Park near Comanche Gap Pavilion, N31 01.07'/W97 36.33'
End: Dana Peak Park near Comanche Gap Pavilion, N31 01.07'/W97 36.33'
Length: 9.9 miles
Float time: 4-8 hours
Difficulty: Moderate due to boat traffic and winds
Rapids: None
River type: Reservoir
Current: None
River gradient: Not applicable
River gauge: Not applicable
Land status: Corps of Engineers park and private

County: Bell
Nearest city/town: Killeen
Boats used: Canoes, kayaks, johnboats, small motorized craft
Season: Spring, summer, and fall
Fees and permits: Park entry fee
Maps: TOPO! Texas; USGS Nolanville TX; DeLorme: Texas Atlas & Gazetteer: page 57
Contact: For information about recreation or water conditions contact the US Army Corps of Engineers at Belton/Stillhouse Hollow Lake at (254) 939-2461.

Put-In and Takeout Information

To put-in/takeout: No shuttle is required. There is only one location for put-in and takeout. From US 190 in Killeen, drive east for 2.3 miles. Take the exit for Farm Road 2410/Knight's Way for 0.2 miles. Merge onto East Central Texas Expressway for 1.7 miles. Turn right onto Farm Road 2410 east for 2.6 miles. Turn right onto Comanche Gap Road for 3 miles. Check in at the guardhouse. Continue until the road dead-ends. Turn right and go 100 yards. Turn left, pulling into the second parking loop on the left.

Overview

The Lampasas River, which is part of the Brazos River basin, begins near the town of Hamilton in Hamilton County. It flows to the southeast for some 100 miles through flat terrain, clay and sandy loams, hardwoods, junipers, and grasses to a confluence with the Leon River. Together, the Lampasas and Leon Rivers help form the Little River. Some 9 miles upstream from the confluence, near the city of Belton, the US Army Corps of Engineers built Stillhouse Hollow Dam (then Lampasas Dam) in

Stillhouse, green hills

1968, thus forming a reservoir. The 6,430-acre reservoir drains some 1,300 square miles of the surrounding countryside. The reservoir plays an important role in flood control, water conservation, fish and wildlife habitat, and local recreation. The 58 miles of shoreline are accessible through four parks, which are operated by the US Army Corps of Engineers: Stillhouse Park, Dana Peak Park, Cedar Gap Park, and Union Grove Park.

Paddle Summary

Before launching, stop by the park guardhouse to pay the fee and ask about the fishing and water conditions. Drive past the playground and swim area and park in the day-use area near Comanche Gap Pavilion, just downhill from a set of restrooms. Unload and carry the boat some 50 yards downhill, across manicured grass, to a narrow stone beach. Launch into shallow, clear water. Turn right. The banks are low. On the right bank the pavilion and several RV sites stand nearby. The hills in the distance resemble the so-called Chocolate Hills in the Philippines. Occasional roads cut white strips through the hillsides.

At 0.5 mile, an inlet is on the right. Across the lake to the left are screened cabins, bass boats, and a park area. Explore the inlet on the right.

At 1.5 miles, reach the point of a small peninsula where 15-foot limestone banks are covered in grass and scrub. Ahead, at the 12 o'clock position, a ridge drops off into flat land. Paddle toward that precipice.

At 1.9 miles, a small island is on the right.

At 2.1 miles, an inlet is on the right.

At 2.6 miles, a large inlet is on the right. Stay left and follow the main body of the lake. Across the lake, a shallow point juts out and holds many birds. As you near a precipice, look left. Three communications towers dominate the horizon. Change direction to head toward them. (*Note:* Beware of speeding boats. Stay to the sides, get your paddle blade high, and keep it moving.)

At 3.5 miles, the shoreline bends to the right. From here, the 3481/Stillhouse Hollow Road bridge is visible for the first time.

At 4.5 miles, a creek enters on the right. Explore the creek. It has lots of flooded timber that, in parts of the year, hold crappie and other fish. Explore as you like before returning to the main lake and continuing the trip to the bridge ahead.

At 5.5 miles, an inlet is on the right. Continue following the right bank toward the boat ramp and bridge ahead.

At 5.9 miles, reach the 3481 Bridge. Follow the bridge from the right bank to the left. Bank anglers cast from beneath the bridge. Birds and boats chase schooling fish.

Turn back (downstream) and head toward the launch/put-in in the most direct route possible, by cutting angles and taking advantage of wind-protected stretches. Be mindful of boat traffic. If you have time and wind permits, follow the right-hand bank back to the put-in. This will add some distance to the trip.

At 9.9 miles, arrive at the put-in on the left.

Paddle Information

Organizations

Central Texas Audubon Society, 1308 Circlewood Dr., Waco, TX 76712; (254) 776-3385; centexaudubon.org.

Contact/Outfitter

US Army Corps of Engineers, Belton/Stillhouse Hollow Lake, 3740 Farm to Market 1670, Belton, TX 76513; (254) 939-2461; swf-wc.usace.army.mil/belton/index.asp.

Austin Canoe & Kayak (ACK), 11604 Stonehollow Dr. #300, Austin, TX 78758; (888) 828-3828; austinkayak.com. Want to rent a boat and take it wherever you decide to go? ACK offers boat rentals from locations in the cities of Austin, Houston, San Marcos, San Antonio, and Spring. "Take it anywhere you like," says one ACK representative, "Just bring it back."

REI Austin-Gateway, 9901 N. Capital of Texas Hwy. Suite 200, Austin, TX 78759; (512) 343-5550; rei.com.

REI Dallas, 4515 LBJ Freeway, Dallas, TX 75244; (972) 490-5989; rei.com.

Comanche Gap Loop (Lampasas River at Stillhouse Hollow Lake)

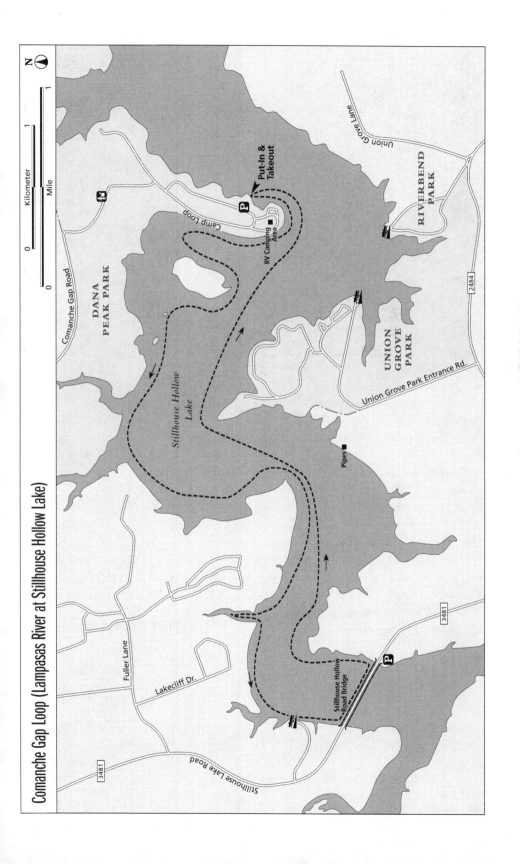

Stillhouse, limestone

Local Events/Attractions

Experience Belton Convention & Visitors Bureau, 412 E. Central Ave. (PO Box 659), Belton, TX 75613; (254) 939-3551; seebelton.com. Belton has rodeos, arts and craft shows, museums, golf, shopping, fine arts, and dining. You can find all the information here.

Texas Ranger Hall of Fame, 100 Texas Ranger Trail, Waco, TX 76706; (254) 750-8631; texasranger.org. Commemorates the Texas Rangers law enforcement agency.

Waco Mammoth Site, 6220 Steinbeck Bend, Waco, TX 76708; (254) 750-7946; wacomammoth.org. The facility offers tours of what they claim is "The nation's first and only recorded discovery of a nursery herd of Pleistocene mammoths."

Balcones Distilling, 212 S. 17th St., Waco, TX 76701; (254) 755-6003; balconesdistilling.com. Try the signature blue corn whisky at Texas's only whisky distillery—well, maybe the only legal one.

Piney Woods

In far east Texas, you'll find the Piney Woods region. Here the Sabine, Cypress, Sulphur, and Red Rivers, as well as other smaller rivers, flow through high pines, hardwood bottoms, and thick stands of elm, oak, mesquite, and ash. You'll also find Spanish moss, cypress trees, alligators, cottonmouth water moccasins, and a cast of other creatures. If you accidentally slip over the state line into Louisiana or Arkansas, you may not notice. Local and state parks in the 23,500-square mile region include Caddo Lake State Park, Huntsville State Park, Lake Bob Sandlin State Park, Lake Livingston State Park, Martin Creek Lake State Park, Martin Dies Jr. State Park, Mission Tejas State Park, Tyler State Park, Village Creek State Park, and others. In this section, you will find some great floats along the Neches and Angelina Rivers.

Davy Crockett, Aaron navigates the stobs

27 Walnut Slough Loop (Neches River on B A Steinhagen Lake)

One of several paddling opportunities offered by Martin Dies Jr. State Park, Walnut Slough Loop gives paddlers 3.3 miles of flat-water paddling through a uniquely east Texas setting. Spanish moss hangs gray like beards from stands of water-sodden cypress. Alligators bake on logs and slip from the muddy banks. Countless birds call, walk, and sail past. And white bass, drum, catfish, and other fish swim beneath your boat.

Start: Walnut Ridge Unit boat ramp, N30 51.76'/W94 10.96'
End: Walnut Ridge Unit boat ramp, N30 51.76'/W94 10.96'
Length: 3.3 miles
Float time: 1-3 hours
Difficulty: Moderate due to the need to pay attention to navigation
Rapids: None
River type: Reservoir
Current: None
River gradient: Not applicable
River gauge: Not applicable
Land status: State park

County: Jasper
Nearest city/town: Jasper
Boats used: Canoes, kayaks, johnboats, small motorized craft
Season: Year-round. Spring and fall offer the mildest temperatures.
Fees and permits: A day-use fee is payable at park headquarters.
Maps: TOPO! Texas; USGS Town Bluff TX; DeLorme: Texas Atlas & Gazetteer: page 73
Contact: For information on recreation or water conditions, call Martin Dies Jr. State Park at (409) 384-5231.

Put-In and Takeout Information

To put-in/takeout: No shuttle is needed. The put-in and takeout are in the same location. From Woodville, drive east on US 190 for 16 miles. Turn left onto Park Road 48. Pass the nature center on the right. Cross a bridge. Stay right and watch for signs for the Walnut Ridge boat ramp.

Overview

The 15,000-acre reservoir now known as B A Steinhagen Lake was created in 1953 with the completion of Dam B, or the Town Bluff Dam, a structure of concrete and compacted earth measuring some 6,700 feet long and as much as 45 feet high. The US Army Corps of Engineers reservoir provides power to Jasper, Liberty, and Livingston, Texas, and Vinton, Louisiana. It provides water for rice production, salinity control, municipal and industrial uses, and other uses. Since

▶ For more information about the Neches River, pick up a copy of Richard Donovan's guidebook *Paddling the Wild Neches,* which was sponsored by The Meadows Center for Water and the Environment.

Walnut Slough, cypress trees

1965, the lake's 705-acre Martin Dies Jr. State Park has been an important recreational destination. The waters of the Angelina and Neches Rivers make the reservoir.

The Angelina River is formed near Laneville by Barnhardt, Scoober, and Shawnee Creeks, and flows through some 120 miles of forest, bottoms, and sandy loam to a confluence with the Neches River near Jasper.

The Neches River flows from near Colfax, through B A Steinhagen Reservoir, and to coastal Sabine Lake. Along the way it drains some 10,000 square miles of east Texas. For much of its 420-mile course, the river forms the shared boundary of neighboring counties as it runs through pines (loblolly, longleaf, and shortleaf), oaks (post, southern, red, and white), cypress and countless other trees, native grasses, and flowering plants.

Paddle Summary

The top five indicators of an upcoming backwater adventure must be green johnboats, old Johnson outboard motors, Spanish moss, alligators, and cypress trees. These things define the paddles at Martin Dies Jr. State Park.

On the way to the Walnut Slough Loop put-in, stop at the guard station/kiosk to pay your fees and ask about fishing and water conditions. The put-in is alongside the boat ramp near a swing set, screened-in structures, and a group dining hall. Two information kiosks mark the launch: "Welcome to the Martin Dies Jr. State Park Paddling Trails," says one, and it offers phone numbers, routes, etc. The other displays general information for the park and waterways. Pull down to the water. Set the boat on a mix of soft mud and gravel. Sit in the boat on the water's edge and scoot out into the calm water.

Turn left out of the launch so the land is on your left. Thick lilies and aquatic grasses transport you to the Amazon, the Pantanal, or maybe to Wonderland. At times, the bald cypresses are fire-red; green moss sways in the wind and dark lines on the pregnant trunks mark the river's drops. Grebes, kingfishers, great blue herons, and various unseen songbirds are everywhere.

At 200 yards, you'll pass a Texas Parks & Wildlife Department (TPWD) trail marker of white PVC pipe and red tape. Follow the bank as it makes a hard left. Explore the stands of cypress knees and lilies. Ahead, beyond the grasses and out of the trail are two bridges for US 190.

At 0.5 mile, a campsite is on the left (N30 51.509'/W94 10.975'). Follow the left bank. Come into an open area. On the left is a stand of water-wading cypress, from which dangling moss obscures the herons that hunt the shadows. The grass beds move, so find a path through.

At 1 mile, an inlet is on the left (N30 51.449'/W94 10.542'). Turn left at the white TPWD buoy marked with a red stripe and a red heart. The trail narrows to about 120 feet.

At 1.1 miles, power lines cross the water. Ducks jump up from water the color of sweet tea. The kayak may be so quiet that wildlife jumps behind you. The grass is thick, so if you get hung up, just keep paddling. Momentum is key.

At 1.7 miles, pass under Park Road 48 (N30 52.055'/W94 10.371') and bear left into a path that is about 45 feet wide. Frogs the size of a thumbnail leap from the floating grasses in a squeak.

At 2 miles, a wooden pedestrian bridge is on the right and another is ahead on the left. Pass under the one on the right and go out into open water. Bear left and follow the bank past a bend to the left, passing cattails, screened structures, a campground, a pier and a metal bulkhead.

At 3.3 miles, arrive back at the put-in.

Paddle Information

Organizations

Jasper–Lake Sam Rayburn Area Chamber of Commerce, 46 E. Milam St., Jasper, TX 75951; (409) 384-2762; jaspercoc.org.

Contact/Outfitter

Martin Dies Jr. State Park, 634 Park Road 48 S., Jasper, TX 75951; (409) 384-5231; tpwd.state.tx.us/state-parks/martin-dies-jr. Call about water conditions and

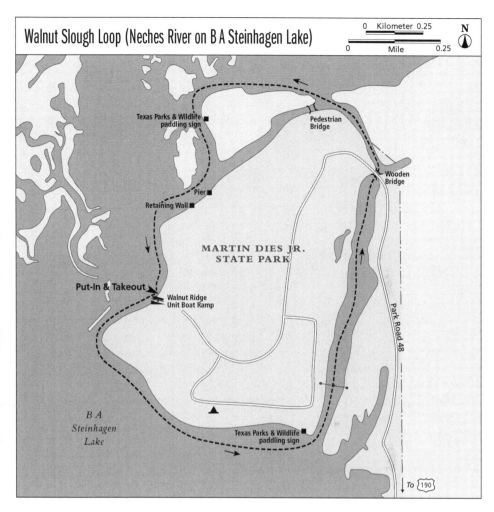

Walnut Slough Loop (Neches River on B A Steinhagen Lake)

0 Kilometer 0.25
0 Mile 0.25

N

Texas Parks & Wildlife paddling sign

Pedestrian Bridge

Wooden Bridge

Pier

Retaining Wall

MARTIN DIES JR. STATE PARK

Put-In & Takeout

Walnut Ridge Unit Boat Ramp

Park Road 48

B A Steinhagen Lake

Texas Parks & Wildlife paddling sign

To 190

activities. Rental boats and lodging are available. Ask about the Texas State Park Pass.

Austin Canoe & Kayak (ACK), 11604 Stonehollow Dr. #300, Austin, TX 78758; (888) 828-3828; austin kayak.com. Want to rent a boat and take it wherever you decide to go? ACK offers boat rentals from locations in Austin, Houston, San Marcos, San Antonio, and Spring. "Take it anywhere you like," says one ACK representative, "Just bring it back."

▶ **Mosquitos are active even at midday in early November. Sunset is worse, so bring your repellant and long sleeves.**

Local Events/Attractions

East Texas Regional Arts Center, 364 N. Austin St., Jasper, TX 75951; (409) 384-2404; easttexasartleague.org. Visit the art gallery and exhibition hall.

Annual Fall Festival, 121 N. Austin St., Jasper, TX 75951; (409) 384-2762; jasper coc.org.

28 Neches River Loop
(Neches River on B A Steinhagen Lake)

One of several paddling opportunities in Martin Dies Jr. State Park, the Neches River Loop gives paddlers 2.7 miles of flat-water paddling through a uniquely east Texas setting. Anglers will have a chance to catch white bass, drum, catfish, and other fish. And, everyone will enjoy the scenery where Spanish moss hangs gray like beards from stands of water-sodden cypress; alligators bake on logs and slip from the muddy banks, and countless birds call, walk, and sail past.

Start: Walnut Ridge Unit boat ramp, N30 51.76'/W94 10.96'
End: Walnut Ridge Unit boat ramp, N30 51.76'/W94 10.96'
Length: 2.7 miles
Float time: 1-3 hours
Difficulty: Moderate due to the need to pay attention to navigation
Rapids: None
River type: Dam-controlled river
Current: None to slow
River gradient: Not applicable
River gauge: Not applicable
Land status: State park

County: Jasper
Nearest city/town: Jasper
Boats used: Canoes, kayaks, johnboats, small motorized craft
Season: Year-round. Spring and fall offer the mildest temperatures.
Fees and permits: A day-use fee is payable at park headquarters.
Maps: TOPO! Texas; USGS Town Bluff TX; DeLorme: Texas Atlas & Gazetteer: page 73
Contact: For information on recreation or water conditions, call Martin Dies, Jr. State Park at (409) 384-5231.

Put-In and Takeout Information

To put-in/takeout: No shuttle is needed. The put-in and takeout are in the same location. From Woodville, drive east on US 190 for 16 miles. Turn left onto Park Road 48. Pass the nature center on the right. Cross a bridge. Stay right and watch for TPWD paddling trails and boat launch signs.

Overview

B A Steinhagen Lake is a 15,000-acre reservoir that dates back to 1953. It formed upon the completion of Dam B, or the Town Bluff Dam, built of compacted earth and concrete. The structure measures some 6,700 feet long and as much as 45 feet high. The waters of the Angelina and Neches Rivers fill the reservoir. Jasper, Liberty, and Livingston, Texas, along with Vinton, Louisiana, rely on this US Army Corps of Engineers reservoir for power. The reservoir also provides water for rice production, salinity control, municipal and industrial uses, fishing, paddling, wildlife viewing, hunting, photography, and other types of recreation.

Neches River, paddling trail put-in

The Angelina River is formed near Laneville by Barnhardt, Scoober, and Shawnee Creeks, and flows through some 120 miles of forest, bottoms, and sandy loam to its confluence with the Neches River near Jasper.

The Neches River flows from near Colfax, through B A Steinhagen Reservoir, to coastal Sabine Lake. Along the way it drains some 10,000 square miles of east Texas. For much of this 420-mile course, the river forms the shared boundary of neighboring counties as it runs through pines (loblolly, longleaf, and shortleaf), oaks (post, southern, red, and white), cypress and countless other trees, native grasses, and flowering plants.

Paddle Summary

This route gives paddlers a chance to experience the creeping shallow backwaters and the easy currents of the Neches River.

Stop at the guard station/kiosk on the way to the Walnut Ridge Unit put-in, to pay your fees and check on fishing and water conditions. The put-in is next to the boat ramp near a swing set, screened-in structures, and a group dining hall. Two information kiosks mark the launch: one is signed "Welcome to the Martin Dies Jr.

Neches River Loop (Neches River on B A Steinhagen Lake)

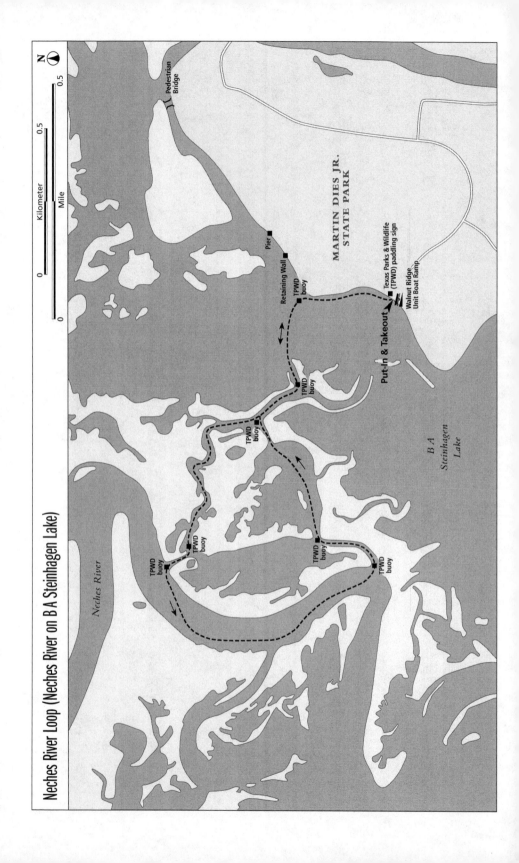

N

0   0.5   Kilometer   0.5
0   0.5   Mile

Pedestrian Bridge

Pier

Retaining Wall

TPWD buoy

MARTIN DIES JR. STATE PARK

Texas Parks & Wildlife (TPWD) paddling sign

Put-In & Takeout

Walnut Ridge Unit Boat Ramp

B A Steinhagen Lake

TPWD buoy

TPWD buoy

TPWD buoy

TPWD buoy

TPWD buoy

TPWD buoy

Neches River

State Park Paddling Trails" and it offers phone numbers, routes, etc. The other displays general information for the park and waterways. Pull down to the water. Set the boat on a mix of soft mud and gravel. Sit in the boat on the water's edge and scoot out into the calm water.

▶ **A novice should do the Neches River Loop paddle with a partner, or early in the morning, and with a GPS unit.**

With a little imagination, this paddle could make you think you're visiting the Amazon, the Pantanal, or maybe Wonderland. Some of the bald cypresses are fire-red; green moss sways in the wind; and a dark line on the pregnant trunks marks the river's drops. Enjoy the sights and sounds of grebes, kingfishers, great blue herons, and various songbirds.

Turn right out of the launch.

At 0.2 mile, go left around a white Texas Parks & Wildlife Department (TPWD) buoy (N30 51.950'/W94 10.978'). You might see a hawk slide just above the tops of high grass. The waterway is about 30 feet wide, with grass and pseudoland on either side.

At 0.4 mile, bear right around a white TPWD buoy with a red stripe and diamond (N30 51.964'/W94 11.159'). The waterway widens to 60 feet or so.

At 0.5 mile, pass a TPWD buoy with a red stripe and crescent moon (N30 52.042'/W94 11.25'). Left and right are options. Go right because later this will allow you to take advantage of the main river current.

At 1 mile, pass a white TPWD buoy with a red stripe and triangle (N30 52.163'/W94 11.540'). Left and right are options. Go right.

At 1.1 miles, pass a white TPWD buoy with a red stripe and square on the side (N30 52.201'/W94 11.582'). Here the waterway joins the Neches River. Left and right are options. Go left. The river is 150 yards wide.

At 1.4 miles, water enters from the right. Stay left.

At 1.6 miles, the river takes a hard right, but on the left bank is a white TPWD buoy with a red stripe and oval (N30 51.830'/W94 11.694'). Turn left. The path narrows to 30 feet or so.

At 1.8 miles, pass a white TPWD buoy with a red stripe and pentagon (N30 51.919'/W94 11.501'). Left and right are options. Go right.

At 2.1 miles, pass a white TPWD buoy with a red stripe and crescent moon. Here you are rejoining the earlier path. Left and right are options. Go right.

At 2.2 miles, pass a white TPWD buoy with a red stripe. Right and left are options. Go right.

At 2.5 miles is a white TPWD buoy with a red stripe and circle. Left and right are options. Go left. The put-in is ahead on the right.

At 2.7 miles, arrive at the put-in on the right.

Paddle Information

Organizations

Jasper–Lake Sam Rayburn Area Chamber of Commerce, 46 E. Milam St., Jasper, TX 75951; (409) 384-2762; jaspercoc.org.

Neches River, canoe dock

Contact / Outfitter

Martin Dies Jr. State Park, 634 Park Road 48 S., Jasper, TX 75951; (409) 384-5231; tpwd.state.tx.us/state-parks/martin-dies-jr. Call about water conditions and activities. Rental boats and lodging are available. Ask about the Texas State Park Pass.

Austin Canoe & Kayak (ACK), 11604 Stonehollow Dr. #300, Austin, TX 78758; (888) 828-3828; austinkayak.com. Want to rent a boat and take it wherever you decide to go? ACK offers boat rentals from locations in Austin, Houston, San Marcos, San Antonio, and Spring. "Take it anywhere you like," says one ACK representative, "Just bring it back."

Local Events / Attractions

East Texas Regional Arts Center, 364 N. Austin St., Jasper, TX 75951; (409) 384-2404; easttexasartleague.org. Visit the art gallery and exhibition hall.

Annual Fall Festival, 121 N. Austin St., Jasper, TX 75951; (409) 384-2762; jasper coc.org.

29 Bevilport to Martin Dies Jr. State Park (Angelina and Neches Rivers)

One of several paddling opportunities offered by Martin Dies Jr. State Park, a trip on the Angelina and Neches Rivers offers paddlers 9.7 miles of flat-water paddling through a uniquely east Texas setting. Spanish moss hangs gray like beards from stands of water-sodden cypress. Alligators bake on logs and slip from the muddy banks. Countless birds call, walk, and sail past. Sunfish pop, pop, pop insects at the water's surface. This stretch offers hunting, fishing, wildlife watching, backcountry camping, and a chance to see remnants of nineteenth-century log rafts.

Start: Bevilport boat ramp, Angelina–Neches/ Dam B Wildlife Management Area, N30 55.43'/W94 09.39'
End: Walnut Ridge Unit boat ramp, N30 51.76'/W94 10.96'
Length: 9.7 miles
Float time: 5–8 hours
Difficulty: Moderate due to distance and navigation
Rapids: None
River type: Dam-controlled river
Current: Mild to moderate
River gradient: 0.41 feet per mile
River gauge: 500–2,000 cubic feet per second to run
Land status: State park and private

County: Jasper
Nearest city/town: Jasper
Boats used: Canoes, kayaks, johnboats, small motorized craft
Season: Year-round. Spring and fall offer the mildest temperatures.
Fees and permits: No charge to launch at Bevilport; a day-use fee is payable at Martin Dies Jr. State Park headquarters at the takeout.
Maps: TOPO! Texas; USGS Pace Hill TX and Town Bluff TX; DeLorme: Texas Atlas & Gazetteer: page 73
Contact: For information on recreation or water conditions, call Martin Dies Jr. State Park at (409) 384-5231.

Put-In and Takeout Information

To shuttle point/takeout: From Jasper, drive west on TX 190 for 11.2 miles. Turn right onto Park Road 48 in the Walnut Ridge Unit. Pass the nature center on the right. Cross a bridge. Stay right and watch for signs for the TPWD paddling trails and the boat launch.

To put-in from takeout: From the Walnut Ridge Unit Boat Ramp, take Park Road 48 to US 190. Turn left and continue on US 190 for 3 miles. Turn left onto Farm Road 1747 and go 4.3 miles. Turn left onto Farm Road 2799 for 1.7 miles. The boat ramp is at the end of the road.

Bevilport, sunning 6-foot gator

River Overview

The Angelina River is formed near Laneville by Barnhardt, Scoober, and Shawnee Creeks; it flows through some 120 miles of forest, bottoms, and sandy loam to its confluence with the Neches River near Jasper.

The Neches River flows from near Colfax, through B A Steinhagen Reservoir, and to coastal Sabine Lake. Along the way it drains some 10,000 square miles of east Texas. For much of its 420-mile course, the river forms the shared boundary of neighboring counties as it runs through pines (loblolly, longleaf, and shortleaf), oaks (post, southern, red, and white), cypress, and countless other trees, native grasses, and flowering plants.

The waters of the Angelina and Neches Rivers converge to form the 15,000–acre reservoir now known as B A Steinhagen Lake behind Dam B or the Town Bluff Dam. Created in 1953, the structure of compacted earth and concrete is some 6,700 feet long and as much as 45 feet high. The US Army Corps of Engineers reservoir provides power to Jasper, Liberty, and Livingston, Texas, and Vinton, Louisiana. It provides water for rice production, salinity control, municipal and industrial uses, and other uses. Since 1965, the lake's 705-acre Martin Dies Jr. State Park has been an important recreational destination. The waters of the Angelina and Neches Rivers make the reservoir.

Paddle Summary

This paddle ends in Martin Dies Jr. State Park, so paddlers must visit the park office before the trip to pay fees and get river information. Farm Road 2799 ends at the Bevilport boat launch. Unload at the concrete boat launch near the wooden dock and rope swing. Parking is available within 100 feet of the put-in. The put-in location is an easy sand slope to the left of the ramp. Slide into a cove off the main current. Take a left out of the cove and head down with the current to the left, along banks that are thick with pines, cypress, and oaks.

Willows and cypress signal incoming backwaters. The river offers too many offshoots to count. The features important for navigation are discussed below. The rules: Stick to the main river. Use a map to plan your paddle. Paddle with a friend. And use a GPS unit.

At 0.5 mile, a brown sign on the right bank reads "Entering Angelina–Neches/ Dam 'B' Wildlife Management Area" (N30 55.120'/W94 09.688').

At 2 miles, a sign on the left reads "Bluff 1 Camping by Permit Call 409-429-3491" (N30 54.174'/W94 10.045'). This site and all subsequent sites have a picnic table, a fire ring, and grate, and a pole with two hooks for hanging garbage bags, food bags, or stringing up deer for cleaning.

At 2.3 miles, a sign on the left reads "Bluff 2."

At 3.1 miles, a sign reads "Hamilton Lake 1" (N30 54.168'/W94 10.125')

At 3.75 miles, a narrow waterway—maybe 20 feet wide—angles in to the river such that it is easily missed. It opens to a secret backwater full of cypress, grass mats, alligators, and other wildlife. Paddle in and around.

At 4.75 miles, an inlet is on the left, and sign reads "Angelina Sites 1–3."

At 5.5 miles, a sign on the left reads "Moon Lake 1."

At 5.7 miles, a sign on the left reads "Moon Lake 2."

At 5.8 miles, a sign on the left reads "Moon Lake 3."

At 7.3 miles, a white Texas Parks & Wildlife Department (TPWD) buoy with a red stripe and half moon (N30 52.729'/W94 11.590') is on the left. Stay right to remain in the main river.

Option: At 7.3 miles, at the white TPWD buoy with a red stripe and half moon, turn left to abandon the main river for a short detour that will cut a bend from the river. The mouth of the waterway is about 20 feet wide. When the water splits, go right into the 10-foot-wide canopied path. Enter an open, grassy area. Paddle for the far bank and turn left into the main river. From there, continue following the directions for this paddle.

At 8.7 miles, reach a white TPWD buoy with a red stripe and half square (N30 52.202'/W94 11.580'). The waterway splits. Bear left. Seventy yards in, reach a white TPWD buoy with a red stripe and triangle. Bear left.

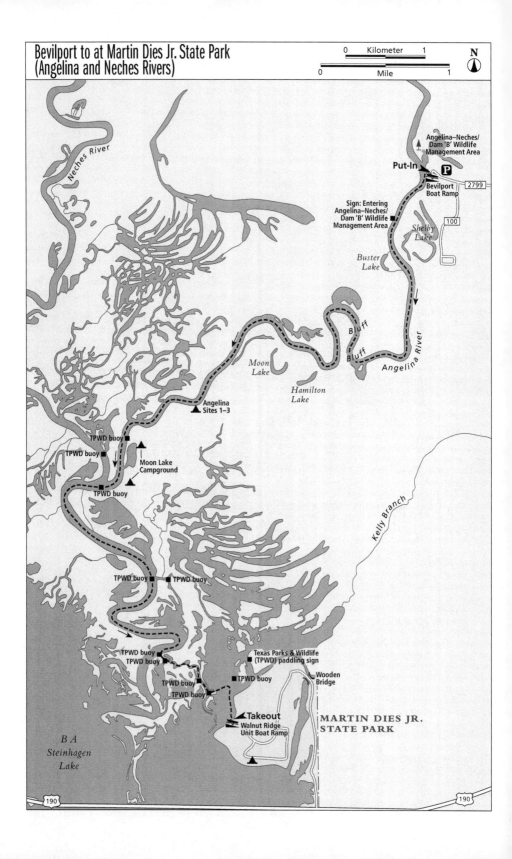

Bevilport to at Martin Dies Jr. State Park
(Angelina and Neches Rivers)

Kilometer

Mile

N

Neches River

Angelina–Neches/
Dam 'B' Wildlife
Management Area

Put-In

Bevilport
Boat Ramp

2799

Sign: Entering
Angelina–Neches/
Dam 'B' Wildlife
Management Area

Shelby
Lake

100

Buster
Lake

Bluff

Moon
Lake

Bluff

Angelina River

Hamilton
Lake

Angelina
Sites 1–3

Kelly Branch

TPWD buoy

TPWD buoy

Moon Lake
Campground

TPWD buoy

TPWD buoy   TPWD buoy

TPWD buoy
TPWD buoy

Texas Parks & Wildlife
(TPWD) paddling sign

Wooden
Bridge

TPWD buoy
TPWD buoy

TPWD buoy

Takeout
Walnut Ridge
Unit Boat Ramp

MARTIN DIES JR.
STATE PARK

B A
Steinhagen
Lake

190

190

At 9.2 miles, reach a white TPWD buoy with a red stripe and crescent moon (N30 52.041'/W94 11.251'). Bear left.

At 9.3 miles, reach a white TPWD buoy with a red stripe and diamond. Bear left. Head for the big pines.

At 9.5 miles, reach a white TPWD buoy with a red stripe (N30 51.960'/W94 10.986') near a pier and metal bulkhead. Bear right. Martin Dies Jr. campground and screened units are on the left. Pass the wooden pier and concrete boat ramp on the left.

At 9.7 miles, arrive at the takeout, alongside the ramp on a bed of mud, gravel, and vegetation.

Paddle Information

Organizations

Jasper–Lake Sam Rayburn Area Chamber of Commerce, 46 E. Milam St., Jasper, TX 75951; (409) 384-2762; jaspercoc.org.

Contact/Outfitter

Martin Dies Jr. State Park, 634 Park Road 48 S., Jasper, TX 75951; (409) 384-5231; tpwd.state.tx.us/state-parks/martin-dies-jr. Call about water conditions and activities. Rental boats and lodging are available. Ask about the Texas State Park Pass.
Austin Canoe & Kayak (ACK), 11604 Stonehollow Dr. #300, Austin, TX 78758; (888) 828-3828; austinkayak.com. Want to rent a boat and take it wherever you decide to go? ACK offers boat rentals from locations in Austin, Houston, San Marcos, San Antonio, and Spring. "Take it anywhere you like," says one ACK representative, "Just bring it back."

Local Events/Attractions

East Texas Regional Arts Center, 364 N. Austin St., Jasper, TX 75951; (409) 384-2404; easttexasartleague.org. Visit the art gallery and exhibition hall.
Annual Fall Festival, 121 N. Austin St., Jasper, TX 75951; (409) 384-2762; jaspercoc.org.

30 B A Steinhagen Lake–Birds to Butch Loop (Neches River)

One of several paddling opportunities offered by Martin Dies Jr. State Park, the Birds to Butch Loop gives paddlers 10.8 miles of flat-water paddling through a uniquely east Texas setting on B A Steinhagen Lake. Chase birds to find schools of fish on the open lake. Work stands of water-sodden cypress. And get a great workout in the process.

Start: Park Road 48 canoe dock, N30 50.61'/W94 10.00'
End: Park Road 48 canoe dock, N30 50.61'/W94 10.00'
Length: 10.8 miles
Float time: 3-8 hours
Difficulty: Moderate to difficult due to distance, wind, chop, and absence of current
Rapids: None
River type: Dammed river/reservoir
Current: None
River gradient: Not applicable
River gauge: Not applicable
Land status: State park and private

County: Jasper, Tyler
Nearest city/town: Jasper
Boats used: Canoes, kayaks, johnboats, small motorized craft
Season: Year-round. Spring and fall offer the mildest temperatures.
Fees and permits: A day-use fee is payable at park headquarters.
Maps: TOPO! Texas; USGS Town Bluff TX; DeLorme: Texas Atlas & Gazetteer: page 73
Contact: For information on recreation or water conditions, call Martin Dies Jr. State Park at (409) 384-5231.

Put-In and Takeout Information

To put-in/takeout: No shuttle is needed. Put-in and takeout are in the same location. From Woodville, drive east on US 190 for 16.2 miles. Turn right onto Park Road 48, which runs through the Hen House Unit. Pass the park headquarters on the right. Park on the right side of the road at the first bridge. The canoe dock is to the right.

Overview

The Angelina and Neches Rivers merge to form the 15,000-acre B A Steinhagen Lake, which provides water for rice production, salinity control, municipal and industrial uses, and more. Dam B or the Town Bluff Dam, which created the lake, provides power to Jasper, Liberty, and Livingston, Texas, and Vinton, Louisiana. The structure of compacted earth and concrete was completed in 1953, and it measures 6,700 feet long and as much as 45 feet high. It's administered by the US Army Corps of Engineers. The surrounding 705-acre Martin Dies Jr. State Park has been an important recreational destination since 1965.

Butch, cypress stand

The Angelina River is formed near Laneville by Barnhardt, Scoober, and Shawnee Creeks, and flows through some 120 miles of forest, bottoms, and sandy loam to its confluence with the Neches River near Jasper.

The Neches River flows from near Colfax to coastal Sabine Lake. Along the way it drains some 10,000 square miles of east Texas. For much of its 420-mile course, the river forms the shared boundary between neighboring counties, and runs through woodlands of pines, oaks, cypress and countless other trees, as well as native grasses and flowering plants.

Paddle Summary

This route takes paddlers from a protected backwater across an open lake and back. The paddle is long and sometimes windy. It is just right for those looking for a beautiful and physically challenging route. (*Note:* This route is not marked on any park signs. To do this route exactly, you'll need a GPS unit. Otherwise, create your own version.)

On the way to the put-in, stop at the park headquarters to pay fees and learn about water conditions. Park on the side of Park Road 48 just before the canoe dock.

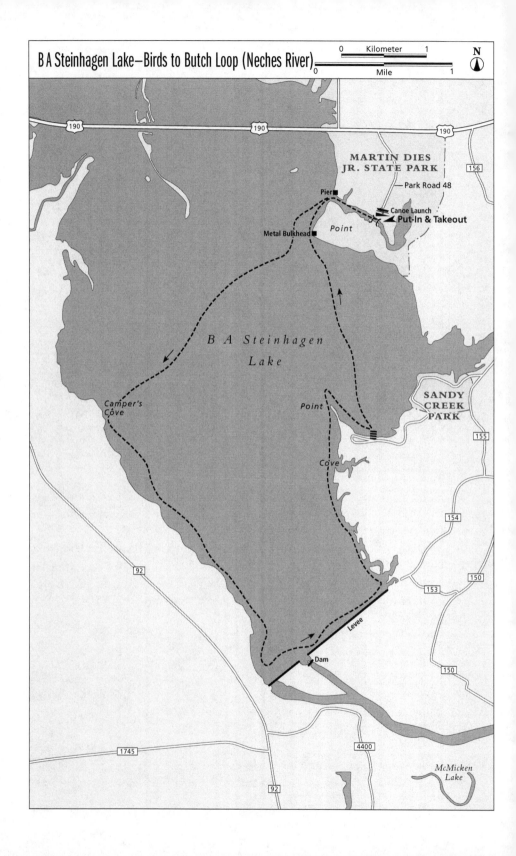

B A Steinhagen Lake–Birds to Butch Loop (Neches River)

0   Kilometer   1

0   Mile   1

N

190

190

190

156

MARTIN DIES
JR. STATE PARK

Park Road 48

Pier

Canoe Launch

Put-In & Takeout

Point

Metal Bulkhead

B A Steinhagen
Lake

Camper's
Cove

Point

SANDY
CREEK
PARK

155

Cove

154

150

92

153

150

Levee

Dam

1745

4400

92

McMicken
Lake

Launch to the left of the floating dock. Take a left out of the launch and pass under the bridge to explore a small cove covered in cypress and grass mats. Turn around, pass back under the bridge, and head out of the slough toward the main lake.

At 0.4 mile, a fishing pier stands on the corner of the open lake. Keep a respectful distance from the anglers. Turn left and follow the bank past the campground, boat ramp, dock, and day-use area. After you pass the concrete boat launch, pull up along the metal bulkhead. Set your sights to the 2 o'clock position, and head across the open lake toward cypress trees. On a clear day, shiny metal roofs are visible on the far bank behind these trees.

At 1.5 miles, at the stand of cypress trees, turn toward the metal roof shining from near Camper's Cove on the far bank (N30 49.423'/W94 12.077'). Paddle to this far bank.

At 2.8 miles, turn left and follow the shoreline through the flooded trees. Keep an eye out for congregating birds. If you find them, fish them. Cast a jig and get ready. The fish are there.

At 5.3 miles, turn left at the foot of the dam (N30 47.822'/W94 10.854') to follow the levee.

At 6.4 miles, the levee ends in cypress trees, aquatic grass, and lily pads. Take a left and continue through shallow water, keeping the bank on your right. Keep an eye out for Butch. He's been running trotlines and fly fishing here for decades. See what he has to say.

At 7.4 miles, a cove is on the right (N30 49.092'/W94 10.337'). The mouth of the cove is 100 yards wide. Follow it through the campground and into a swampy area with lots of flooded timber. When the path ends at about 7.6 miles turn around and head back to the main lake, continuing with the bank on your right.

At 8.2 miles, round the point to the right, and continue with the bank on the right.

At 8.6 miles, a boardwalk and a dumpster are on the right (N30 49.283'/W94 10.091'). From here, turn left and aim for the water tower. As you approach, watch for the point you departed from.

At 10 miles, reach the point where you departed. Follow the wall, keeping it on the right.

At 10.4 miles, pass the fishing pier on the right. Take a right into the cove.

At 10.8 miles, arrive back at the put-in.

Paddle Information

Organizations

Jasper–Lake Sam Rayburn Area Chamber of Commerce, 46 E. Milam St., Jasper, TX 75951; (409) 384-2762; jaspercoc.org.

Contact/Outfitter

Martin Dies Jr. State Park, 634 Park Road 48 S., Jasper, TX 75951; (409) 384-5231; tpwd.state.tx.us/state-parks/martin-dies-jr. Call about water conditions and activities. Rental boats and lodging are available. Ask about the Texas State Park Pass.

Butch, calm put-in

Austin Canoe & Kayak (ACK), 11604 Stonehollow Dr. #300, Austin, TX 78758; (888) 828-3828; austinkayak.com, Want to rent a boat and take it wherever you decide to go? ACK offers boat rentals from locations in Austin, Houston, San Marcos, San Antonio, and Spring. "Take it anywhere you like," says one ACK representative, "Just bring it back."

Local Events / Attractions

East Texas Regional Arts Center, 364 N. Austin St., Jasper, TX 75951; (409) 384-2404; easttexasartleague.org. Visit the art gallery and exhibition hall.

Annual Fall Festival, 121 N. Austin St., Jasper, TX 75951; (409) 384-2762; jasper coc.org.

31 Davy Crockett National Forest Paddling Trail (Neches River)

This 9.6-mile stretch of the Neches River takes paddlers through the Davy Crockett National Forest. The river runs a secluded course so filled with stobs that paddlers leave the river as well-practiced navigators. Common companions along this stretch include owls, hawks, wild turkeys, deer, kingfishers, and wild hogs. The banks and bluffs are home to pine, oak, hickory, dogwood, hackberry, and pecan.

Start: CR 2829 Bridge, N31 26.67'/W95 02.04'

End: TX 7 Bridge, N31 23.79'/W94 57.93'

Length: 9.6 miles

Float time: 4–6 hours

Difficulty: Moderate due to many river obstructions

Rapids: Countless Class I. If the water is high, all the felled timber could make this a treacherous run.

River type: Dam-controlled river

Current: Moderate

River gradient: 1.15 feet per mile

River gauge: 200–2,000 cubic feet per second to run

Land status: Private

County: Angelina

Nearest city/town: Lufkin

Boats used: Canoes, kayaks, johnboats, small motorized craft. For much of the trip, only canoes and kayaks are appropriate.

Season: Year-round

Fees and permits: None

Maps: TOPO! Texas; USGS Weches TX, Forest TX, Kennard NE TX, Centralia TX; DeLorme: Texas Atlas & Gazetteer: page 60

Contact: For information on river conditions contact the Angelina & Neches River Authority at (936) 632-7795

Put-In and Takeout Information

To shuttle point/takeout: From Lufkin, drive west on TX 103/Farm Road 706 for 11.3 miles. Continue straight to merge with TX 7 west. Continue for 0.6 mile. Take the driveway to the left immediately before the TX 7 bridge over the Neches River. **To put-in from takeout:** From the TX 7 Bridge, drive west on TX 7 for 4.6 miles. Watch for brown signs for the paddling trail. Turn right onto FS 511-1 for 2.2 miles. Turn right onto CR 1155 for 2.4 miles. Take a right on CR 2729 for 0.3 mile. Look for a Davy Crockett Paddling Trail kiosk before a metal bridge with high sides and a wooden floor. Park before the bridge.

River Overview

The Neches River has long played a role in local history. Archaeologists have determined that native peoples were living in the area as early as 12,000 years ago. Spanish explorer Alonso De León led several expeditions to the area in the 1680s. Beginning in the 1830s, flat-bottomed barges were used to float goods down to Sabine Bay.

Davy Crockett, after river bass

The river remained important in commerce until the proliferation of railways in the 1870s.

The Neches River flows from near Colfax, through Lake Palestine and B A Steinhagen Reservoir, and on to coastal Sabine Lake. For much of its 420-mile course, the river forms the shared boundary of neighboring counties, and runs through woodlands of pine (loblolly, longleaf, and shortleaf), oak (post, southern, red, and white), cypress, and countless other trees, native grasses, and flowering plants. It drains some 10,000 square miles of east Texas.

Paddle Summary

There are no fees or permits for this paddle, so just head to the river. Park alongside the road near the informational paddle sign. There is a house nearby, so be respectful of private property. Carry your boat down the dirt road that runs down a steep embankment alongside the metal bridge. This is a precarious put-in, so look for the spot that suits you best. Turn downstream to the right and prepare to cruise the forest. The river is full of stobs, flooded timber, felled trees, and other obstacles that—by paying attention—are easy enough to navigate. The City of Lufkin cuts paths through the fallen trees so paddlers have a clear path. The current is such that you can just steer in most places, except when headwinds pick up. The water is muddy, so you'll have to read it well to detect sandbars, stobs, and so on. Wild pigs and deer, as well as kingfishers, ducks, owls, hawks, turkeys, and countless other birds, are common companions.

At 0.2 mile, a private dock is on the left. Butterflies and falling leaves mimic one another on their descent to the river's surface.

At 1.8 miles, a Class I rapid (N31 24.830'/W94 59.339') runs some 100 yards. It is shallow and there are many downed logs.

At 2 miles, the water slows, a cattle gate stands on the left, and a creek enters on the left.

At 4.1 miles, a Class I rapid stretches some 50 yards.

At 4.7 miles, a small dry creek enters from the right.

VULTURES: YOU ARE NEVER TRULY ALONE IN TEXAS

Texas covers some 268,820 square miles. That—says TexasAlmanac.com—is enough to cover Maine, New Hampshire, Vermont, Massachusetts, Rhode Island, Connecticut, New York, Pennsylvania, Ohio, and North Carolina.

The area includes every manner of landscape, from mountains to sea, swamps to desert, high plains to sandy beaches. And no matter where you are in the state, you are never alone. Buzzards are always looking over your shoulder, hovering, waiting for you to slip up, and reminding you not to.

"Buzzard" is a misnomer that came to the United States with European settlers. Texas has vultures: turkey vultures (*Cathartes aura*) and black vultures (*Coragyps atratus*). People confuse the two, in no small part because black vultures and turkey vultures roost and eat carrion together. And though they both may inspire recollections of Beaky Buzzard from the old-school Looney Tunes cartoons, or perhaps thoughts of impending doom, these birds are unique. Black vultures, for example, don't have a very good sense of smell, so they follow turkey vultures to carcasses. Then the black vultures bully the turkey vultures away from the food.

Here are a few tips for distinguishing the two.

	Size	Coloration	Wings	Tail	Head
Black Vulture	Smaller	White wing tip	Straight across in flight	Tail less obvious	Black
Turkey Vulture	Larger	White trailing edge of wing	Forward in a slight V shape	Prominent tail	Red

Davy Crockett National Forest Paddling Trail (Neches River)

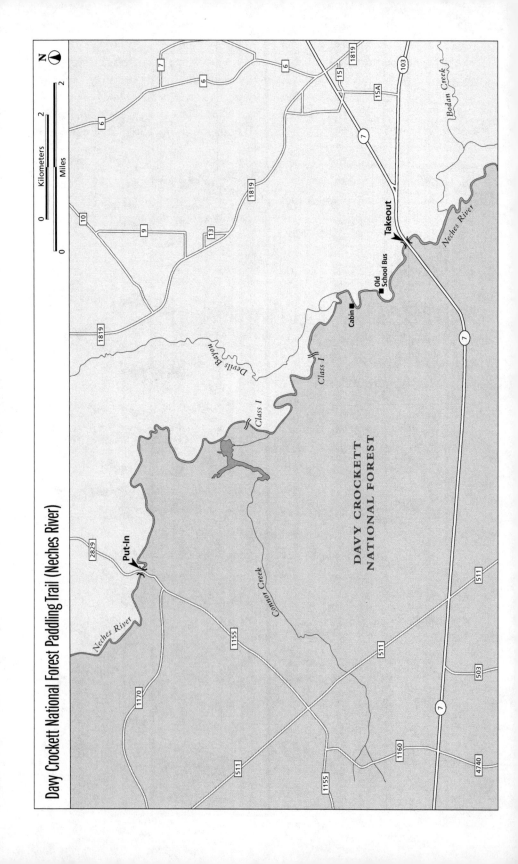

At 6.3 miles, a fence stands on the right. A Class I rapid runs some 50 yards.

At 6.7 miles, stairs climb the bluff to an old house and a camp on the left. Water pours from a 2-inch PVC pipe into the river.

At 7.1 miles, an old cabin with broken screens and a tin roof is on the left. The bend looks like a catfish honey hole.

At 7.4 miles, water comes in from the left. Some 75 yards upstream in that small creek is a metal pedestrian bridge.

At 8.2 miles, an old school bus is on the left bank (N31 24.114'/W94 58.559'). The sounds of cars and signs of trotlines mark that you're nearing the takeout.

At 9.6 miles, reach the takeout. From the river you can see a green Angelina County Line sign and a white sign for TX 7. Pass under the bridge and take out on the left, on a gravel patch near the concrete boat ramp.

Paddle Information

Contact / Outfitter

Lufkin Convention & Visitors Bureau, 1615 S. Chestnut St., Lufkin, TX 75901; (936) 633-0349; visitlufkin.com/play. Call and ask about paddling outfitters, events, and water conditions.

Austin Canoe & Kayak (ACK), 11604 Stonehollow Dr. #300, Austin, TX 78758; (888) 828-3828; austinkayak.com. Want to rent a boat and take it wherever you decide to go? ACK offers boat rentals from locations in Austin, Houston, San Marcos, San Antonio, and Spring. "Take it anywhere you like," says one ACK representative, "Just bring it back."

Local Events / Attractions

Davy Crockett National Forest, 18551 TX 7 E., Kennard, TX 75847; (936) 655-2299; fs.usda.gov/detail/texas/about-forest/districts/?cid=fswdev3_008441. This public forest contains more than 160,000 acres of East Texas woodlands, streams, recreation areas, and wildlife habitat.

Neches River Rendezvous, Lufkin Convention & Visitors Bureau, 1615 S. Chestnut St., Lufkin, TX 75901; (936) 634-6035; visitlufkin.com/events/annual/neches river. This community paddling event runs 10 miles of the Neches River.

Gulf Coast

The Texas Gulf Coast stretches about 360 miles, from near Beaumont at the Louisiana border to near Brownsville at the Mexico border. Between those two points are some 3,300 miles of Texas shoreline. You'll find estuaries, barrier islands, bays, rivers, and streams. In short, this region offers a lifetime of paddling, wildlife watching, and fishing.

In this 21,000-square mile region, you'll find Houston and Corpus Christi, and a string of quirky coastal communities like Port Aransas. You'll also find Battleship Texas State Historic Site, Galveston Island State Park, Goose Island State Park, Lake Corpus Christi State Park, Texana Park and Campground, Mustang Island State Park, Port Isabel Lighthouse State Historic Site, Sea Rim State Park, Sheldon Lake State Park & Environmental Learning Center, and more.

In this section, you will find fresh and saltwater floats and fishing trips in Galveston Bay, Corpus Christi Bay, the Tres Palacios River, and more. If you love fishing or birding, this is the region for you.

Jenkins, coming in at sunset

32 Oak Bayou Loop (Galveston Bay)

One of many paddling opportunities offered by Galveston Island State Park, the Oak Bayou Loop offers 4.2 miles of paddling through one of the best areas for fishing and birding in Galveston Bay, which is the largest estuary in the state of Texas.

Start: Oak Bayou kayak launch, N29 12.29'/W94 57.44'
End: Oak Bayou kayak launch, N29 12.29'/W94 57.44'
Length: 4.2 miles
Float time: 2–4 hours
Difficulty: Easy to moderate, depending upon headwinds
Rapids: None
River type: Bayou and bay
Current: Tidal area
River gradient: Not applicable
River gauge: Not applicable
Land status: State park and private

County: Galveston
Nearest city/town: Galveston
Boats used: Kayaks, johnboats, motorized craft
Season: Year-round. Spring and fall offer the mildest temperatures.
Fees and permits: Galveston Island State Park charges an entrance fee for adults. If you have a Texas State Park Pass, you and your guests can enter at no charge.
Maps: TOPO! Texas; USGS Lake Como TX; DeLorme: Texas Atlas & Gazetteer: page 81
Contact: For information about recreation or water conditions, contact Galveston Island State Park at (409) 737-1222.

Put-In and Takeout Information

To put-in/takeout: No shuttle is necessary. The put-in and takeout are in the same location. From Galveston, take I-45 south to exit 1A. Continue on TX 342 Spur south/Broadway Street for 0.4 mile. Turn right onto 61st Street for 1.6 miles. Turn right onto Seawall Boulevard for 2.5 miles and continue when it becomes Termini San Luis Pass Road. Continue for 6.8 miles. At Galveston Island State Park headquarters (on the left), turn right onto Park Road 66, and head toward the launch. Pass one road on the right and another on the left. After 0.7 mile, a series of covered picnic tables stand on the right, between the road and a small pond. On the left is a wooden boardwalk. This is the put-in.

▶ At the time of this writing, paddling trail buoy markers had been damaged or destroyed by a storm. No timeline for the replacement of the buoys was available, according to the Texas Parks & Wildlife Department. Contact Galveston Island State Park for an update.

Overview

Galveston Bay estuary, near the cities of Galveston and Houston, is a semi-enclosed coastal body of water where seawater and freshwater mix. The Trinity River and San Jacinto River provide the freshwater. The Gulf of Mexico provides the saltwater. A few bits of land stand between the bay and the Gulf: Galveston Island, Bolivar

Oak Bayou, campsite for the night

Peninsula, and Follets Island. The bay has a muddy bottom, is 7 to 9 feet deep and, with some 600 square miles of surface water, is the largest estuary in Texas. It is said to host, at least for a time, some 75 percent of the bird species in North America. For this reason, the Environmental Protection Agency has declared Galveston Bay an estuary of national significance. The bay is divided into East Bay, Galveston Bay, Trinity Bay, and West Bay. It has long been an important waterway for commerce, culture, and recreation.

Paddle Summary

Before heading out to the launch, stop at Galveston Island State Park headquarters to pay fees, get a map, and ask questions about the water and weather conditions. The office has lots of information about birding, fishing, paddling, and other activities in the park and the surrounding area. Head down Park Road 66 to the Oak Bayou Loop put-in, which is marked with a Texas Parks & Wildlife Department (TPWD) Paddling Trails kiosk.

Park on the right shoulder and carry gear across the marsh grass to the shallow, sandy shore. Scoot out into the protected bayou, which is about 200 yards wide. The bayou continues for a time to the left. But, for this paddle, take a right and follow the main bayou toward the bay. Note the "Jamaica Beach" water tower on the left in the distance. Use it for your bearings.

Roseate spoonbills and white egrets may stalk the shallows. During my paddle, a hawk cruised the tops of marsh grass on the right bank, a sand hill crane stood in the marsh, and two birders squatted and watched the show.

At 0.2 mile, the bayou bears left. Redfish and speckled trout hold in this area at times. As you continue, note the series of grass islands some hundred yards away on the left. You'll explore those shortly.

At 0.8 mile, the bayou meets the bay (N29 12.693'/W94 58.071'). The location is marked by PVC TPWD buoy 23. Winds and waves here can be significant. Turn left and head to the shallow, sheltered network of submerged grasses and grass islands. Birds and fish hold in this grassy area. It extends back toward the put-in. Explore as far back as the depth will allow.

▶ **The TexasKayakFisherman community forum is a great place to hear who's paddling and what's biting. Check it out at texaskayakfisherman.com/ forum.**

At 1.1 miles, among the grass islands and grass flats (N29 12.500'/W94 58.008'), turn around and follow the bank on the left, heading toward the bay.

At 1.7 miles, reach a point (N29 12.633'/W94 58.475'). Take a left. Some 200 yards out is a line of Submerged Breakwater signs. Stay inside these signs and use them for navigation if you want to explore. The water tower is still on your left. *Note:* The breakwaters are made of cloth and will steal your lures.

As you round the point, an island is ahead on the right and the mouth of Butterowe Bayou is on the left. Continue ahead toward the water tower and enter the heart of Carancahua Cove. Watch for birds and fish feeding in the shallows. Squadrons of eastern brown pelicans cruise over like fighter pilots in formation. Shorebirds scurry shin deep.

Watch for rays slipping by under the boat, kicking up sand and speckled trout trailing close behind searching for an easy meal. To the right, on the far bank, is a row of beach houses. To the left is undisturbed sandy beach. Continue through the heart of the cove. To the north is a string of small islands protecting the cove from the bay. To the south is a checkerboard network of marsh terraces constructed by Galveston Island State Park Wetlands Restoration Project. To the west is a string of beach homes. You can extend this paddle by exploring any of these options. Otherwise, from the center of the cove at 2.8 miles, turn around, head back around the point, and return to the put-in as you came. Pass Butterowe Bayou on the right. Take a right at the point. Take a right at TPWD buoy 23. Follow the bayou back to the put-in. On the return, a headwind may slow progress.

At 4.2 miles, arrive back at the put-in/takeout on the left.

Oak Bayou Loop (Galveston Bay)

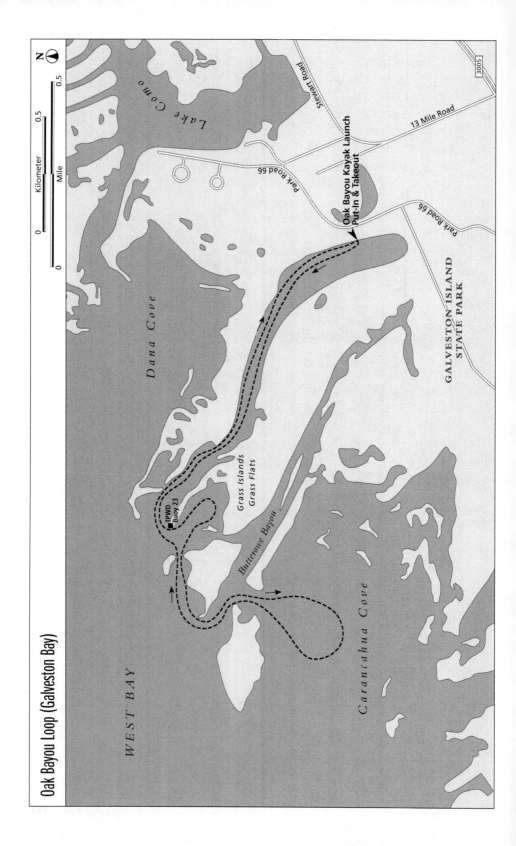

Paddle Information

Organizations

Coastal Conservation Association, 6919 Portwest Dr. Suite 100, Houston, TX 77024; (800) 201-FISH; ccatexas.org. Members saved the redfish. And they're still hard at work.

Houston Association of Sea Kayakers, 12601 Boheme Dr., Houston, TX 77024; (713) 899-2144; hask.org. This organization is "dedicated to the safe enjoyment of the sport of sea kayaking."

▶ For a Galveston Island State Park bird list, see npwrc.usgs .gov/resource/birds/chekbird/ r2/galvesto.htm.

Contact/Outfitter

Austin Canoe & Kayak (ACK), 11604 Stonehollow Dr. #300, Austin, TX 78758; (888) 828-3828; austinkayak.com Want to rent a boat and take it wherever you decide to go? ACK offers boat rentals from locations in the cities of Austin, Houston, San Marcos, San Antonio, and Spring. "Take it anywhere you like," says one ACK representative, "Just bring it back."

Local Information

Galveston Island State Park, 14901 Farm Rd. 3005, Galveston, TX 77554; (409) 737-1222; tpwd.state.tx.us/state-parks/galveston-island. Come for paddling, fishing, camping, birding, nature study, hiking, mountain biking, and beach swimming.

Local Events/Attractions

Galveston Island Visitors Center, 2328 Broadway St., Galveston, TX 77550; (888) 425-4753; galveston.com/visitorscenter.

Texas Seaport Museum, 2200 Harborside Dr., Galveston, TX 77550; (409) 763-1877; galvestonhistory.org/attractions/maritime-heritage/texas-seaport-museum. Experience the adventure of the high seas aboard the *Elissa*, a vessel from 1877 that has been designated a National Historic Landmark.

33 Jenkins Bayou Loop (Galveston Bay)

One of many paddling opportunities offered by the Galveston Island State Park, Jenkins Bay Loop offers 4.3 miles of paddling through part of the largest estuary in Texas. The trip explores marsh grass-lined bayous, the edge of the open bay, a maze of grass islands, and the docks of waterfront homes. The paddle offers access to many bird and fish species.

Start: Jenkins Bayou kayak launch, N29 11.84' / W94 57.98'
End: Jenkins Bayou kayak launch, N29 11.84' / W94 57.98'
Length: 4.3 miles
Float time: 2–4 hours
Difficulty: Moderate due to headwinds
Rapids: None
River type: Bayou and bay
Current: Tidal area
River gradient: Not applicable
River gauge: Not applicable
Land status: State park and private
County: Galveston

Nearest city/town: Galveston
Boats used: Kayaks, johnboats, motorized craft
Season: Year-round. Spring and fall offer the mildest temperatures.
Fees and permits: Galveston Island State Park charges an entrance fee for adults. If you have a Texas State Park Pass, you and your guests can enter at no charge.
Maps: TOPO! Texas; USGS Lake Como TX; DeLorme: Texas Atlas & Gazetteer: page 81
Contact: For information about recreation or water conditions, contact Galveston Island State Park at (409) 737-1222.

Put-In and Takeout Information

To put-in/takeout: No shuttle is needed. Put-in and takeout are in the same location. From Galveston take I-45 south to exit 1A for Texas 342 Spur south/Broadway Street, continuing toward 61st Street for 0.4 mile. Turn right onto 61st Street for 1.6 miles. Turn right onto Seawall Boulevard for 2.5 miles. This road becomes Termini San Luis Pass Road, continue and go 6.8 miles. At Galveston Island State Park headquarters (on the left), turn right onto Park Road 66, and head toward the launch. Pass a road on the right. At 0.6 mile, turn left. Continue 0.6 mile, past a parking lot and observation deck, to a parking lot at the end of the road. A Texas Parks & Wildlife Department (TPWD) paddling kiosk marks the location.

Overview

Seawater and freshwater combine to form this semi-enclosed coastal body of water, Galveston Bay. The Gulf of Mexico provides the saltwater. The Trinity River and San Jacinto River provide the freshwater. A few bits of land stand between the bay and the Gulf: Galveston Island, Bolivar Peninsula, and Follets Island. The 7- to 9-foot deep bay has a muddy bottom and, with some 600 square miles of surface water, is the largest estuary in Texas. It is said to host, at least for a time, some 75 percent of the

Jenkins, a little bayou for paddling

bird species in North America. For this reason, the Environmental Protection Agency has declared Galveston Bay an estuary of national significance. The bay is divided into East Bay, Galveston Bay, Trinity Bay, and West Bay. It has long been an important waterway for commerce, culture, and recreation.

Paddle Summary

Before heading out to the launch, stop at Galveston Island State Park headquarters to pay fees, get a map, and ask questions about the water and weather conditions. The office has lots of information about birding, fishing, paddling, and other activities in the park and the surrounding area.

A sand road runs past the Jenkins Bayou paddling kiosk at the parking lot. Continue down this sand road to unload, then return to the lot to park. Launch from the gradual sandy slope into a narrow, shallow, and sheltered bayou surrounded by acres of marsh grasses. To the left, the bayou continues for short while before ending.

Note the "Jamaica Beach" water tower on the left, useful for your bearings. Beach homes are ahead on the horizon. White ibis walk shin deep in shallows, doing ibis things.

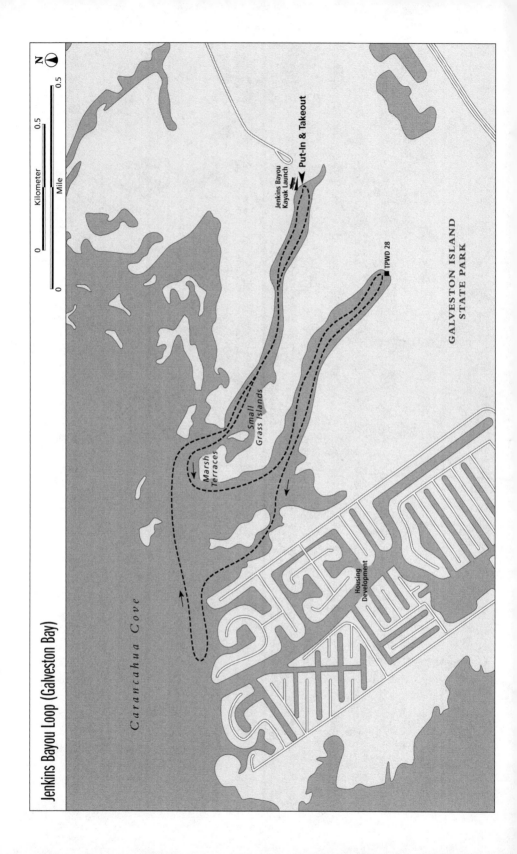

Jenkins Bayou Loop (Galveston Bay)

Carancahua Cove

Marsh Terraces

Small Grass Islands

Jenkins Bayou Kayak Launch

Put-In & Takeout

TPWD 28

GALVESTON ISLAND STATE PARK

Housing Development

N

Kilometer 0   0.5   0.5

Mile 0   0.5

This paddle follows the bayou along a finger of marshland out to the western edge of Carancahua Cove. It then makes a U-turn and doubles back to follow a second bayou on the other side of the same finger of marshland, before returning to the put-in. Along the way, the trip offers an opportunity to explore a checkerboard network of marsh terraces constructed by the Galveston Island State Park Wetlands Restoration Project.

Turn right out of the launch and head toward the bay. The bayou is some 40 yards wide.

At 0.4 mile, an island (N29 11.906'/W94 58.326') is in the middle of the bayou. The right path is shallow.

At 0.7 mile, an inlet and a network of small grass islands (N29 12.056'/W94 58.663') are on the right. These islands are part of the wetlands restoration project. Continue ahead.

At 1 mile, a point (N29 12.175'/W94 58.753') is on the left as the bayou centers Carancahua Cove. Ahead lie a string of small islands, a line of submerged breakwaters, and the bay. Turn left. Turn left again within a few yards and follow the bayou back into an expanse of marshland. Along the right bank ahead is the maze of grass islands created by the Galveston Island State Park Wetlands Restoration Project. Ahead, on the horizon, are power lines and the occasional passing vehicle, which betrays the road passing through the marsh. Continue along the left bank to the end of the bayou.

Anglers note: If you're trolling, try paddling zigzag patterns across the bayou to find the fish.

At 2 miles, TPWD sign 28 (N29 11.662'/W94 58.216') marks the end of the bayou. Many birds are in the area. Turn around and head back the way you came. Explore the restoration project and watch birds as you go.

At 3 miles, turn right at the point on the left to return to the put-in/takeout.

At 3.3 miles, turn right at the point on the right to return to the put-in/takeout.

At 4.3 miles, arrive at the put-in/takeout on the left.

Paddle Information

Organizations

Coastal Conservation Association, 6919 Portwest Dr. Suite 100, Houston, TX 77024; (800) 201-FISH; ccatexas.org. Members saved the redfish. And they're still hard at work.

Houston Association of Sea Kayakers, 12601 Boheme Dr., Houston, TX 77024; (713) 899-2144; hask.org. The organization is "dedicated to the safe enjoyment of the sport of sea kayaking."

Contact/Outfitter

Austin Canoe & Kayak (ACK), 11604 Stonehollow Dr. #300, Austin, TX 78758; (888) 828-3828; austinkayak.com. Want to rent a boat and take it wherever you decide to go? ACK offers boat rentals from locations in the cities of Austin, Houston, San Marcos, San Antonio, and Spring. "Take it anywhere you like," says one ACK representative, "Just bring it back."

Local Information

Galveston Island State Park, 14901 Farm Rd. 3005, Galveston, TX 77554; (409) 737-1222; tpwd.state.tx.us/state-parks/galveston-island. Come for paddling, fishing, camping, birding, nature study, hiking, mountain biking, and beach swimming.

Local Events/Attractions

Galveston Island Visitors Center, 2328 Broadway St., Galveston, TX 77550; (888) 425-4753; galveston.com/visitorscenter.

Texas Seaport Museum, 2200 Harborside Dr., Galveston, TX 77550; (409) 763-1877; galvestonhistory.org/attractions/maritime-heritage/texas-seaport-museum. Experience the adventure of the high seas aboard the *Elissa,* a vessel from 1877 that has been designated a National Historic Landmark.

34 Dana Cove Loop (Galveston Bay)

Dana Cove Loop offers 5.1 miles of paddling through part of the largest estuary in Texas. The trip begins and ends in a protected cove, runs along a string of grass islands and waterfront homes, and offers access to many bird and fish species.

Start: Dana Cove kayak launch, N29 12.77'/W94 57.20'
End: Dana Cove kayak launch, N29 12.77'/W94 57.20'
Length: 5.1 miles
Float time: 3–5 hours
Difficulty: Easy to moderate depending on headwinds.
Rapids: None
River type: Bayou and bay
Current: Tidal area
River gradient: Not applicable
River gauge: Not applicable
Land status: State park and private

County: Galveston
Nearest city/town: Galveston
Boats used: Kayaks, johnboats, motorized craft
Season: Year-round. Spring and fall offer the mildest temperatures.
Fees and permits: Galveston Island State Park charges an entrance fee for adults. If you have a Texas State Park Pass, you and your guests can enter at no charge.
Maps: TOPO! Texas; USGS Lake Como TX; DeLorme: Texas Atlas & Gazetteer: page 81
Contact: For information about recreation or water conditions, contact Galveston Island State Park at (409) 737-1222.

Put-In and Takeout Information

To put-in/takeout: No shuttle is needed. Put-in and takeout are in the same location. From Galveston, take I-45 south to exit 1A for Texas 342 Spur South/Broadway Street. Continue toward 61st Street for 0.4 mile. Turn right onto 61st Street for 1.6 miles. Turn right onto Seawall Boulevard for 2.5 miles. The road becomes Termini San Luis Pass Road; continue for 6.8 miles. At Galveston Island State Park headquarters (on the left), turn right onto Park Road 66 and follow it for 1.4 miles. The put-in location is at the end of the road.

Overview

Galveston Bay estuary is a semi-enclosed coastal body of water, where seawater and freshwater mix, near Galveston and Houston. The Trinity and San Jacinto Rivers provide the freshwater; the Gulf of Mexico provides the saltwater. A few bits of land stand between the bay and the Gulf: Galveston Island, Bolivar Peninsula, and Follets Island. The bay has a muddy bottom, is 7 to 9 feet deep, and with some 600 square miles of surface water, is the largest estuary in Texas. It is said to host, at least for a time, some 75 percent of the bird species in North America. For this reason, the Environmental Protection Agency has declared Galveston Bay an estuary of national significance. The bay is divided into East Bay, Galveston Bay, Trinity Bay, and West Bay. It has long been an important waterway for commerce, culture, and recreation.

Dana Cove, launching at sunrise

Paddle Summary

Before heading out to the launch, stop at Galveston Island State Park headquarters to pay fees, get a map, and ask questions about the water and weather conditions. The office has lots of information about birding, fishing, paddling, and other activities in the park and the surrounding area. Then head down Park Road 66 to the Dana Cove Loop put-in, which is marked with a Texas Parks & Wildlife Department (TPWD) Paddling Trails kiosk.

Park and unload near the paddling trail information kiosk. On the left is a fish cleaning station and ample parking. This place is popular with bank anglers and kayak anglers. Walk some 30 yards along a sandy path to the water's edge at Lake Como, a small saltwater lake lined with homes. Note the cell tower behind the lake, which is useful for your bearings. Scoot from the easy sandy slope into the shallow water of a cove lined with beach homes and private docks. Leave the launch and turn left toward the bay.

At 0.1 mile, a grass island (N29 12.888'/W94 57.176') is guarded by great blue herons and kingfishers. Bear right. White herons may wade in the grass banks on the right, out in front of beach homes. Follow the string of grass islands ahead on the left (toward the west). The islands are covered with birds. White PVC markers and crab pots mark the way out. They run parallel to the string of grass islands. The right bank peels off into a row of beach homes and docks. You'll check those out later. The winds can be quite strong here, and the waves can work into a chop that will get you wet. If you're paddling in the winter, consider a skirt. (*Note:* This is a great place to troll for redfish and speckled trout as you paddle.)

▶ **Remember to mind the tides and the winds when planning your coastal paddling trip.**

At 0.6 mile, the last in the string of small islands is on the left (N29 13.158' / W94 57.713'). Round it to the left tightly, and continue down those islands with their other side on your left. Cormorants, pelicans, gulls, shorebirds and others cover the islands, crash into the water in pursuit of fish, and work the sky. Paddle toward the tower ahead, which stands behind the launch.

There will be boats out, floating and fishing and running full speed. Flash your paddles and pay attention. Also, stick close to the islands for protection.

At 1 mile, reach the mouth of Lake Como from which you launched. Bear right and work through shallows and grassy islands. Watch for redfish working in the shallows, and look out to see birds working. Head back out, following the grass islands toward the island you rounded earlier.

At 1.5 miles, round it to the right and turn back toward the cove from which you launched.

At 1.9 miles, turn left. A string of five houses is ahead. Paddle to the last house in the row (N29 13.182' / W94 57.033'). Boats will be zipping to and from the marina, so be mindful.

At 2.2 miles, pass the last house in the string at Dalehite Cove. If the winds permit, float with the wind to end of the string of homes. Fish the docks as you go. Then paddle back to this point. Do this until you get no bites, and then do it once more. At the end of the string of homes, turn left to head back toward the put-in. Follow the left bank of Lake Como and return to the put-in.

At 5.1 miles, arrive back at the put-in on the left.

Paddle Information

Organizations

Coastal Conservation Association, 6919 Portwest Dr. Suite 100, Houston, TX 77024; (800) 201-FISH; ccatexas.org. Members saved the redfish. And they're still hard at work.

Houston Association of Sea Kayakers, 12601 Boheme Dr., Houston, TX 77024; (713) 899-2144; hask.org. This organization is "dedicated to the safe enjoyment of the sport of sea kayaking."

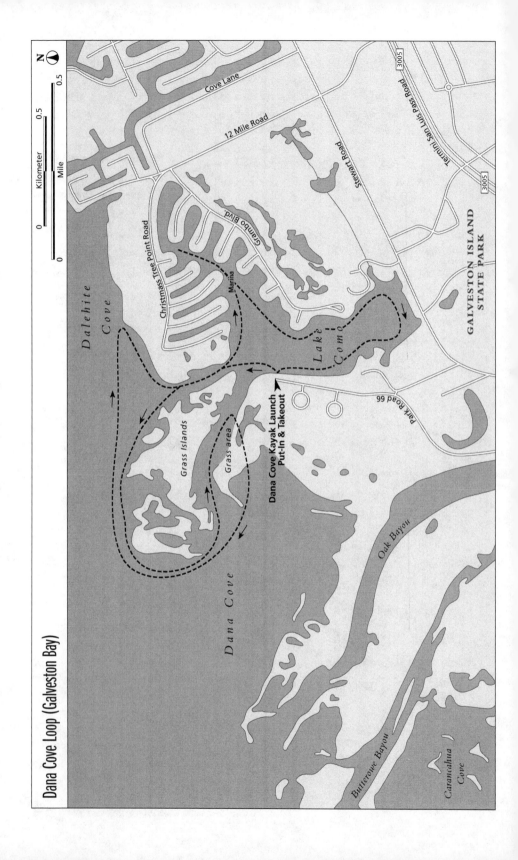

Dana Cove Loop (Galveston Bay)

N

Kilometer 0 0.5
Mile 0 0.5

Cove Lane

12 Mile Road

Stewart Road

Grambo Blvd.

Christmass Tree Point Road

Marina

Dalehite Cove

Lake Como

Park Road 66

Dana Cove Kayak Launch
Put-In & Takeout

Grass Islands

Grass area

Dana Cove

Oak Bayou

Butterowe Bayou

Caracahua Cove

GALVESTON ISLAND
STATE PARK

Termini San Luis pass Road

3005

3005

Dana Cove, the put-in

Contact/Outfitter

Austin Canoe & Kayak (ACK), 11604 Stonehollow Dr. #300, Austin, TX 78758; (888) 828-3828; austinkayak.com. Want to rent a boat and take it wherever you decide to go? ACK offers boat rentals from locations in the cities of Austin, Houston, San Marcos, San Antonio, and Spring. "Take it anywhere you like," says one ACK representative, "Just bring it back."

Local Information

Galveston Island State Park, 14901 Farm Rd. 3005, Galveston, TX 77554; (409) 737-1222; tpwd.state.tx.us/state-parks/galveston-island. Come for paddling, fishing, camping, birding, nature study, hiking, mountain biking, and beach swimming.

Local Events/Attractions

Galveston Island Visitors Center, 2328 Broadway St., Galveston, TX 77550; (888) 425-4753; galveston.com/visitorscenter.

Texas Seaport Museum, 2200 Harborside Dr., Galveston, TX 77550; (409) 763-1877; galvestonhistory.org/attractions/maritime-heritage/texas-seaport-museum. Experience the adventure of the high seas aboard the *Elissa,* a vessel from 1877 that has been designated a National Historic Landmark.

35 Wilson's Cut Loop (Corpus Christi Bay)

With this launch location, weather is everything. When the bay is calm, it offers a 7.7-mile loop around a bird sanctuary, through mangrove tangles, across flats, and back. In high winds, it offers a 5-mile exploratory loop through mangrove tangles, prime bird habitat, over grassy flats, and back. Spend a day fishing and exploring the mangroves, or make this one of a pair of local paddle trips on the day.

Start: Wilson's Cut, N27 44.25'/W97 08.20'
End: Wilson's Cut, N27 44.25'/W97 08.20'
Length: 5 miles; 7.7 miles for alternate route
Float time: 2–5 hours
Difficulty: Easy to moderate, depending on wind, tides, and navigation
Rapids: None
River type: Bay and mangrove
Current: Tidal area
River gradient: Not applicable

River gauge: Paddle at high tide
Land status: Municipal property and private
County: Nueces
Nearest city/town: Port Aransas
Boats used: Kayaks, johnboats, small motorized craft
Season: Year-round
Fees and permits: None
Maps: TOPO! Texas; USGS Port Ingleside TX; DeLorme: Texas Atlas & Gazetteer: page 85

Put-In and Takeout Information

To put-in/takeout: No shuttle is needed. Put-in and takeout are in the same location. From Port Aransas, take TX 361 south for 6.8 miles. Look for two tall condominiums on the left: the Sandpiper and the Seagull. After you pass Seacomber Drive on the left, look right. Turn right onto an unmarked road of packed sand. Take the first right onto an unmarked path. Follow this road to the launch and parking area. (*Note:* This area is tidal, so park on the edge of the lot that is nearest the main road and condos.)

River Overview

Corpus Christi Bay—one of the few natural harbors along the Texas coast—is a large estuary located near the city of Corpus Christi. The area is environmentally important in that it hosts some 490 species of birds and 234 species of fish. In recognition of its importance, the Environmental Protection Agency has designated the 190-square-mile bay as an estuary of national significance. The Nueces River and Oso Creek flow into the bay, and provide freshwater. Mustang Island and North Padre Island protect the shallow, 20-foot-deep bay from the Gulf of Mexico. The Gulf Intracoastal Waterway crosses Corpus Christi Bay, which further contributes to the bay's importance in commerce.

▶ **Be sure to wear sturdy water shoes on the Wilson's Cut Loop: A battle between oyster beds and soggy feet is no battle at all.**

Wilson's Cut, trail marker

Paddle Summary

On the way to the launch, stop by Mustang Island State Park and pick up a laminated "Mustang Island Paddling Trails Aerial Photocard," which shows some possible routes in the area.

The put-in location is situated on a gradual sandy slope that acts as a popular launch for boats of all types. Drive to the water's edge and unload. Park at the edge of the lot nearest the main road.

Slide out into the end of a 60-yard wide canal that is lined on both sides by marsh grasses. The birding begins here, and continues for the rest of the day. On the horizon ahead, pelicans and gulls may be working, signifying fish and calling your name. Beyond them is Corpus Christi Bay. Head down the canal toward them. (**Note:** For navigation, note the two condominium buildings directly behind the launch. As long as you can see those, you can get back to the launch.)

On the left, immediately after the launch, is a white sign labeled "6." As the bayou opens the wind intensifies.

▶ The only wild flock of whooping cranes in Texas winters is on this stretch of Texas coast. Learn more at fws.gov/refuge/Aransas/wildlife_and_habitat/index.html.

At 0.4 mile continue straight ahead, passing a white sign marked "7" on your right (N27 44.404'/W97 8.602'). Pelicans and other birds will likely be gathered ahead near the bay.

At 1.4 miles, an industrial area of some sort, with commercial vessels, many tanks, and other materials, is on the left (N27 44.698'/W97 9.478'). On some days, this portion of the paddle is into a severe headwind. Any inch won with a stroke is lost immediately in a pause.

(*Note*: Ahead, the cut meets Corpus Christi Bay. Just beyond is Shamrock Island Bird Sanctuary. Beyond the protection of the mangroves, the water can change in an instant. One moment there's only a headwind to contend with, and the next waves threaten to swamp the boat. On a calm day, consider altering this trip with a loop around the island. This route keeps paddlers in protected waters. On such a shallow paddle route, the tides determine the path and how much walking you'll do.)

On the right, a path at N27 44.73'/W97 09.44' runs through the mangroves. Turn right and follow the path.

At 1.6 miles (N27 44.81'/W97 09.37') enter a broad, shallow, open lake. Paddle to the middle of the lake. The bay is on the left in the distance. Paddle to the edge of the bay and turn right to put the mangroves on your left shoulder, staying in protected water. Ahead, on the horizon, is a light blue water tower. Paddle toward that.

At 1.9 miles (N27 45.00'/W97 09.22') going left, right, and center are all options. Paddle to the north-northwest. A tan house is ahead. Paddle toward that. Pass through a chain of small grass islands. It may be very windy here. A pink house and a green house soon emerge too. The tan house is built near a small hill, which can provide a windbreak for a paddler in need of a rest.

At 2.4 miles, reach the tan house labeled PC1579 (N27 45.288'/W97 08.865'). This is one of several houses here. On the horizon a string of buildings shine white with the occasional pink accent. Head for that.

At 2.7 miles, a white-and-orange sign labeled "11" is on the left (N27 45.431'/W97 08.631'). Visible on the horizon to the right are a white-and-blue beach development and the two condos near the launch. Take aim with the bow and head for the water that lies between the development and the condos.

At 3 miles, a white-and-orange sign marked "10" is at the edge of the mangroves (N27 45.220'/W97 08.362'). Go left. The next sign is visible ahead on the right.

At 3.2 miles, sign "9" is on the left (N27 45.270'/W97 08.167'). Go right. Head toward the two marked condos and the put-in. Paddle parallel to TX 361, which is on the left.

At 4.3 miles, sign "8" (N27 44.73'/W97 08.33') is on the right. Continue onward to a second sign marked "8"—just for the sake of confusion (N27 44.66'/W97 08.34'). There are opportunities to

▶ Stop by Island Tackle, at 207 W Avenue G in Port Aransas, to pick up tackle, tips, and a Hook-N-Line bay fishing map. Tell Leland that Shane sent you.

Wilson's Cut Loop (Corpus Christi Bay)

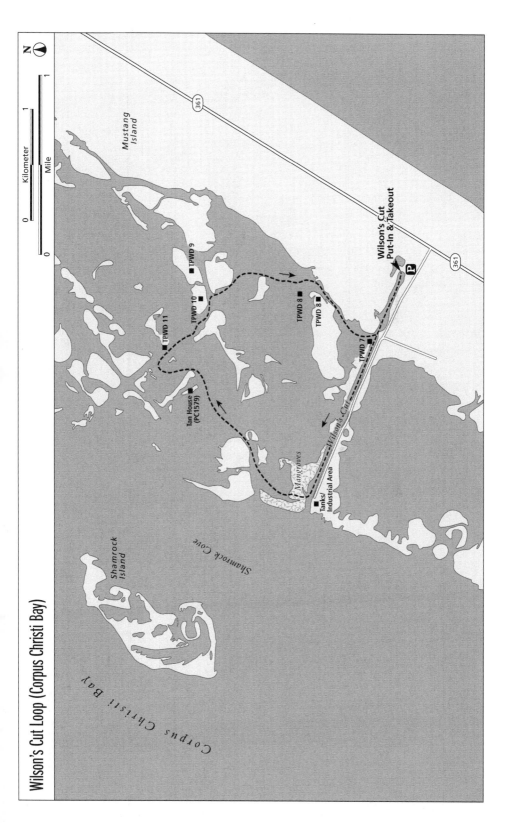

explore the mangroves through little paths that are only a couple of feet wide. The bottom is muddy here. The utility poles and metal tanks near the launch are visible ahead.

At 4.7 miles, turn left at white sign labeled "7" to reenter the bayou from which you launched.

At 5 miles, arrive back at the put-in/takeout.

Paddle Information

Organizations

Coastal Conservation Association, 6919 Portwest Dr. Suite 100, Houston, TX 77024; (800) 201-FISH; ccatexas.org. Members saved the redfish. And they're still hard at work.

Coastal Bend Bays Foundation, 1231 Agnes St. Suite 100, Corpus Christi, TX 78401; (361) 882-3439; baysfoundation.org.

▶ This is a popular hunting location during duck season. Be respectful of the blinds and of the tiny, steel ball bearings that will burst forth and fall on your head.

Contact/Outfitter

Slowride Guide Services, 821 S. Commercial St., Aransas Pass, TX 78336; (361) 758-0463; slowrideguide.com. "Catch fish, see birds, pick up shells, take a gut-wrenching paddle, or just enjoy nature. We can do it all," says one representative.

Austin Canoe & Kayak (ACK), 11604 Stonehollow Dr. #300, Austin, TX 78758; (888) 828-3828; austinkayak.com. Want to rent a boat and take it wherever you decide to go? ACK offers boat rentals from locations in the cities of Austin, Houston, San Marcos, San Antonio, and Spring. "Take it anywhere you like," says one ACK representative, "Just bring it back."

Local Information

Port Aransas Visitors Center, 403 W. Cotter St., Port Aransas, TX 78373; (361) 749-5919; portaransas.org. Stop by.

Local Events/Attractions

Mustang Island State Park, 17047 TX 361, Port Aransas, TX 78373; (361) 749-5246; tpwd.state.tx.us/state-parks/mustang-island. Come for paddling, fishing, camping, picnicking, swimming, cycling, and birding.

Shrimporee, 130 W. Goodnight Ave., Aransas Pass, TX 78336; (361) 758-2750; aransaspass.org. Their sign claims it to be "Home of the largest shrimp festival in Texas."

Earth Day–Bay Day, Heritage Park, 1581 N. Chaparral St., Corpus Christi, TX 78401; (361) 882-3439; baysfoundation.org. This free annual conservation event hosts some 10,000 visitors and features a catch-and-release fishing tank, a rock-climbing wall, and more.

36 Redfish Loop (Redfish Bay)

This 6.6-mile loop allows paddlers to explore a maze of mangroves, shallow lakes, and oyster bars that is reminiscent of some of the quiet reserves of Quintana Roo, Mexico. To paddle here is to enter a beautiful, intriguing, secret place. Paddle alongside a pod of dolphins. Set up and photograph countless birds. Or, take on one of the best fishing spots in Texas. This place is well worth a visit.

Start: Lighthouse Lakes Paddling Trails Park, N27 51.96'/W97 05.00'
End: Lighthouse Lakes Paddling Trails Park, N27 51.96'/W97 05.00'
Length: 6.6 miles
Float time: 3-5 hours
Difficulty: Easy to moderate, depending on navigation, planning for tides, and wind
Rapids: None
River type: Bay and mangroves
Current: Tidal area
River gradient: Not applicable

River gauge: Do not paddle at low tide. If you paddle at lower tides, prepare to portage over sand, mud, and sharp oysters.
Land status: Municipal park and private
County: Aransas
Nearest city/town: Aransas Pass
Boats used: Kayaks, motorized craft, airboats, shipping vessels in the channel
Season: Year-round
Fees and permits: None
Maps: TOPO! Texas; USGS Port Aransas TX; DeLorme: Texas Atlas & Gazetteer: page 85

Put-In and Takeout Information

To put-in/takeout: No shuttle is needed. Put-in and takeout are in the same location. From Aransas Pass, take TX 361 south for 4.2 miles. Turn left at the Lighthouse Trails sign. Turn right at the Lighthouse Lakes Texas Paddling Trails information kiosk. Continue past a wooden pier and park to where the road ends.

River Overview

The Port Aransas bay estuarine nursery includes Copano Bay, Mission Bay, St. Charles Bay, and Redfish Bay. It lies between Corpus Christi Bay and the San Antonio Bay estuarine areas. The Aransas and Mission Rivers and Copano Creek flow into the bay, and are the sources of freshwater for the estuary. San Jose Island protects the bay from the Gulf of Mexico. The Gulf Intracoastal Waterway and Aransas Pass offer access to Aransas Bay. The 70-square mile bay has an average depth of 10 feet. The bay is an important area for local fisheries, birds, and sea grasses—all of which are protected

▶ Be sure to wear sturdy water shoes on this trip. The battle between oyster beds and soggy feet is short and decisive.

through the efforts of the nearby 59,000-acre Aransas National Wildlife Refuge and the Mission–Aransas National Estuarine Research Reserve.

Redfish Loop, decoys and blind

Paddle Summary

Every spot is a potential launch spot along the easy sandy slope, which is dotted with mangroves and sea grass near a deep-water channel. On the left is a green, square, channel marker marked "3." The sky is as big as any Montana has ever seen. Take a right out of the launch to head toward Port Aransas. TX 361 will be on your right shoulder. On the left is an expanse of mangroves, shallows, oyster beds, and prime bird and fish habitat. A pod of dolphins works the waters here.

Toward Port Aransas, the channel ahead disappears into the sky on the horizon like no infinity pool ever could. Many boats zip, limp, or growl past. Pelicans, shorebirds, cormorants, and others line the sandbars, stand guard atop the mangroves, and wade across the shallows. A few hundred yards on is an orange triangular sign marked "4."

At 0.6 mile, turn left into an inlet at a white Texas Parks & Wildlife Department (TPWD) sign labeled "1" in orange lettering (N27 51.729'/W97 04.544'). The sign stands some 5 feet high and is hung on a white post. It is visible at a great distance. Use these signs to help navigate the mangroves and lakes. There are few other landmarks. Leave the channel and enter the shallow mangroves.

(*Note*: At and near low tide, the water in the mangroves is very shallow. The oyster beds, grass beds, and sandbars are such that you will have to portage often, which is okay if that's what you want to do. The best time to paddle this route is near high tide. However, if you don't mind the walk, the birding is fantastic at low tide as well. Wear good, strong, durable footwear that will stand up to the razor edges of the oyster beds. They can be hidden beneath the mud; and they will slice your feet like sandwich meat. Closed-toe shoes are best.)

Enter a large, shallow lake and look across to the next sign. An orange-and-white post and white TPWD sign marked "2" are at 0.9 mile (N27 51.909'/W97 04.374'). (At low tide, you can't get in here.) Paddle to the sign. Paddle the main passage that runs to the north-northeast through the mangroves.

At 1.1 miles, enter a small lake. Continue ahead.

At 1.2 miles, the lake disappears and the main trail turns to the right. Follow it.

At 1.3 miles, enter another small lake

At 1.4 miles, enter a large lake. A TPWD sign is to the north-northeast. Paddle to it.

At 1.5 miles, reach TPWD sign "10" (N27 52.237'/W97 04.026'). Take a left into a narrow pass immediately before the sign. Pass through a series of shallow lakes by heading to the north-northwest.

At 1.8 miles, enter a large lake. Look to the north-northwest for the TPWD sign.

At 2.1 miles, reach TPWD sign "44" (N27 52.588'/W97 04.391'). Enter the 20-foot cut through the mangroves. TPWD sign "43" is not far beyond. Paddle toward the middle of the large shallow lake. Scan the right side of the lake for the next sign and head to it.

At 2.4 miles, reach TPWD sign "42" (N27 52.839'/W97 04.385'). Pass through a narrow, deep pass.

At 2.5 miles, reach TPWD sign "41," at the edge of a large open lake. Directly ahead is a high point of mangrove, land, and vegetation. Head toward that. On the horizon, at 9 o'clock, you can see the white water tower. The light blue water tower is at 11 o'clock. Paddle past the high point and continue on the same line, heading north-northeast.

At 3.1 miles, reach TPWD sign "62" (N27 53.169'/W97 03.968'). Paddle into a narrow path through the mangrove to leave the lake.

At 3.3 miles, reach TPWD sign "63" (N27 53.010'/W97 03.976'). Two brown condos stand on the horizon. Paddle toward those. Look for a yellow post at 11 o'clock. Adjust and paddle to that.

At 3.6 miles, reach TPWD sign "64" (N27 52.780'/W97 03.869'). Enter the narrow path through the mangrove.

At 3.7 miles, reach TPWD sign "65" (N27 52.728'/W97 03.810'). Enter an open lake. At 2 o'clock are two small islands and, behind them, a large tan barn and a red lighthouse, which was under repair when I paddled here.

At 4.3 miles, to the left, you'll see TPWD sign "20" (N27 52.247'/W97 03.486'). Turn right and follow the bank on your left shoulder.

At 4.5 miles, at N27 52.18'/W97 03.62' is the post for TPWD sign "21," but the sign is missing. Bear right. There is an oyster bed here.

At 4.75 miles, reach TPWD sign "12" (N27 52.011'/W97 03.753').

Redfish Loop (Redfish Bay)

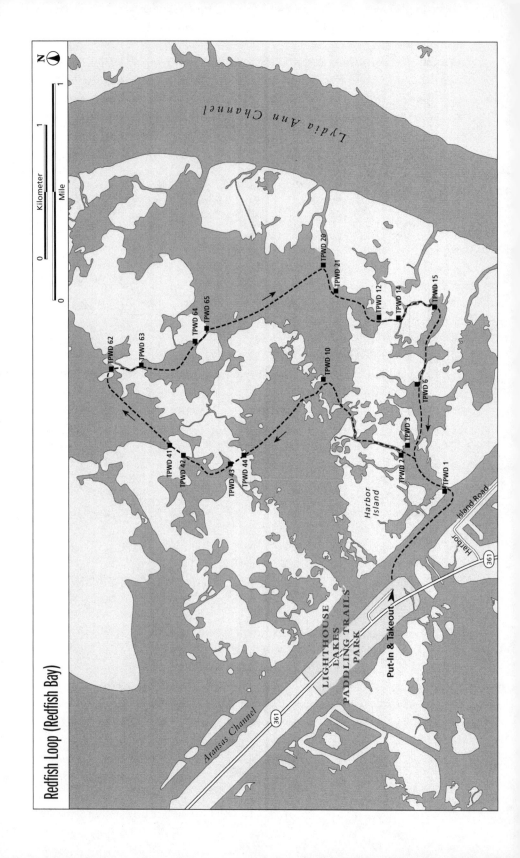

At 4.9 miles, reach TPWD sign "14" (N27 51.931'/W97 03.757'). Go left.

At 5.1 miles, reach TPWD sign "15" (N27 51.780'/W97 03.685'). Paddle west. Follow the left bank, while minding the deepest path.

At 5.3 miles, paddle west across a large lake.

At 5.4 miles, enter another narrow pass. Continue west.

At 5.5 miles, reach TPWD sign "6" (N27 51.849'/W97 04.065'.) Paddle into the middle of the large lake ahead. Look to the west for the yellow post of TPWD sign "3."

At 5.8 miles, reach sign "3" (N27 51.885'/W97 04.335'). From here, sign "2" is visible.

At 5.9 miles, reach sign "2." Turn south. Look for sign "1" and head for it.

At 6.3 miles, enter the channel at TPWD sign "1." Turn right at the channel. Pass the TX 361 bridge on the left.

At 6.6 miles, arrive back at the put-in/takeout.

Paddle Information

Organizations

Coastal Conservation Association, 6919 Portwest Dr. Suite 100, Houston, TX 77024; (800) 201-FISH; ccatexas.org. Members saved the redfish. And they're still hard at work.

PADDLE ROCKPORT—IF ONLY FOR THE BIRDS

The town of Rockport is at the heart of one of the best bird-watching areas in the United States. The area's 400 species of birds range from the endangered and towering whooping crane to the miniscule and equally amazing ruby-throated hummingbird. Combine that avian diversity with a beautiful seascape, charming accommodations, and a storied local history, and you have one of the best destinations along the Great Texas Coastal Birding Trail and the famed Central Flyway.

Aransas Pathways, a project of the county of Aransas and the towns of Rockport and Fulton, recognizes the unique natural resources and the growing interest of bird watchers and paddlers in that resource. The organization is investing in the future by planning trail systems and launch spots, identifying birding sites, building boardwalks and photography blinds, and laying out walking paths and biking trails.

Birding in the Rockport area is great year-round. And there is no better way to get up close and personal with birds than with a small boat and a quiet stroke.

For more information see the Rockport Fulton Chamber of Commerce, Tour Rockport-Fulton app on iTunes: itunes.apple.com/us/app/tour-rockport-fulton-texas/id518106584?mt=8, or aransaspathways.com.

Coastal Bend Bays Foundation, 1231 Agnes St. Suite 100, Corpus Christi, TX 78401; (361) 882-3439; baysfoundation.org.

Contact / Outfitter

Slowride Guide Services, 821 S. Commercial St., Aransas Pass, TX 78336; (361) 758-0463; slowrideguide.com. The company promises that you'll "catch fish, see birds, pick up shells, take a gut-wrenching paddle, or just enjoy nature. We can do it all."

Austin Canoe & Kayak (ACK), 11604 Stonehollow Dr. #300, Austin, TX 78758; (888) 828-3828; austinkayak.com. Want to rent a boat and take it wherever you decide to go? ACK offers boat rentals from locations in the cities of Austin, Houston, San Marcos, San Antonio, and Spring. "Take it anywhere you like," says one ACK representative, "Just bring it back."

Local Information

Aransas Pass Visitors Center, 130 W. Goodnight Ave., Aransas Pass, TX 78336; (361) 758-2750; aransaspass.org. Stop by.

Local Events / Attractions

Shrimporee, 130 W. Goodnight Ave., Aransas Pass, TX 78336; (361) 758-2750; aransaspass.org. Their sign claims "Home of the largest shrimp festival in Texas."

Earth Day–Bay Day, Heritage Park, 1581 N. Chaparral St., Corpus Christi, TX 78401; (361) 882-3439; baysfoundation.org. This free annual conservation event hosts some 10,000 visitors and features a catch-and-release fishing tank, rock-climbing wall, and more.

37 Electric Loop (Corpus Christi Bay)

This 3.4-mile paddle gives but a taste of a beautiful, intriguing, secret place. This is a shorter version of other paddles here. But, it still allows you to experience a maze of mangroves, shallow lakes, and oyster bars that is reminiscent of some of the quiet reserves of Quintana Roo, Mexico. Paddle alongside a pod of dolphins. Set up and photograph countless birds. Or, take on one of the best fishing spots in Texas. This place is well worth a visit.

Start: Lighthouse Lakes Paddling Trails Park, N27 51.96'/W97 05.00'
End: Lighthouse Lakes Paddling Trails Park, N27 51.96'/W97 05.00'
Length: 3.4 miles
Float time: 1.5–3 hours
Difficulty: Easy to moderate, depending on navigation, planning for tides, and wind
Rapids: None
River type: Bay and mangroves
Current: Tidal area
River gradient: Not applicable

River gauge: This is a high-tide paddle. If you paddle at lower tides, prepare to portage.
Land status: Municipal and private
County: Aransas
Nearest city/town: Aransas Pass
Boats used: Kayaks, motorized craft, airboats, shipping vessels in the channel
Season: Year-round
Fees and permits: None
Maps: TOPO! Texas; USGS Port Aransas TX; DeLorme: Texas Atlas & Gazetteer: page 85

Put-In and Takeout Information

To put-in/takeout: No shuttle is needed. Put-in and takeout are in the same location. From Aransas Pass, take TX 361 south for 4.2 miles. Turn left at the Lighthouse Trails sign. Turn right at the Lighthouse Lakes Texas Paddling Trails information kiosk. Continue past a wooden pier and park where the road ends. Put in on the left.

River Overview

The Port Aransas bay estuarine nursery includes Copano Bay, Mission Bay, St. Charles Bay, and Redfish Bay. It lies between Corpus Christi Bay and the San Antonio Bay estuarine areas. The Aransas and Mission Rivers and Copano Creek flow into the bay and are the freshwater sources for the estuary. San Jose Island protects the bay from the Gulf of Mexico. The Gulf Intracoastal Waterway and Aransas Pass offer access to Aransas Bay. The 70-square mile bay has an average depth of 10 feet. The bay is important for local

▶ The Hook-N-Line bay fishing map for the Rockport area is waterproof, has GPS coordinates of Texas Parks & Wildlife mile markers, and has detailed information for kayaking and fishing. Map number F130 covers the Lighthouse Lakes and the Mustang Island Trails. See HookNLine.com.

Electric Loop, hunting the shallows

fisheries, birds, and sea grasses—all of which are protected through the efforts of the nearby 59,000-acre Aransas National Wildlife Refuge and the Mission–Aransas National Estuarine Research Reserve.

Paddle Summary

Every spot is a potential launch spot along the easy sandy slope dotted with mangroves and sea grass at the edge of Aransas Channel. A green, square channel marker marked "3" is on the left. Take a right out of the launch to head toward Port Aransas. TX 361 is on your right shoulder. On the left is an expanse of mangroves, shallows, oyster beds, and prime bird and fish habitat.

Toward Port Aransas, the channel ahead disappears into the sky. Boats zip past. Pelicans, cormorants, and other birds line the sandbars, stand atop mangroves, and wade across the shallows. A few hundred yards on is an orange triangular sign with marked "4."

At 0.6 mile, turn left into an inlet at a white TPWD sign labeled "1" in orange lettering (N27 51.729'/W97 04.544'). (**Note:** The sign stands 5 feet high and is hung on a white post. It is visible at a great distance. Use these signs to help navigate the mangroves and lakes. There are few other landmarks.) Leave the channel and enter the shallow mangroves.

(**Note:** At and near low tide, the water in the mangroves is very shallow. The oyster beds, grass beds, and sandbars are such that you will have to portage often, which is okay if that's what you want to do. The best time to paddle this route is near high tide. However, if you don't mind the walk, the birding is fantastic at low tide as well. Wear good, strong, durable footwear that will stand up to the razor edges of oyster beds. They can be unseen beneath the mud; and will slice your feet like sandwich meat. Closed-toe shoes are best.)

Look across the shallow lake to see the next paddle point: TPWD sign "2." As you paddle to that, note the many oyster beds, duck blinds, and communities of decoys.

At 0.9 mile, look for TPWD sign "3" (N27 51.885' / W97 4.335'). Paddle to that. Reach it at 1 mile. Pass the sign on the left and continue across the open water. Watch for the next TPWD sign.

At 1.2 miles, reach TPWD sign "4" (N27 51.745' / W97 4.111'). Continue along the long narrow stretch through the mangroves.

TARPON, TEXAS, AND FARLEY BOAT WORKS

Port Aransas, Texas, was once known as "Tarpon," in honor of the game fish at the center of the local culture and economy. In 1937, siren stories of monster tarpon lured President Franklin Delano Roosevelt to join a Port Aransas guide aboard a locally built wooden craft for a day of fishing. Their success ensured the President's return. It also anchored the legacy of Farley Boat Works, local boatbuilders who had revolutionized tarpon fishing by designing what may have been the first pure sport-fishing vessel on the Gulf of Mexico—some say in the United States.

By the time Farley Boat Works closed in 1973, the Texas tarpon fishery had collapsed and wooden boats were moved to the wayside for craft constructed of fiberglass and aluminum. Local knowledge of wooden boat building began to disappear.

As of 2014, the still fragile tarpon fishery shows some signs of recovery, thanks to regulations, conservation efforts, and research programs. One such effort engages anglers as citizen scientists as they help track, catch, and release the tarpon unharmed. The old Farley Boat Works is reborn as a nonprofit community center where expert boatbuilders share their craft and preserve the local boat-building tradition. Students pay only for materials. The shop, which is staffed primarily by volunteers, is said to be the only school building wooden boats on the coast of the Gulf of Mexico.

For more information about participating or building your own boat, contact Farley Boat Works at Port Aransas Museum at portaransasmuseum.org, or call director Rick Pratt at (361) 749-3800 or (361) 549-6328.

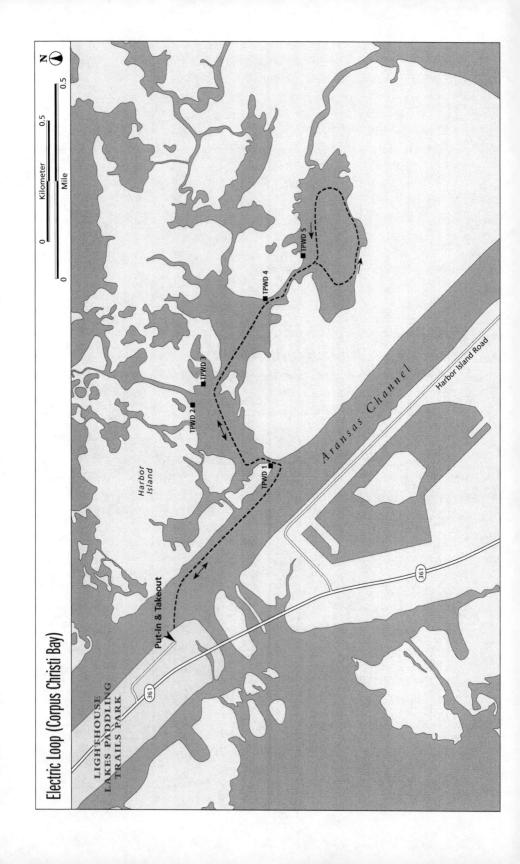

Electric Loop (Corpus Christi Bay)

LIGHTHOUSE
LAKES PADDLING
TRAILS PARK

N

0   Kilometer   0.5

0   Mile   0.5

Put-in & Takeout

Harbor
Island

TPWD 1
TPWD 2
TPWD 3
TPWD 4
TPWD 5

Aransas Channel

Harbor Island Road

361

361

At 1.4 miles, reach TPWD sign "5" (N27 51.650'/W97 3.994'). Here the pass enters a large shallow lake. Turn right. Make a loop around the lake. Exit the way you entered. From TPWD sign "5," look straight across the lake to the channel from which you entered.

Paddle to TPWD sign "3." From here, TPWD sign "2" is visible.

Head back to the channel and TPWD sign "1." Turn right at the channel. Head toward the TX 361 bridge ahead on the left, and the launch site.

At 3.4 miles, arrive back at the put-in location on the left.

Paddle Information

Organizations

Coastal Conservation Association, 6919 Portwest Dr. Suite 100, Houston, TX 77024; (800) 201-FISH; ccatexas.org, Members saved the redfish, some say. And, they're still hard at work.

Coastal Bend Bays Foundation, 1231 Agnes St. Suite 100, Corpus Christi, TX 78401; (361) 882-3439; baysfoundation.org.

Contact/Outfitter

Slowride Guide Services, 821 S. Commercial St., Aransas Pass, TX 78336; (361) 758-0463; slowrideguide.com. "Catch fish, see birds, pick up shells, take a gut-wrenching paddle, or just enjoy nature. We can do it all, " says one representative.

Austin Canoe & Kayak (ACK), 11604 Stonehollow Dr. #300, Austin, TX 78758; (888) 828-3828; austinkayak.com. Want to rent a boat and take it wherever you decide to go? ACK offers boat rentals from locations in the cities of Austin, Houston, San Marcos, San Antonio, and Spring. "Take it anywhere you like," says one ACK representative, "Just bring it back."

▶ Winds and tides are your best friends or your worst enemies when paddling along coastal areas with mangroves, oyster beds, and sandbars. Plan to take advantage of the wind, rather than fighting it. Make sure you have enough water to get into and out of your paddle destination. Read tide forecasts.

Local Information

Aransas Pass Visitors Center, 130 W. Goodnight Ave., Aransas Pass, TX 78336; (361) 758-2750; aransaspass.org. Stop by.

Local Events/Attractions

Shrimporee, 130 W. Goodnight Ave., Aransas Pass, TX 78336; (361) 758-2750; aransaspass.org. Organizers call it the "Home of the largest shrimp festival in Texas."

Earth Day–Bay Day, Heritage Park, 1581 N. Chaparral St., Corpus Christi, TX 78401; (361) 882-3439; baysfoundation.org. This free annual conservation event hosts some 10,000 visitors and features a catch-and-release fishing tank, rock-climbing wall, and more.

38 Island Moorings-Little Flats Loop (Corpus Christi Bay)

This 7.1-mile paddle offers mangroves, grass and sand flats, oyster beds and birds, Caribbean-clear water, and bully redfish that taunt you at every turn. You'll earn it. The winds that push you out of the protected harbor will dare you to paddle back in and, at times, leave you no choice but to lean forward, dig in, and paddle as hard as you ever have. This is an absolutely wonderful paddle for those who are fit and up to the challenge.

Start: Island Moorings Yacht Club and Marina, N27 48.39'/W97 5.20'
End: Island Moorings Yacht Club and Marina, N27 48.39'/W97 5.20'
Length: 7.1 miles
Float time: 4-7 hours
Difficulty: Moderate to difficult, depending on wind
Rapids: None
River type: Bay and mangroves
Current: Tidal area
River gradient: Not applicable
River gauge: At lower tides, there will likely be some portaging involved.

Land status: Municipal and private
County: Nueces
Nearest city/town: Port Aransas
Boats used: Kayaks, johnboats, motorized craft
Season: Year-round
Fees and permits: Ask at the front desk if there is a fee.
Maps: TOPO! Texas; USGS Port Aransas TX; DeLorme: Texas Atlas & Gazetteer: page 85
Contact: Call Island Moorings Marina at (888) 749-9030 to ask about fees and weather.

Put-In and Takeout Information

To put-in/takeout: No shuttle is needed. Put-in and takeout are in the same location. From Port Aransas, take TX 361 south for 1 mile. Turn right onto Piper Boulevard and go 0.1 mile. Turn left onto Island Moorings Parkway. The launch is at a concrete boat ramp on the left side of the parking lot.

Overview

One of the few natural harbors along the Texas coast, Corpus Christi Bay is a large estuary located near the city of Corpus Christi. The Nueces River and Oso Creek flow into the bay and provide freshwater. Mustang Island and North Padre Island protect the 20-foot-deep bay from the Gulf of Mexico. The Gulf Intracoastal Waterway crosses Corpus Christi Bay, which further contributes to the bay's commercial vitality. The area is environmentally important, hosting some 490 species of birds and 234 species of fish. In

▶ While wading, stingrays will be attracted to the mud you kick up. Watch your step, slide your feet, and don't harass them. Let them pass. They are docile.

Little Flats, fish camp

recognition of its value, the Environmental Protection Agency has designated the 190-square-mile bay an estuary of national significance.

Paddle Summary

The Island Moorings Yacht Club and Marina's private boat launch is accessible to the public for kayakers and stand-up paddlers, if you call ahead. The Mustang Beach Airport occupies the adjacent property.

Unload the boat at an edge of the concrete ramp so as not to clog the ramp. The ramp is steep and can be slick, so a loaded boat may slide into the water if left unattended. The club asks paddlers to park at the front edge of the lot, well away from the ramp and the clubhouse.

Slide into the harbor, which is lined with wooden docks, yachts, live-aboard sailing vessels, and million-dollar homes. Paddle toward the houses on the far bank and bear right to follow the water out of the harbor.

At 0.6 mile, a large boathouse stands on the right and the water turns left toward a long stretch of homes. Ahead, the white-and-red triangular sign marked "24" stands alongside the white-and-green square marked "23." Bear left to remain in calmer water. On the right stands a wooden platform and post.

At 0.9 miles, reach a white-and-orange post and white Texas Parks & Wildlife Department (TPWD) sign with orange letters reading "21" (N27 48.499'/W97 5.721'). Bear right through the cut. Oyster beds are on either side. These are exposed at low tide. Many birds peruse the exposed oyster beds. Redfish shine from the sand and grassy shallows, pushing wakes with their heads, shining fins, and kicking up sandy swirls. Airplanes take off and land at the airport. Note this for navigational reference. Follow the left bank. Ahead, an orange-and-white sign shines from a point across a large open flat.

At 1.5 miles, reach TPWD sign "20" (N27 48.410'/W97 6.296'). Bear right. White stakes mark the border of a large oyster bed.

Continue ahead to TPWD sign "19" (N27 48.306'/W97 06.652') at 2 miles. This stretch may need to be portaged. A walk in the shallows is a great experience. Bear right at sign "19," and turn due west. Ahead, on the horizon, is the city skyline. Head toward that. The water opens up as the shallows drop into the Corpus Christi Bay.

At 2.4 miles, near N27 48.29'/W97 07.07', or when you start to see redfish, step out of the boat, and start casting and easing across the flats. Slide your feet to avoid stingrays. A weedless silver spoon is a very effective lure here. The mixed grass-and-sand bottom holds fish. Ahead, to the left, a string of islands marks the edge of the deep water, where waves pick up significantly. Pelicans and other birds hold on islands and hunt the drop-off. To the right, a house is on wooden pilings.

After fishing a while, paddle out just past the islands and bear left to put the islands on your left shoulder. Ahead, on the horizon, are two condos and a light blue water tower. Dolphins play on the right, in the deeper water between you and the Corpus Christi skyline.

At 3.3 miles, TPWD sign "17" (N27 47.581'/W97 07.183') marks a cut between two islands that begs to be explored and fished. When you are done, turn around and head back along the islands, keeping them on your right shoulder. The aforementioned house is ahead. Directly behind it, from this angle, is a utility pole with a blinking light. Head toward that light.

At 4.5 miles, pass the three houses (PC1573, PC1561, and PC1559). Pelicans sit on the docks near No Trespassing signs. Just past the third house (PC1559, N27 48.580'/W97 07.157'), bear right and head toward the water tower and the multicolored houses that line the banks in the distance. Paddle across a wide expanse of shallow flats.

At 5.5 miles, look near the island for a path through the shallow oyster reef. It will curve around to the channel between you and marker "18." At the 10 o'clock position from the water tower, there are two channel markers: a green square "17," and a red triangle "18." They stand at 5.8 miles (N27 49.003'/W97 06.116'). Between the flats and the channel markers is a large oyster bed. When the water is low, the bed will likely be exposed. Look to the left for a path through. Again, this route is sensitive to the tides. The winds can be strong heading across these flats.

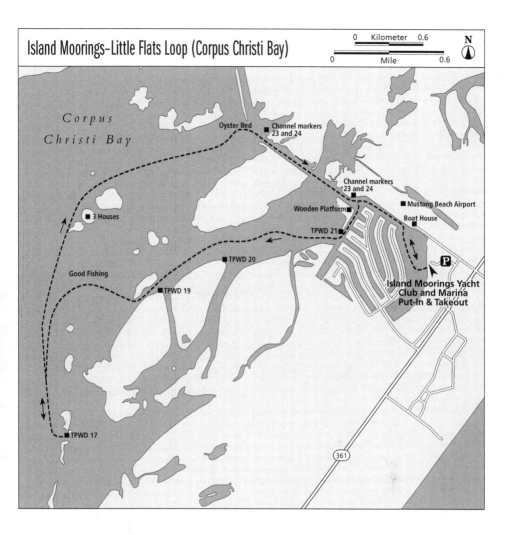

Island Moorings-Little Flats Loop (Corpus Christi Bay)

Corpus Christi Bay

Oyster Bed

Channel markers 23 and 24

Channel markers 23 and 24

Wooden Platform

Mustang Beach Airport

Boat House

TPWD 21

3 Houses

TPWD 20

Good Fishing

TPWD 19

Island Moorings Yacht Club and Marina
Put-In & Takeout

TPWD 17

361

From channel markers "17" and "18," look right. A line of wooden pilings and channel markers lead to the return to the harbor. The headwinds can be really strong here. This is where you prove your paddle prowess. It can be a grind.

At 6.4 miles, be sure to slow down for the no-wake zone, at green square channel marker "23" and red triangle channel marker "24." The boathouse is ahead. Reenter the harbor and return to the launch.

At 7.1 miles, arrive back at the launch on the left.

Paddle Information

Organizations

Coastal Conservation Association, 6919 Portwest Dr. Suite 100, Houston, TX 77024; (800) 201-FISH; ccatexas.org. Members saved the redfish. And they're still hard at work.

Coastal Bend Bays Foundation, 1231 Agnes St. Suite 100, Corpus Christi, TX 78401; (361) 882-3439; baysfoundation.org.

Contact / Outfitter

Slowride Guide Services, 821 South Commercial St., Aransas Pass, TX 78336; (361) 758-0463; slowrideguide.com. "Catch fish, see birds, pick up shells, take a gut-wrenching paddle, or just enjoy nature. We can do it all, "says one representative.

Austin Canoe & Kayak (ACK), 11604 Stonehollow Dr. #300, Austin, TX 78758; (888) 828-3828; austinkayak.com. Want to rent a boat and take it wherever you decide to go? ACK offers boat rentals from locations in the cities of Austin, Houston, San Marcos, San Antonio, and Spring. "Take it anywhere you like," says one ACK representative, "Just bring it back."

Local Information

Island Moorings Yacht Club and Marina, 3500 Island Moorings Pkwy., Port Aransas, TX 78373; (888) 749-9030; islandmoorings.com.

Port Aransas Visitors Center, 403 W. Cotter St., Port Aransas, Texas 78373; (361) 749-5919; portaransas.org. Stop by.

Local Events / Attractions

Mustang Island State Park, 17047 TX 361, Port Aransas, TX 78373; (361) 749-5246; tpwd.state.tx.us/state-parks/mustang-island. Come for paddling, fishing, camping, picnicking, swimming, cycling, and birding.

Shrimporee, 130 W. Goodnight Ave., Aransas Pass, TX 78336; (361) 758-2750; aransaspass.org. Their sign proclaims, "Home of the largest shrimp festival in Texas."

Earth Day–Bay Day, Heritage Park, 1581 N. Chaparral St., Corpus Christi, TX 78401; (361) 882-3439; baysfoundation.org. This free annual conservation event hosts some 10,000 visitors and features a catch-and-release fishing tank, rock-climbing wall and more.

39 Hampton's Landing-Ransom Island Loop (Corpus Christi Bay)

This 5.4-mile loop gives paddlers an up close and personal view of impressive maritime vessels, mangrove islands, and Caribbean-clear waters. The birding is good. The fishing is great. And the paddling is even better. The route takes paddlers from a protected marina across a shipping channel, through a chain of islands, over grass flats, and back again. High winds (up to 20 miles per hour) are not uncommon on this trip, and it is largely in the open water. Plan so that you go into the winds when they are at their lowest and you are at your freshest. As with any trip, try to plan such that the winds help push you back into the launch site whenever possible. Otherwise you may be phoning a friend for an unexpected ride. The good news: This can be paddled at any tide.

Start: San Patricio municipal boat ramp aka Hampton's Landing, N27 53.34'/W97 08.81'
End: San Patricio municipal boat ramp aka Hampton's Landing, N27 53.34'/W97 08.81'
Length: 5.4 miles
Float time: 3-5 hours
Difficulty: Moderate due to length, tides, and winds
Rapids: None
River type: Bay and mangroves
Current: Tidal area
River gradient: Not applicable

River gauge: Good at low tide as well as high tide
Land status: Municipal and private
County: Nueces
Nearest city/town: Aransas Pass
Boats used: Kayaks, johnboats, motorized craft, shipping vessels in the channel
Season: Year-round
Fees and permits: None
Maps: TOPO! Texas; USGS Aransas Pass TX; DeLorme: Texas Atlas & Gazetteer: page 85

Put-In and Takeout Information

To put-in/takeout: No shuttle is needed. Put-in and takeout are in the same location. From Aransas Pass, drive southwest on South Commercial Street for 0.9 mile. Turn left onto Ransom Road for 0.4 mile. Turn left to stay on Ransom Road for 0.1 mile. Pass campers, sailboats, and other vessels on the left. The road ends in San Patricio municipal boat ramp aka Hampton's Landing.

Overview

Corpus Christi Bay is one of the few natural harbors along the Texas coast. Within sight of the city of Corpus Christi, the large estuary hosts some 490 species of birds and 234 species of fish. Such is its importance that the Environmental Protection Agency designated the 190-square-mile bay as an estuary of national significance. The Nueces River and Oso Creek flow into the bay and provide freshwater. Mustang

Island and North Padre Island protect the shallow, 20-foot-deep bay from the Gulf of Mexico. Corpus Christi Bay also hosts a stretch of the Gulf Intracoastal Waterway.

Paddle Summary

The launch is at the San Patricio County boat ramp, known locally as Hampton's Landing. The area has public restrooms, a wooden pier, boat launch facilities, ample parking, and picnic areas. Launch the kayak to the left of the concrete boat ramp, on a sandy beach, so as to avoid the heavy boat traffic. Park in the nearby lot. No Paddling signs mark the location.

Hamptons Landing, Ransom Island wreck

Push out into the water. To the left is a marina. Turn right, and follow the narrow channel that runs straight out into Corpus Christi Bay. On the point on the left, directly across from the boat ramp, is the Shoal Grass Lodge & Conference Center. Note this for navigation. Paddle past the conference center. Pass a cut to the left. Paddle through the mangrove and marsh grass islands as you head into the bay. On the left is the TX 361 bridge. On the right, a string of wooden pilings stand along the bank.

At 0.5 mile, pass a green square channel marker labeled "41" (N27 52.963'/W97 08.5465'). Paddle across the shipping channel that runs from Corpus Christi. Be aware of shipping traffic here. Some of the vessels seem the size of city blocks. Stay out of the way. On the right, a sign announces a state scientific area where sea grass is protected. Shrimp boats pass on the left.

At low tide, sand islands are exposed on the left of the channel. They host a surf-and-turf gathering of birds: pelicans, gulls, grackles, cormorants, and others. On the right are a chain of sand islands, oyster beds, and mangroves. Ahead across the bay on the horizon, is a water tower. Aim for that.

At 1.2 miles, in the middle of an island to the right, is a concrete structure. Follow the chain of small islands as they bear to the right. Monitor water depth as you go and

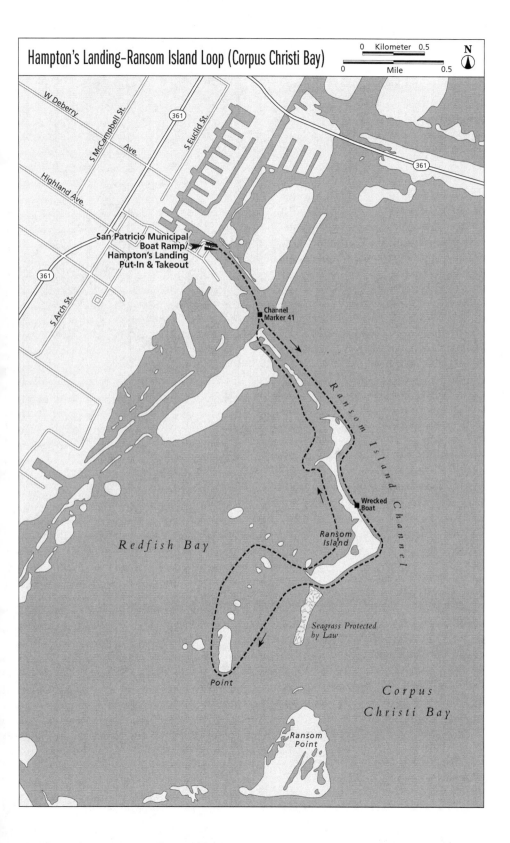

Hampton's Landing–Ransom Island Loop (Corpus Christi Bay)

0   Kilometer   0.5

0   Mile   0.5

N

361

W Deberry

S McCampbell St.

Ave.

361

S Euclid St.

Highland Ave.

361

S Arch St.

San Patricio Municipal
Boat Ramp/
Hampton's Landing
Put-In & Takeout

Channel
Marker 41

Ransom Island Channel

Wrecked
Boat

Ransom
Island

Redfish Bay

Seagrass Protected
by Law

Point

Corpus
Christi Bay

Ransom
Point

be careful not to damage the sea grass beds. A condo is at the 1 o'clock position from the water tower. Redirect and aim at that. Ahead, on the right, is a white boat beached on a rocky point (N27 52.125'/W97 07.977') near a sandy cove. Head to that. On my paddle, loons called and dolphins swam past. Follow the island and the beach to that wreck.

At 1.7 miles, reach the wrecked boat on a point at Ransom Island. Leave the point and continue down the beach, with the beach on your right.

At 1.8 miles, a white-and-blue sign on the right is marked "Warning Pipeline." Continue, keeping the island on the right.

At 2.2 miles, N27 51.85'/W97 08.23' a sign is marked "Seagrass Pro-

Hampton's Landing, perfect find

tected by Law." From here, look straight ahead (at the 4 o'clock position from the water tower) to a strip of mangrove and grass islands. Aim at the tip of the farthest island. Cross a broad shallow area with sand-and-grass bottom.

At 2.8 miles, arrive at the tip of a small island at N27 51.48'/W97 08.65'. Continue around the point, with the island on your right shoulder, and head back along the opposite side of the island chain. You'll be heading back toward the put-in to the north. The island chain curves around and directs you back toward the launch. Between the launch and the TX 361 bridge, a white water tower should be visible. Note that for navigation on the return. The masts of the sailing vessels stand behind the put-in/takeout.

At 4.8 miles, at green square channel marker "41," pass through the island chain. The rooftop sign for Mickeys Bar & Grill is visible ahead. Paddle to that. Watch for boat traffic.

At 5.4 miles, arrive back at the put-in/takeout on the left.

Paddle Information

Organizations

Coastal Conservation Association, 6919 Portwest Dr. Suite 100, Houston, TX 77024; (800) 201-FISH; ccatexas.org. Members saved the redfish, some say. And they're still hard at work.

Coastal Bend Bays Foundation, 1231 Agnes St. Suite 100, Corpus Christi, TX 78401; (361) 882-3439; baysfoundation.org

Contact/Outfitter

Slowride Guide Services, 821 S. Commercial St., Aransas Pass, TX 78336; (361) 758-0463; slowrideguide.com, "Catch fish, see birds, pick up shells, take a gut-wrenching paddle, or just enjoy nature. We can do it all," says one representative.

Austin Canoe & Kayak (ACK), 11604 Stonehollow Dr. #300, Austin, TX 78758; (888) 828-3828; austinkayak.com. Want to rent a boat and take it wherever you decide to go? ACK offers boat rentals from locations in the cities of Austin, Houston, San Marcos, San Antonio, and Spring. "Take it anywhere you like," says one ACK representative, "Just bring it back."

Local Information

Aransas Pass Visitors Center, 130 W. Goodnight Ave., Aransas Pass, TX 78336; (361) 758-2750; aransaspass.org. Stop by.

Local Events/Attractions

Shrimporee, 130 W. Goodnight Ave., Aransas Pass, TX 78336; (361) 758-2750; aransaspass.org. Organizers call it the "Home of the largest shrimp festival in Texas."

Earth Day–Bay Day, Heritage Park, 1581 N. Chaparral St., Corpus Christi, TX 78401; (361) 882-3439; baysfoundation.org. This free annual conservation event hosts some 10,000 visitors and features a catch-and-release fishing tank, rock-climbing wall and more.

40 JB Hunting Ranch to Carl Park (Tres Palacios River)

This 8.1-mile stretch of tidal river begins among scenery reminiscent of riverscapes in Bolivia's Amazonia, and takes paddlers along a crawling path toward the Gulf of Mexico. The current on the tides is noticeable, but you can easily paddle in either direction. Even at low tide, the river offers plenty of water to float. JB Hunting Ranch offers a Texas original: Hunt feral pigs in the morning and spend the rest of the day paddling the Palacios, watching wildlife, and fishing for redfish.

Start: JB Hunting Ranch, N28 52.06' / W96 9.79'
End: Carl Park, N28 47.18' / W96 9.01'
Length: 8.1 miles
Float time: 4–7 hours
Difficulty: Moderate due to distance
Rapids: None
River type: Tidal river
Current: Mild to slow, depending upon tides
River gradient: Less than 1 foot per mile
River gauge: Not applicable
Land status: Municipal park and private
County: Matagorda

Nearest city/town: Palacios
Boats used: Canoes, kayaks, johnboats, small motorized craft
Season: Year-round. Spring and fall offer milder temperatures.
Fees and permits: A fee is charged per person for the shuttle.
Maps: TOPO! Texas; USGS Blessing TX; DeLorme: Texas Atlas & Gazetteer: page 80
Contact: Call JB Hunting Ranch about details and water conditions: (361) 588-6845 or (979) 240-9445.

Put-In and Takeout Information

To shuttle point/takeout: From Palacios, take TX 35 north for 5.2 miles. Turn right onto Farm Road 521 east for 3.4 miles. Turn right at signs for Carl Park. Follow the park road to the ramp downstream of the bridge.

To put-in from takeout: From Carl Park, turn left onto Farm Road 521 and go west for 3.4 miles. Turn right onto TX 35 and go north for 8 miles. Turn right onto Farm Road 459. Cross train tracks and follow the road to the left and along the train tracks. Follow for 0.6 mile. The road turns into Hicki Road ahead, but turn right to follow Farm Road 459. When Farm Road 459 turns left, a small dirt road continues straight. This is Hahn Road. Follow it for a few hundred yards. Take the gravel driveway to the left before the dead end. Follow the road to the high fence and gate. Press the button to ring the office of JB Hunting Ranch.

Overview

Despite its regal name, "Three Palaces" of Spanish origin, the Tres Palacios River would be easy to miss. It runs slow. It doesn't raise a ruckus or offer up towering bluffs or whirling rapids. And it's a meager 46 miles long. But this tidal river is a great paddle,

Palacios, Shane catching mullet in a cast net

and it offers some good fishing for redfish as well. The Tres Palacios River begins near El Campo in Wharton County and runs southeast to the Tres Palacios Bay. Along the way, it runs through hardwoods, pines, cypress, marsh grasses, and other flora. Several residential developments are present along the path of the river.

Paddle Summary

As soon as you enter the JB Hunting Ranch, someone will welcome you and show you where to park. The put-in location is situated at the bottom of a hill. Unload at the top of the hill and carry the boat down to a wooden boat dock. Launch the boat into deep water and step in. (**Note:** The proprietor was looking into building a boat launch specifically for kayaks at the time of publication.)

The slow river is some 35 feet wide here. The visibility is low. If you sit here for a day, you can watch the tide push water up the river, then stop, then pull the water out again. The low, 5-foot banks are earthen and lined with live oaks, palmettos, cypress, wood debris, and many felled trees—a combination that changes with the tide.

For the duration of the trip, jug lines, feral hogs, deer, kingfishers, great blue herons, white egrets, and many other birds are common companions.

At 0.2 mile, a boat ramp is on the right.

At 0.5 mile, Briar Creek comes in on the left, from the dense woods. Logs are wedged into the branches of trees some 8 feet overhead—reminder of the last flood.

At 1.1 miles, a gazebo is on the right.

At 1.2 miles, a dock is on the right.

At 1.4 miles, pass an old bridge and five pilings.

At 1.6 miles, pass a string of several homes and manicured banks.

FERAL HOGS AND THE FARM-FUR-FIN-AND-FEATHER-TO-FORK-FOODCHAIN

A credit card's slide, beep, and "Sign here" distract us from the math of our money. But try to hand over dollars, and there's nothing between them and you but the memory of all it took to earn them.

Food is similar. It has math.

I recently threw out half a roast. "Boy," said my memory in my grandmother's voice. I was ashamed to have forgotten the arithmetic of food: Someone has to kill an animal, clean it, and cook it. Vegetables, fruit, and so on require a similar investment. The more of that we outsource, the less our connection. When our only investment comes in a "slide, beep, sign here," we haven't invested in our food at all.

So, what do we do? Reclaim a place in the farm-fur-fin-and-feather-to-fork-foodchain. Participation therein is a prophylaxis to waste. We can't all revert to subsistence livelihoods. And, of course, some abhor gardening as much as others disdain hunting. Fair enough. But we can all find a way to reconnect to our food. In Texas, those interested can also help the state with an invasive plague: the feral pig.

After the roast debacle, two friends—one of whom had never before hunted—and I did just that. We drove for four hours; hunted for four more; shot, skinned, and quartered three feral hogs (turning them into meat); drove four hours home; cured the hogs for three days; wrapped them in freezer paper and froze them. One shoulder I brined and spent fourteen hours cooking in a smoker.

It's a hell of an investment for meat. And it was a blast. We had good times with good friends. And we recalled the hard work that goes into every piece of meat, vegetable, shrimp, and swaggle of tofu we eat. Those who do that hard work for us are feeding us. There's something to be said for feeding ourselves.

A version of this was published in the March 2014 edition of GAFF Magazine.

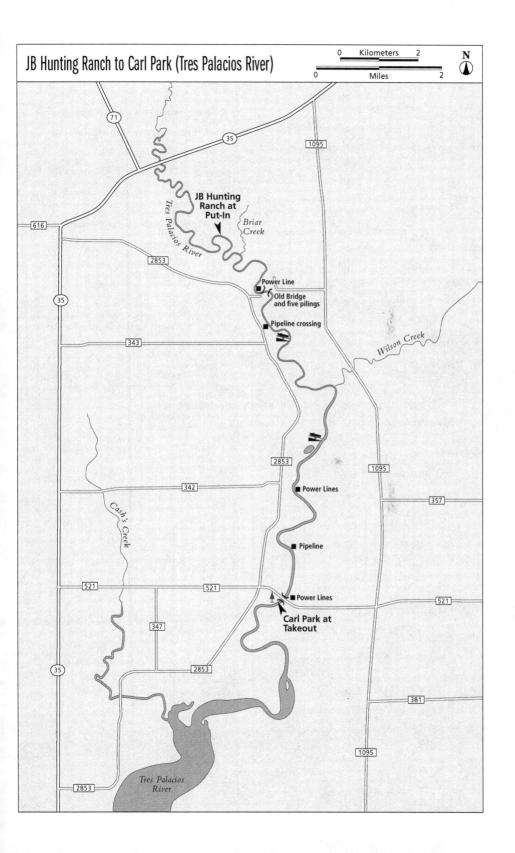

JB Hunting Ranch to Carl Park (Tres Palacios River)

At 1.9 miles, the river is now some 60 feet wide, double its width at the launch.

At 2 miles, a wooden dock and two boat ramps are on the right.

At 2.4 miles, a string of homes, bulkheads, docks, fishing lights, boats, and grills continues to the takeout.

At 2.6 miles, the Tidewater Oaks subdivision boat ramp is on the right. Paddle down the center of river to avoid the tangles near the riverbanks. Listen for outboard motors and prepare to share the river.

At 3 miles, a seemingly misplaced ridge reaches some 30 feet high and is topped with live oaks.

At 3.1 miles, a creek comes in from the left.

At 3.5 miles, the river is some 80 feet wide.

At 4.7 miles, reach the Tres Palacios Oaks subdivision boat ramp.

At 4.2 miles, Wilson Creek is on the left.

At 4.3 miles, the first marsh grass appears on left, and continues to the takeout.

By 5.1 miles, many sloughs are running in and out of the marsh grass.

At 5.6 miles, open grassland stretches out along both sides of the river.

At 5.7 miles, power lines cross the river.

At 5.8 miles, cattails begin.

At 5.9 miles, power lines cross the river.

At 6.1 miles, power lines cross the river. Ahead stands a communications tower.

At 7 miles, a boat dock is on the right.

At 7.4 miles, a pipeline sign is on left.

At 7.7 miles, a road, bridge, power lines, and abandoned bridge are visible. The river is some 100 feet wide. Pass under the Farm Road 521 bridge.

At 8.1 miles, the takeout is at the concrete boat ramp on the right, in Carl Park.

▶ For shrimping communities all along the Gulf Coast, the "Blessing of the Fleet" is one of the most important days of the year. In Palacios, the "Shrimp Capital of Texas," St. Anthony's Church hosts an annual Shrimporee and Blessing of the Fleet to ensure a safe and bountiful season. Contact the Palacios Chamber of Commerce for more information at 420 Main St, Palacios TX 77465 or (361) 972-2615.

Paddle Information

Organizations

Texas State Marine Education Center, 100 Marine Center Dr., Palacios, Texas 77465; (361) 972-5370; gulfbase.org/organization/view.php?oid=tsmec. The center is located on 27 acres of pristine shoreline west of the Port of Palacios.

Coastal Conservation Association, 6919 Portwest Dr. Suite 100, Houston, TX 77024; (800) 201-FISH; ccatexas.org. Members saved the redfish. And they're still hard at work.

Palacios, dolphin

Contact / Outfitter

JB Hunting Ranch, 229 JB Ranch Rd., Palacios, TX 77465; (361) 588-6845 or (979) 240-9445, (979) 240-5569. The launch is on the ranch. The ranch offers shuttles, parking, more. Call for information.

Austin Canoe & Kayak (ACK), 11604 Stonehollow Dr. #300, Austin, TX 78758; (888) 828-3828; austinkayak.com. Want to rent a boat and take it wherever you decide to go? ACK offers boat rentals from locations in the cities of Austin, Houston, San Marcos, San Antonio, and Spring. "Take it anywhere you like," says one ACK representative, "Just bring it back."

Local Events / Attractions

Luther Hotel, 408 S. Bay Boulevard, Palacios, TX 77465; (361) 972-2312; facebook .com/lutherhotel. The Luther opened its doors in 1903 and has hosted Rita Hayworth, Lyndon Johnson, and others. This quirky spot should not be missed.

Pedal Palacios, Palacios; (361) 972-2136; pedalpalacios.org. Twelve miles, 30 miles, 60 miles—pick your pedal poison.

Paddle Index

About the Author

Shane Townsend was raised in the family boarding house at the edge of the Pascagoula River Swamp. He has hiked the Andes, fished with machetes in the Amazon basin, and paddled dugout canoes deep within Southeast Asia's Ring of Fire. He's a lifelong outdoorsman and a former Peace Corps volunteer. His writing has appeared in *Field & Stream, USA Today's Hunt & Fish, Quail Forever Journal, Southwest Fly Fishing, GAFF Magazine, Native Peoples, Mississippi Magazine, Kayak Angler, Canoe & Kayak, Americas,* the Matador Network, *SHOT Daily, SHOT Business, National Shooting Sports Foundation Range Report,* and other outlets. The Outdoor Writers Association of America and the Texas Outdoor Writers Association have each recognized his work with Excellence in Craft awards.

Shane and his family live in Austin, where he serves as senior program adviser for The Meadows Center for Water and the Environment, and as a member of the boards of directors for the Texas Outdoor Writers Association and the Coastal Conservation Association–Austin.

Find him at BatCityOutdoors.com, BatCityOutdoors@gmail.com, linkedin.com/in/jshanetownsend, or in the *Last Cast* in each GAFF Magazine.

Your next adventure begins here.

falcon.com